THE LIFE OF
SIR WALTER SCOTT, Bart.

ABRIDGED

Macmillan's Pocket American and English Classics

A Series of English Texts, edited for use in Elementary and Secondary Schools, with Critical Introductions, Notes, etc.

16mo   Cloth   25 cents each

Addison's Sir Roger de Coverley.
Andersen's Fairy Tales.
Arabian Nights' Entertainments.
Arnold's Sohrab and Rustum.
Austen's Pride and Prejudice.
Austen's Sense and Sensibility.
Bacon's Essays.
Baker's Out of the Northland.
Bible (Memorable Passages).
Blackmore's Lorna Doone.
Boswell's Life of Johnson. Abridged.
Browning's Shorter Poems.
Browning, Mrs., Poems (Selected).
Bryant's Thanatopsis, etc.
Bulwer's Last Days of Pompeii.
Bunyan's The Pilgrim's Progress.
Burke's Speech on Conciliation.
Burns' Poems (Selections).
Byron's Childe Harold's Pilgrimage.
Byron's Shorter Poems.
Carlyle's Essay on Burns.
Carlyle's Heroes and Hero Worship.
Carroll's Alice's Adventures in Wonderland (Illustrated).
Chaucer's Prologue and Knight's Tale.
Church's The Story of the Iliad.
Church's The Story of the Odyssey.
Coleridge's The Ancient Mariner.
Cooper's The Deerslayer.
Cooper's The Last of the Mohicans.
Cooper's The Spy.
Dana's Two Years Before the Mast.
Defoe's Robinson Crusoe. Part I.
Defoe's Robinson Crusoe. Abridged.
De Quincey's Confessions of an English Opium-Eater.
De Quincey's Joan of Arc, and The English Mail-Coach.
Dickens' A Christmas Carol, and The Cricket on the Hearth.
Dickens' A Tale of Two Cities.
Dickens' David Copperfield. (Two vols.)
Dryden's Palamon and Arcite.
Early American Orations, 1760-1824.
Edwards' (Jonathan) Sermons.
Eliot's Mill on the Floss.
Eliot's Silas Marner.

Emerson's Essays.
Emerson's Early Poems.
Emerson's Representative Men.
English Narrative Poems.
Epoch-making Papers in U. S. History.
Franklin's Autobiography.
Gaskell's Cranford.
Goldsmith's The Deserted Village, and Other Poems.
Goldsmith's The Vicar of Wakefield.
Gray's Elegy, etc., and Cowper's John Gilpin, etc.
Grimm's Fairy Tales.
Hale's The Man Without a Country.
Hawthorne's Grandfather's Chair.
Hawthorne's Mosses from an Old Manse.
Hawthorne's Tanglewood Tales.
Hawthorne's The House of the Seven Gables.
Hawthorne's Twice-told Tales (Selections).
Hawthorne's Wonder-Book.
Holmes' Poems.
Holmes' Autocrat of the Breakfast Table.
Homer's Iliad (Translated).
Homer's Odyssey (Translated).
Hughes' Tom Brown's School Days.
Huxley's Selected Essays and Addresses.
Irving's Life of Goldsmith.
Irving's Knickerbocker's History.
Irving's Sketch Book.
Irving's The Alhambra.
Irving's Tales of a Traveller.
Keary's Heroes of Asgard.
à Kempis : The Imitation of Christ.
Kingsley's The Heroes.
Lamb's The Essays of Elia.
Lamb's Tales from Shakespeare.
Lincoln's Addresses, Inaugurals, and Letters.
Lockhart's Life of Scott. Abridged.
Longfellow's Evangeline.
Longfellow's Hiawatha.
Longfellow's Miles Standish.
Longfellow's Miles Standish and Minor Poems.

Macmillan's Pocket American and English Classics

A Series of English Texts, edited for use in Elementary and Secondary Schools, with Critical Introductions, Notes, etc.

16mo   Cloth   25 cents each

Longfellow's Tales of a Wayside Inn.
Lowell's The Vision of Sir Launfal.
Macaulay's Essay on Addison.
Macaulay's Essay on Hastings.
Macaulay's Essay on Lord Clive.
Macaulay's Essay on Milton.
Macaulay's Lays of Ancient Rome.
Macaulay's Life of Samuel Johnson.
Malory's Le Morte d'Arthur.
Milton's Minor Poems.
Milton's Paradise Lost, Books I and II.
Old English Ballads.
Old Testament Selections.
Palgrave's Golden Treasury.
Parkman's Oregon Trail.
Plutarch's Lives (Cæsar, Brutus, and Mark Antony).
Poe's Poems.
Poe's Prose Tales (Selections).
Poems, Narrative and Lyrical.
Pope's Homer's Iliad.
Pope's Homer's Odyssey.
Pope's The Rape of the Lock.
Rossetti (Christina), Selected Poems.
Ruskin's Sesame and Lilies.
Ruskin's The Crown of Wild Olive and Queen of the Air.
Scott's Ivanhoe.
Scott's Kenilworth.
Scott's Lady of the Lake.
Scott's Lay of the Last Minstrel.
Scott's Marmion.
Scott's Quentin Durward.
Scott's The Talisman.
Select Orations.
Selected Poems, for Required Reading in Secondary Schools.
Selections for Oral Reading.
Shakespeare's As You Like It.

Shakespeare's Hamlet.
Shakespeare's Henry V.
Shakespeare's Julius Cæsar.
Shakespeare's King Lear.
Shakespeare's Macbeth.
Shakespeare's Merchant of Venice.
Shakespeare's Midsummer Night's Dream.
Shakespeare's Richard II.
Shakespeare's The Tempest.
Shakespeare's Twelfth Night.
Shelley and Keats: Poems (Selections).
Sheridan's The Rivals and The School for Scandal.
Short Stories. A collection.
Southern Orators (Selections).
Southern Poets (Selections).
Spenser's Faerie Queene, Book I.
Stevenson's Kidnapped.
Stevenson's The Master of Ballantrae.
Stevenson's Travels with a Donkey, and An Inland Voyage.
Stevenson's Treasure Island.
Swift's Gulliver's Travels.
Tennyson's Idylls of the King.
Tennyson's In Memoriam.
Tennyson's The Princess.
Tennyson's Shorter Poems.
Thackeray's English Humourists.
Thackeray's Henry Esmond.
Thoreau's Walden.
Trevelyan's Life of Macaulay. Abridged.
Virgil's Æneid.
Washington's Farewell Address, and Webster's First Bunker Hill Oration.
Whittier's Snow-Bound and Other Early Poems.
Woolman's Journal.
Wordsworth's Shorter Poems.

THE MACMILLAN COMPANY
NEW YORK · BOSTON · CHICAGO · DALLAS
ATLANTA · SAN FRANCISCO

MACMILLAN & CO., Limited
LONDON · BOMBAY · CALCUTTA
MELBOURNE

THE MACMILLAN CO. OF CANADA, Ltd.
TORONTO

SIR WALTER SCOTT

LOCKHART'S

LIFE OF SCOTT

ABRIDGED AND EDITED WITH INTRODUCTION
AND NOTES

BY

O. LEON REID

PRINCIPAL OF THE GIRLS' HIGH SCHOOL
LOUISVILLE, KENTUCKY

New York

THE MACMILLAN COMPANY

1914

TABLE OF CONTENTS

PREFACE

JOHN GIBSON LOCKHART's *Life of Sir Walter Scott* has ranked since its publication in 1838 among the few great biographies of the English language. It first appeared in seven volumes, abridged by the author in 1848 to two volumes. The present edition is an abridgment of that of 1848. The text follows Lockhart's edition closely, the English spellings of Scott and Lockhart being allowed to stand so as to preserve so far as possible the flavor of the original. It is the hope of the editor that many young readers may be inspired by this introduction to a great and good man to read more of Lockhart's larger work and to rejoice in the poems and stories of the Mighty Minstrel so constantly referred to in these pages.

With the exception of less than a score of italicized link phrases or sentences, inserted to join the severed threads of Lockhart's narrative, the following abridgment is restricted to the original sentences of the author. Notes have been given only where the context does not furnish an enlightening hint concerning the person or matter with which high school boys and girls of to-day may be supposed to be unfamiliar.

Writing of his childhood enjoyment of the knights and ladies and dragons and giants of Spenser, Scott says, "God only knows how delighted I was to find myself in such society." How many readers throughout the world can echo that sentiment in connection with the goodly society created by Scott! In Lockhart's pages we may take the long sea-trail back to Scotland and find ourselves a fellow guest with Irving at Abbotsford. We may linger there through those joyous years of success and, at last, in rapt and pitying admiration watch the mighty struggle of the true knight, Sir Walter Scott, a struggle against a debt more than six times as large as that over which our own Mark Twain triumphed. We shall be very proud of our friend, Walter Scott, and because he fought the good fight we shall be the stronger.

O. L. REID.

The Girls' High School,
Louisville, Kentucky,
    May 15, 1913.

INTRODUCTION

IN the closing pages of Lockhart's *Life of Scott* we read, "Abbotsford, after his own immortal works, is the best monument of its founder." We now know that next to Scott's immortal works the *Life* written by his devoted son-in-law, John Gibson Lockhart, has done most for the fame of Scotland's greatest story-teller.

At a social affair in Edinburgh in 1818 Lockhart, then in his twenty-fourth year, was presented to his great countryman, Walter Scott. As a brilliant young Tory writer whose satires had been appearing for some time in *Blackwood's Magazine*, Lockhart had attracted Scott's attention. An additional bond between them was the fact that the younger man was of the body of Edinburgh advocates, and, as Scott had done some years earlier, was gradually drifting into the profession of literature.

Scott was ever alert to the attractions of keen young minds. Here was a handsome young scholar, tall and slight, proud and reserved, yet willing to meet all advances of the older man. As to his intellectual ability, he had entered the University of Glasgow before his twelfth birthday. Because of his ability in Greek he was recommended for a scholarship at Balliol College, Oxford, and was graduated from there as one of the honor men in the classics in his nineteenth year. During these years he had also mastered the reading of German, French, Italian, and Spanish. The three years after his graduation were occupied in preparation for the bar, to which he was admitted as an advocate in 1816. He had further enriched his training by a season in Germany during which he had met the great poet Goethe. But much learning had not made him mad. He could accept another's point of view. While not enjoying sports himself, he seems to delight in recounting stories to illustrate Sir Walter's pleasure in them. He could listen quite as well as talk. In all the seven volumes of the unabridged *Life* there are few foreign phrases, just enough to indicate the scholar's self-restraint rather than the pedant's indulgence.

The acquaintance with Scott rapidly ripened into deep friendship. In an intimate circle Lockhart's reserve passed gently into pleasing gayety, and it is not difficult to understand how Sir Walter's daughter, Sophia, of the four Scott children the one most like her father, found in her father's young friend the man to whom she could give her deepest love. They were married in 1820.

Five years later Lockhart was called to London to the editorship of the *Quarterly Review* at a yearly salary of £1000. Until a short time before his death he continued to maintain the high standards of editorship that had always characterized the *Quarterly*. In the discharge of this office he refused to publish Carlyle's essay on "Chartism." Yet Carlyle always felt kindly toward him. In his review of the *Life* Carlyle seemed more willing to do justice to the biographer than to the subject of his work. The *Encyclopædia Britannica* refers to this review as "peevish," but many admirers of Scott find pleasure in reading the estimate of that other great Scotchman. His limitations on Scott's greatness do not lessen our regard for the man who has become a hero for many of us, as he had for Lockhart.

Lockhart was not a success as a novelist, but his *Life of Burns* established his right to be termed one of the greatest of biographers. His *Scott* is second only to — Boswell's *Johnson*. By some it is ranked first among English biographies.

As we read this great life and admire its author's splendid narrative style, we may note from time to time some slight references to himself. By piecing these together and by considering how great his part was in Scott's affairs, we shall better understand Lockhart's true character. Nor shall we be surprised to learn that the large sums realized from the sale of his most important work, *The Life of Scott*, were applied to the discharge of his hero's debts.

In 1854, broken in health, Lockhart went to live with his daughter, Mrs. Hope-Scott, at Abbotsford. His was the room next to that one in which Sir Walter had passed away so peacefully while his beloved Tweed rippled its music that September day twenty-two years before. The Tweed country was a bit bleak in November when Lockhart died. They buried him in old Dryburgh at Scott's feet.

LIFE OF SIR WALTER SCOTT

CHAPTER I

MEMOIR OF HIS EARLY YEARS, WRITTEN BY HIMSELF

Ashestiel, April 26th, 1808.

THE present age has discovered a desire, or rather a rage, for literary anecdote and private history, that may be well permitted to alarm one who has engaged in a certain degree the attention of the public. That I have 5 had more than my own share of popularity, my contemporaries will be as ready to admit as I am to confess that its measure has exceeded not only my hopes, but my merits, and even wishes. I may be therefore permitted, without an extraordinary degree of vanity, to take the 10 precaution of recording a few leading circumstances (they do not merit the name of events) of a very quiet and uniform life — that, should my literary reputation survive my temporal existence, the public may know from good authority all that they are entitled to know of an indi- 15 vidual who has contributed to their amusement.

From the lives of some poets a most important moral lesson may doubtless be derived, and few sermons can be read with so much profit as the Memoirs of Burns,° of Chatterton,° or of Savage.° Were I conscious of any 20 thing peculiar in my own moral character which could render such developement necessary or useful, I would as

B   1

readily consent to it as I would bequeath my body to
dissection, if the operation could tend to point out the
nature and the means of curing any peculiar malady.
But as my habits of thinking and acting, as well as my
5 rank in society, were fixed long before I had attained, or
even pretended to, any poetical reputation, and as it
produced, when acquired, no remarkable change upon
either, it is hardly to be expected that much information
can be derived from minutely investigating frailties,
10 follies, or vices, not very different in number or degree
from those of other men in my situation. As I have not
been blessed with the talents of Burns or Chatterton, I
have been happily exempted from the influence of their
violent passions, exasperated by the struggle of feelings
15 which rose up against the unjust decrees of fortune. Yet,
although I cannot tell of difficulties vanquished, and
distance of rank annihilated by the strength of genius,
those who shall hereafter read this little Memoir may find
in it some hints to be improved, for the regulation of their
20 own minds, or the training those of others.

Every Scottishman has a pedigree. It is a national
prerogative, as unalienable as his pride and his poverty.
My birth was neither distinguished nor sordid. According to the prejudices of my country, it was esteemed
25 *gentle*, as I was connected, though remotely, with ancient
families both by my father's and mother's side. My
father's grandfather was Walter Scott, well known in
Teviotdale° by the surname of *Beardie*. He was the
second son of Walter Scott, first Laird of Raeburn, who
30 was third son of Sir William Scott, and the grandson of
Walter Scott, commonly called in tradition *Auld Watt* of
Harden. I am therefore lineally descended from that
ancient chieftain, whose name I have made to ring in

many a ditty, and from his fair dame, the Flower of
Yarrow° — no bad genealogy for a Border minstrel.
Beardie, my great-grandfather aforesaid, derived his
cognomen from a venerable beard, which he wore unblem-
ished by razor or scissors, in token of his regret for the 5
banished dynasty of Stuart.° It would have been well
that his zeal had stopped there. But he took arms, and
intrigued in their cause, until he lost all he had in the
world, and, as I have heard, run a narrow risk of being
hanged, had it not been for the interference of Anne, 10
Duchess of Buccleuch and Monmouth.

He left three sons. The second, Robert Scott, was my
grandfather. He was originally bred to the sea; but,
being shipwrecked near Dundee in his trial-voyage, he
took such a sincere dislike to that element, that he could 15
not be persuaded to a second attempt. This occasioned
a quarrel between him and his father, who left him to
shift for himself. Robert was one of those active spirits
to whom this was no misfortune. He turned Whig upon
the spot, and fairly abjured his father's politics, and his 20
learned poverty. His chief and relative, Mr. Scott of
Harden, gave him a lease of the farm of Sandy-Knowe,
comprehending the rocks in the centre of which Smailholm
or Sandy-Knowe Tower is situated.

Robert Scott of Sandy-Knowe, married, in 1728, Bar- 25
bara Haliburton, daughter of Thomas Haliburton of Newmains, an ancient and respectable family in Berwickshire.
Among other patrimonial possessions, they enjoyed the
part of Dryburgh, now the property of the Earl of Buchan,
comprehending the ruins of the Abbey. My granduncle, 30
Robert Haliburton, having no male heirs, this estate, as
well as the representation of the family, would have devolved upon my father, and indeed Old Newmains had

settled it upon him; but this was prevented by the misfortunes of my granduncle, a weak silly man, who engaged
in trade, for which he had neither stock nor talents, and
became bankrupt.   The ancient patrimony was sold for a
5 trifle (about £3000), and my father, who might have purchased it with ease, was dissuaded by my grandfather,
who at that time believed a more advantageous purchase
might have been made of some lands which Raeburn
thought of selling.   And thus we have nothing left of
10 Dryburgh, although my father's maternal inheritance, but
the right of stretching our bones where mine may perhaps
be laid ere any· eye but my own glances over these pages.

Walter Scott, my father, was born in 1729, and educated
to the profession of a Writer to the Signet.   In April
15 1758, he married Anne Rutherford, eldest daughter of
Dr. John Rutherford, professor of medicine in the University of Edinburgh.   He was one of those pupils of
Boerhaave,° to whom the school of medicine in our northern metropolis owes its rise, and a man distinguished for
20 professional talent, for lively wit, and for literary acquire-
ments.

My father and mother had a very numerous family,
no fewer, I believe, than twelve children, of whom
many were highly promising, though only five survived
25 very early youth.   I was born, as I believe, on the 15th
August 1771, in a house belonging to my father, at the
head of the College Wynd.   It was pulled down, with
others, to make room for the northern front of the new
College.   I was an uncommonly healthy child, but had
30 nearly died in consequence of my first nurse being ill of a
consumption, a circumstance which she chose to conceal,
though to do so was murder to both herself and me.   She
went privately to consult Dr. Black, the celebrated pro-

fessor of chemistry, who put my father on his guard. The woman was dismissed, and I was consigned to a healthy peasant, who is still alive to boast of her *laddie* being what she calls *a grand gentleman*. I shewed every sign of health and strength until I was about eighteen months old. One night, I have been often told, I shewed great reluctance to be caught and put to bed; and after being chased about the room, was apprehended and consigned to my dormitory with some difficulty. It was the last time I was to shew such personal agility. In the morning, I was discovered to be affected with the fever which often accompanies the cutting of large teeth. It held me three days. On the fourth, when they went to bathe me as usual, they discovered that I had lost the power of my right leg. My grandfather, an excellent anatomist as well as physician, the late worthy Alexander Wood, and many others of the most respectable of the faculty, were consulted. There appeared to be no dislocation or sprain; blisters and other topical remedies were applied in vain. When the efforts of regular physicians had been exhausted, without the slightest success, my anxious parents, during the course of many years, eagerly grasped at every prospect of cure which was held out by the promise of empirics, or of ancient ladies or gentlemen who conceived themselves entitled to recommend various remedies, some of which were of a nature sufficiently singular. But the advice of my grandfather, Dr. Rutherford, that I should be sent to reside in the country, to give the chance of natural exertion, excited by free air and liberty, was first resorted to; and before I have the recollection of the slightest event, I was, agreeably to this friendly counsel, an inmate in the farm-house of Sandy-Knowe.

It is here at Sandy-Knowe, in the residence of my paternal grandfather, already mentioned, that I have the first consciousness of existence; and I recollect distinctly that my situation and appearance were a little whimsical.
5 Among the odd remedies recurred to to aid my lameness, some one had recommended, that so often as a sheep was killed for the use of the family, I should be stripped, and swathed up in the skin, warm as it was flayed from the carcase of the animal. In this Tartar-like habiliment I
10 well remember lying upon the floor of the little parlour in the farm-house, while my grandfather, a venerable old man with white hair, used every excitement to make me try to crawl. This must have happened about my third year, for my grandfather died shortly after that
15 period.

My grandmother continued for some years to take charge of the farm, assisted by my father's second brother, Mr. Thomas Scott, who resided at Crailing, as factor or land-steward for Mr. Scott of Danesfield, then proprietor of
20 that estate. This was during the heat of the American war, and I remember being as anxious on my uncle's weekly visits (for we heard news at no other time) to hear of the defeat of Washington, as if I had had some deep and per-sonal cause of antipathy to him. I know not how this
25 was combined with a very strong prejudice in favour of the Stuart family, which I had originally imbibed from the songs and tales of the Jacobites.° This latter political propensity was deeply confirmed by the stories told in my hearing of the cruelties exercised in the executions at Car-
30 lisle, and in the Highlands, after the battle of Culloden.°
One or two of our own distant relations had fallen on that occasion, and I remember of detesting the name of Cum-berland with more than infant hatred. Mr. Curle, farmer

at Yetbyre, husband of one of my aunts, had been present at their execution; and it was probably from him that I first heard these tragic tales which made so great an impression on me. The local information, which I conceive had some share in forming my future taste and pursuits, 5 I derived from the old songs and tales which then formed the amusement of a retired country family. My grandmother, in whose youth the old Border depredations were matter of recent tradition, used to tell me many a tale of Watt of Harden, Wight Willie of Aikwood, Jamie Telfer of 10 the fair Dodhead, and other heroes — merry men all of the persuasion° and calling of Robin Hood° and Little John.° A more recent hero, but not of less note, was the celebrated *Diel of Littledean*, whom she well remembered, as he had married her mother's sister. Of this extraordinary 15 person I learned many a story, grave and gay, comic and warlike. Two or three old books which lay in the window-seat were explored for my amusement in the tedious winter-days. Automathes,° and Ramsay's° Tea-table Miscellany were my favourites, although at a later period an 20 odd volume of Josephus's° Wars of the Jews divided my partiality.

My kind and affectionate aunt, Miss Janet Scott, whose memory will ever be dear to me, used to read these works to me with admirable patience, until I could repeat long 25 passages by heart. The ballad of Hardyknute I was early master of, to the great annoyance of almost our only visitor, the worthy clergyman of the parish, Dr. Duncan, who had not patience to have a sober chat interrupted by my shouting forth this ditty. Methinks I now see his tall 30 thin emaciated figure, his legs cased in clasped gambadoes, and his face of a length that would have rivalled the Knight of La Mancha's,° and hear him exclaiming, "One may as well speak in the mouth of a cannon as where that child is." With this little acidity, which was natural to him, he was a most excellent and benevolent man, a gentleman in every feeling, and altogether different from those of his 5 order who cringe at the tables of the gentry, or domineer and riot at those of the yeomanry.

I was in my fourth year when my father was advised that the Bath° waters might be of some advantage to my lameness. My affectionate aunt, although such a journey 10 promised to a person of her retired habits any thing but pleasure or amusement, undertook as readily to accompany me to the wells of Bladud,° as if she had expected all the delight that ever the prospect of a watering-place held out to its most impatient visitants. My health was by this 15 time a good deal confirmed by the country air, and the influence of that imperceptible and unfatiguing exercise to which the good sense of my grandfather had subjected me; for when the day was fine, I was usually carried out and laid down beside the old shepherd, among the crags or 20 rocks round which he fed his sheep. The impatience of a child soon inclined me to struggle with my infirmity, and I began by degrees to stand, to walk, and to run. Although the limb affected was much shrunk and contracted, my general health, which was of more importance, 25 was much strengthened by being frequently in the open air; and, in a word, I who in a city had probably been condemned to hopeless and helpless decrepitude, was now a healthy, high-spirited, and, my lameness apart, a sturdy child — *non sine diis animosus infans.*°

30 We went to London by sea, and it may gratify the curiosity of minute biographers to learn that our voyage was performed in the Duchess of Buccleuch, Captain Beatson, master. At London we made a short stay, and saw some

of the common shows exhibited to strangers. When, twenty-five years afterwards, I visited the Tower of London and Westminster Abbey, I was astonished to find how accurate my recollections of these celebrated places of visitation proved to be, and I have ever since trusted 5 more implicitly to my juvenile reminiscences. At Bath, where I lived about a year, I went through all the usual discipline of the pump-room and baths, but I believe without the least advantage to my lameness. During my residence at Bath, I acquired the rudiments of reading 10 at a day-school, kept by an old dame near our lodgings, and I had never a more regular teacher, although I think I did not attend her a quarter of a year. An occasional lesson from my aunt supplied the rest. Afterwards, when grown a big boy, I had a few lessons from Mr. Stalker of 15 Edinburgh, and finally from the Rev. Mr. Cleeve. But I never acquired a just pronunciation, nor could I read with much propriety.

In other respects my residence at Bath is marked by very pleasing recollections. The venerable John Home,° 20 author of Douglas, was then at the watering-place, and paid much attention to my aunt and to me. His wife, who has survived him, was then an invalid, and used to take the air in her carriage on the Downs,° when I was often invited to accompany her. But the most delightful recollections 25 of Bath are dated after the arrival of my uncle, Captain Robert Scott, who introduced me to all the little amusements which suited my age, and above all, to the theatre. The play was As You Like It; and the witchery of the whole scene is alive in my mind at this moment. I made, 30 I believe, noise more than enough, and remember being so much scandalized at the quarrel between Orlando and his brother in the first scene, that I screamed out, "A'n't they brothers?" A few weeks' residence at home convinced me, who had till then been an only child in the house of my grandfather, that a quarrel between brothers was a very natural event.

5 After being a year at Bath, I returned first to Edinburgh, and afterwards for a season to Sandy-Knowe; — and thus the time whiled away till about my eighth year, when it was thought sea-bathing might be of service to my lameness.

10 For this purpose, still under my aunt's protection, I remained some weeks at Prestonpans; a circumstance not worth mentioning, excepting to record my juvenile intimacy with an old military veteran, Dalgetty by name, who had pitched his tent in that little village, after all his 15 campaigns, subsisting upon an ensign's half-pay, though called by courtesy a Captain. As this old gentleman, who had been in all the German wars, found very few to listen to his tales of military feats, he formed a sort of alliance with me, and I used invariably to attend him for the pleas-20 ure of hearing those communications. Sometimes our conversation turned on the American war, which was then raging. It was about the time of Burgoyne's unfortunate expedition, to which my Captain and I augured different conclusions. Somebody had shewed me a map of North 25 America, and, struck with the rugged appearance of the country, and the quantity of lakes, I expressed some doubts on the subject of the General's arriving safely at the end of his journey, which were very indignantly refuted by the Captain. The news of the Saratoga disaster, 30 while it gave me a little triumph, rather shook my intimacy with the veteran.

From Prestonpans I was transported back to my father's house in George's Square, which continued to be my most established place of residence, until my marriage in 1797. I felt the change from being a single indulged brat, to becoming a member of a large family, very severely; for under the gentle government of my kind grandmother, who was meekness itself, and of my aunt, who, though of 5 an higher temper, was exceedingly attached to me, I had acquired a degree of licence which could not be permitted in a large family. I had sense enough, however, to bend my temper to my new circumstances; but such was the agony which I internally experienced, that I have guarded 10 against nothing more in the education of my own family, than against their acquiring habits of self-willed caprice and domination. I found much consolation during this period of mortification, in the partiality of my mother. She joined to a light and happy temper of mind a strong 15 turn to study poetry and works of imagination. She was sincerely devout, but her religion was, as became her sex, of a cast less austere than my father's. Still, the discipline of the Presbyterian Sabbath was severely strict, and I think injudiciously so. Although Bunyan's° Pil- 20 grim, Gesner's° Death of Abel, Rowe's° Letters, and one or two other books, which, for that reason, I still have a favour for, were admitted to relieve the gloom of one dull sermon succeeding to another — there was far too much tedium annexed to the duties of the day; and in the end 25 it did none of us any good.

My week-day tasks were more agreeable. My lameness and my solitary habits had made me a tolerable reader, and my hours of leisure were usually spent in reading aloud to my mother Pope's° translation of Homer,° which, ex- 30 cepting a few traditionary ballads, and the songs in Allan Ramsay's Evergreen, was the first poetry which I perused. My mother had good natural taste and great feeling: she

used to make me pause upon those passages which expressed generous and worthy sentiments, and if she could not divert me from those which were descriptive of battle and tumult, she contrived at least to divide my atten-
5 tion between them. My own enthusiasm, however, was chiefly awakened by the wonderful and the terrible — the common taste of children, but in which I have remained a child even unto this day. I got by heart, not as a task, but almost without intending it, the passages with which
10 I was most pleased, and used to recite them aloud, both when alone and to others — more willingly, however, in my hours of solitude, for I had observed some auditors smile, and I dreaded ridicule at that time of life more than I have ever done since.

15 In [1778] I was sent to the second class of the Grammar School, or High School of Edinburgh, then taught by Mr. Luke Fraser, a good Latin scholar and a very worthy man. Though I had received, with my brothers, in private, lessons of Latin from Mr. James French, now a
20 minister of the Kirk of Scotland, I was nevertheless rather behind the class in which I was placed both in years and in progress. This was a real disadvantage, and one to which a boy of lively temper and talents ought to be as little exposed as one who might be less expected to make
25 up his lee-way, as it is called. The situation has the unfortunate effect of reconciling a boy of the former character (which in a posthumous work I may claim for my own) to holding a subordinate station among his class-fellows — to which he would otherwise affix disgrace. There is also,
30 from the constitution of the High School, a certain danger not sufficiently attended to. The boys take precedence in their *places*, as they are called, according to their merit, and it requires a long while, in general, before even a

clever boy, if he falls behind the class, or is put into one for which he is not quite ready, can force his way to the situation which his abilities really entitle him to hold. But, in the meanwhile, he is necessarily led to be the associate and companion of those inferior spirits with whom he is placed; for the system of precedence, though it does not limit the general intercourse among the boys, has nevertheless the effect of throwing them into clubs and coteries, according to the vicinity of the seats they hold. A boy of good talents, therefore, placed even for a time among his inferiors, especially if they be also his elders, learns to participate in their pursuits and objects of ambition, which are usually very distinct from the acquisition of learning; and it will be well if he does not also imitate them in that indifference which is contented with bustling over a lesson so as to avoid punishment, without affecting superiority or aiming at reward. It was probably owing to this circumstance, that, although at a more advanced period of life I have enjoyed considerable facility in acquiring languages, I did not make any great figure at the High School — or, at least, any exertions which I made were desultory and little to be depended on.

Our class contained some very excellent scholars. As for myself, I glanced like a meteor from one end of the class to the other, and commonly disgusted my kind master as much by negligence and frivolity, as I occasionally pleased him by flashes of intellect and talent. Among my companions, my good-nature and a flow of ready imagination rendered me very popular. Boys are uncommonly just in their feelings, and at least equally generous. My lameness, and the efforts which I made to supply that disadvantage, by making up in address what I wanted in activity, engaged the latter principle in my favour; and

in the winter play hours, when hard exercise was impossible, my tales used to assemble an admiring audience round Lucky Brown's fire-side, and happy was he that could sit next to the inexhaustible narrator.   I was also,
5 though often negligent of my own task, always ready to assist my friends; and hence I had a little party of staunch partisans and adherents, stout of hand and heart, though somewhat dull of head — the very tools for raising a hero to eminence.   So, on the whole, I made a brighter figure
10 in the *yards* than in the *class*.

After having been three years under Mr. Fraser, our class was, in the usual routine of the school, turned over to Dr. Adam, the Rector.   It was from this respectable man that I first learned the value of the knowledge I had
15 hitherto considered only as a burdensome task.   It was the fashion to remain two years at his class, where we read Cæsar, and Livy, and Sallust, in prose; Virgil, Horace, and Terence, in verse.   I had by this time mastered, in some degree, the difficulties of the language, and began to
20 be sensible of its beauties.   This was really gathering grapes from thistles; nor shall I soon forget the swelling of my little pride when the Rector pronounced, that though many of my school-fellows understood the Latin better, *Gualterus Scott* was behind few in following and enjoying
25 the author's meaning.   Thus encouraged, I distinguished myself by some attempts at poetical versions from Horace and Virgil.   Dr. Adam used to invite his scholars to such essays, but never made them tasks.   I gained some distinction upon these occasions, and the Rector in future took
30 much notice of me; and his judicious mixture of censure and praise went far to counterbalance my habits of indolence and inattention.   I saw I was expected to do well, and I was piqued in honour to vindicate my master's

favourable opinion. I climbed, therefore, to the first form; and, though I never made a first-rate Latinist, my school-fellows, and what was of more consequence, I myself, considered that I had a character of learning to maintain. Dr. Adam, to whom I owed so much, never 5 failed to remind me of my obligations when I had made some figure in the literary world. He was, indeed, deeply imbued with that fortunate vanity which alone could induce a man who has arms to pare and burn a muir,° to submit to the yet more toilsome task of cultivating youth. 10

From Dr. Adam's class I should, according to the usual routine, have proceeded immediately to college. But, fortunately, I was not yet to lose, by a total dismission from constraint, the acquaintance with the Latin which I had acquired. My health had become rather delicate from 15 rapid growth, and my father was easily persuaded to allow me to spend half-a-year at Kelso with my kind aunt, Miss Janet Scott, whose inmate I again became. It was hardly worth mentioning that I had frequently visited her during our short vacations. 20

At this time she resided in a small house, situated very pleasantly in a large garden, to the eastward of the church-yard of Kelso, which extended down to the Tweed. My time was here left entirely to my own disposal excepting for about four hours in the day, when I was expected to 25 attend the Grammar-school of the village. The teacher, at that time, was Mr. Lancelot Whale, an excellent classical scholar, a humourist, and a worthy man.

In the mean while my acquaintance with English litera-ture was gradually extending itself. In the intervals of 30 my school hours I had always perused with avidity such books of history or poetry or voyages and travels as chance presented to me — not forgetting the usual, or rather ten

times the usual, quantity of fairy tales, eastern stories,
romances, &c.   These studies were totally unregulated and
undirected.   My tutor thought it almost a sin to open a
profane play or poem; and my mother, besides that she
5 might be in some degree trammelled by the religious
scruples which he suggested, had no longer the opportunity to hear me read poetry as formerly.   I found, however, in her dressing-room (where I slept at one time) some
odd volumes of Shakspeare, nor can I easily forget the
10 rapture with which I sate up in my shirt reading them by
the light of a fire in her apartment, until the bustle of the
family rising from supper warned me it was time to creep
back to my bed, where I was supposed to have been safely
deposited since nine o'clock.   Chance, however, threw in
15 my way a poetical preceptor.   This was no other than the
excellent and benevolent Dr. Blacklock, well known at that
time as a literary character.   I know not how I attracted
his attention, and that of some of the young men who
boarded in his family; but so it was that I became a fre-
20 quent and favoured guest.   The kind old man opened to
me the stores of his library, and through his recommendation I became intimate with Ossian° and Spenser.°   I was
delighted with both, yet I think chiefly with the latter
poet.   The tawdry repetitions of the Ossianic phraseology
25 disgusted me rather sooner than might have been expected
from my age.   But Spenser I could have read for ever.
Too young to trouble myself about the allegory, I considered all the knights and ladies and dragons and giants
in their outward and exoteric sense, and God only knows
30 how delighted I was to find myself in such society.   As I
had always a wonderful facility in retaining in my memory
whatever verses pleased me, the quantity of Spenser's
stanzas which I could repeat was really marvellous.   But

this memory of mine was a very fickle ally, and has through my whole life acted merely upon its own capricious motion, and might have enabled me to adopt old Beattie of Meikledale's answer, when complimented by a certain reverend divine on the strength of the same faculty : — "No, sir," answered the old Borderer, "I have no command of my memory. It only retains what hits my fancy, and probably, sir, if you were to preach to me for two hours, I would not be able when you finished to remember a word you had been saying." My memory was precisely of the same kind : it seldom failed to preserve most tenaciously a favourite passage of poetry, a play-house ditty, or, above all, a Border-raid ballad ; but names, dates, and the other technicalities of history, escaped me in a most melancholy degree. The philosophy of history, a much more important subject, was also a sealed book at this period of my life ; but I gradually assembled much of what was striking and picturesque in historical narrative ; and when, in riper years, I attended more to the deduction of general principles, I was furnished with a powerful host of examples in illustration of them. I was, in short, like an ignorant gamester, who kept up a good hand until he knew how to play it.

I left the High School, therefore, with a great quantity of general information, ill arranged, indeed, and collected without system, yet deeply impressed upon my mind ; readily assorted by my power of connexion and memory, and gilded, if I may be permitted to say so, by a vivid and active imagination. If my studies were not under any direction at Edinburgh, in the country, it may be well imagined, they were less so. A respectable subscription library, a circulating library of ancient standing, and some private book-shelves, were open to my random perusal,

c

and I waded into the stream like a blind man into a ford, without the power of searching my way, unless by grop-ing for it.   My appetite for books was as ample and in-discriminating as it was indefatigable, and I since have
5 had too frequently reason to repent that few ever read so much, and to so little purpose.

Among the valuable acquisitions I made about this time, was an acquaintance with Tasso's° Jerusalem Delivered, through the flat medium of Mr. Hoole's° translation.   But
10 above all, I then first became acquainted with Bishop Percy's° Reliques of Ancient Poetry.   As I had been from infancy devoted to legendary lore of this nature, and only reluctantly withdrew my attention, from the scarcity of materials and the rudeness of those which I possessed, it
15 may be imagined, but cannot be described, with what de-light I saw pieces of the same kind which had amused my childhood, and still continued in secret the Delilahs° of my imagination, considered as the subject of sober research, grave commentary, and apt illustration, by an editor who
20 shewed his poetical genius was capable of emulating the best qualities of what his pious labour preserved.   I re-member well the spot where I read these volumes for the first time.   It was beneath a huge platanus-tree, in the ruins of what had been intended for an old-fashioned ar-
25 bour in the *garden* I have mentioned.   The summer-day sped onward so fast, that notwithstanding the sharp ap-petite of thirteen, I forgot the hour of dinner, was sought for with anxiety, and was still found entranced in my in-tellectual banquet.   To read and to remember was in this
30 instance the same thing, and henceforth I overwhelmed my school-fellows, and all who would hearken to me, with tragical recitations from the ballads of Bishop Percy.   The first time, too, I could scrape a few shillings together,

which were not common occurrences with me, I bought unto myself a copy of these beloved volumes; nor do I believe I ever read a book half so frequently, or with half the enthusiasm. About this period also I became acquainted with the works of Richardson,° and those of 5 Mackenzie° — (whom in later years I became entitled to call my friend) — with Fielding,° Smollet,° and some others of our best novelists.

To this period also I can trace distinctly the awaking of that delightful feeling for the beauties of natural objects 10 which has never since deserted me. The neighbourhood of Kelso, the most beautiful, if not the most romantic village in Scotland, is eminently calculated to awaken these ideas. It presents objects, not only grand in themselves, but venerable from their association. The meeting of two 15 superb rivers, the Tweed and the Teviot, both renowned in song — the ruins of an ancient Abbey — the more distant vestiges of Roxburgh Castle — the modern mansion of Fleurs, which is so situated as to combine the ideas of ancient baronial grandeur with those of modern taste — 20 are in themselves objects of the first class; yet are so mixed, united, and melted among a thousand other beauties of a less prominent description, that they harmonize into one general picture, and please rather by unison than by concord. I believe I have written unintelligibly upon 25 this subject, but it is fitter for the pencil than the pen. The romantic feelings which I have described as predominating in my mind, naturally rested upon and associated themselves with these grand features of the landscape around me; and the historical incidents, or traditional 30 legends connected with many of them, gave to my admiration a sort of intense impression of reverence, which at times made my heart feel too big for its bosom. From this time the love of natural beauty, more especially when combined with ancient ruins, or remains of our fathers' piety or splendour, became with me an insatiable passion, which, if circumstances had permitted, I would willingly 5 have gratified by travelling over half the globe.

I was recalled to Edinburgh about the time when the College meets, and put at once to the Humanity class, under Mr. Hill, and the first Greek class, taught by Mr. Dalzell. The former held the reins of discipline very 10 loosely, and though beloved by his students — for he was a good-natured man as well as a good scholar — he had not the art of exciting our attention as well as liking. This was a dangerous character with whom to trust one who relished labour as little as I did; and amid the riot of his 15 class I speedily lost much of what I had learned under Adam and Whale. At the Greek class, I might have made a better figure, for Professor Dalzell maintained a great deal of authority, and was not only himself an admirable scholar, but was always deeply interested in the progress of 20 his students. But here lay the villany. Almost all my companions who had left the High School at the same time with myself, had acquired a smattering of Greek before they came to College. I, alas! had none; and finding myself far inferior to all my fellow-students, I could hit 25 upon no better mode of vindicating my equality than by professing my contempt for the language, and my resolution not to learn it. A youth who died early, himself an excellent Greek scholar, saw my negligence and folly with pain, instead of contempt. He came to call on me in 30 George's Square, and pointed out in the strongest terms the silliness of the conduct I had adopted, told me I was distinguished by the name of the *Greek Blockhead*, and exhorted me to redeem my reputation while it was called

to-day. My stubborn pride received this advice with
sulky civility; the birth of my Mentor (whose name was
Archibald, the son of an inn-keeper) did not, as I thought
in my folly, authorize him to intrude upon me his advice.
The other was not sharp-sighted, or his consciousness of a 5
generous intention overcame his resentment. He offered
me his daily and nightly assistance, and pledged himself
to bring me forward with the foremost of my class. I felt
some twinges of conscience, but they were unable to pre-
vail over my pride and self-conceit. The poor lad left me 10
more in sorrow than in anger, nor did we ever meet again.
All hopes of my progress in the Greek were now over;
insomuch that when we were required to write essays on
the authors we had studied, I had the audacity to produce
a composition in which I weighed Homer against Ariosto, 15
and pronounced him wanting in the balance. I supported
this heresy by a profusion of bad reading and flimsy argument. The wrath of the Professor was extreme, while
at the same time he could not suppress his surprise at the
quantity of out-of-the-way knowledge which I displayed. 20
He pronounced upon me the severe sentence — that dunce
I was, and dunce was to remain — which, however, my
excellent and learned friend lived to revoke over a bottle
of Burgundy, at our literary Club at Fortune's, of which
he was a distinguished member. 25
Meanwhile, as if to eradicate my slightest tincture of
Greek, I fell ill during the middle of Mr. Dalzell's second
class, and migrated a second time to Kelso — where I again
continued a long time reading what and how I pleased, and
of course reading nothing but what afforded me immediate 30
entertainment. The only thing which saved my mind
from utter dissipation, was that turn for historical pursuit,
which never abandoned me even at the idlest period. I

had forsworn the Latin classics for no reason I know of,
unless because they were akin to the Greek; but the occasional perusal of Buchanan's° history, that of Mathew
of Paris,° and other monkish chronicles, kept up a kind of
5 familiarity with the language even in its rudest state.
But I forgot the very letters of the Greek alphabet; a
loss never to be repaired, considering what that language
is, and who they were who employed it in their compositions.

10   About this period — or soon afterwards — my father
judged it proper I should study mathematics; a study
upon which I entered with all the ardour of novelty. My
tutor was an aged person, Dr. MacFait, who had in his
time been distinguished as a teacher of this science. Age,
15 however, and some domestic inconveniences, had diminished his pupils, and lessened his authority amongst the few
who remained. I think, that had I been more fortunately
placed for instruction, or had I had the spur of emulation,
I might have made some progress in this science, of which,
20 under the circumstances I have mentioned, I only acquired
a very superficial smattering.

    In other studies I was rather more fortunate. I made
some progress in Ethics under Professor John Bruce, and
was selected as one of his students whose progress he ap-
25 proved, to read an essay, before Principal Robertson. I
was farther instructed in Moral Philosophy at the class of
Mr. Dugald Stewart, whose striking and impressive elo-
quence riveted the attention even of the most volatile
student. To sum up my academical studies, I attended
30 the class of History, then taught by the present Lord
Woodhouselee, and, as far as I remember, no others, excepting those of the Civil and Municipal Law. So that, if
my learning be flimsy and inaccurate, the reader must

have some compassion even for an idle workman who had so narrow a foundation to build upon. If, however, it should ever fall to the lot of youth to peruse these pages — let such a reader remember, that it is with the deepest regret that I recollect in my manhood the opportunities of learning which I neglected in my youth; that through every part of my literary career I have felt pinched and hampered by my own ignorance; and that I would at this moment give half the reputation I have had the good fortune to acquire, if by doing so I could rest the remaining part upon a sound foundation of learning and science.

I imagine my father's reason for sending me to so few classes in the College, was a desire that I should apply myself particularly to my legal studies. He had not determined whether I should fill the situation of an Advocate or a Writer; but judiciously considering the technical knowledge of the latter to be useful at least, if not essential, to a barrister, he resolved I should serve the ordinary apprenticeship of five years to his own profession. I accordingly entered into indentures with my father about 1785–6, and entered upon the dry and barren wilderness of forms and conveyances.

I cannot reproach myself with being entirely an idle apprentice — far less, as the reader might reasonably have expected,

"A clerk foredoom'd my father's soul to cross."

The drudgery, indeed, of the office I disliked, and the confinement I altogether detested; but I loved my father, and I felt the rational pride and pleasure of rendering myself useful to him. I was ambitious also; and among my companions in labour, the only way to gratify ambition was to labour hard and well. Other circumstances reconciled

me in some measure to the confinement. The allowance
for copy-money furnished a little fund for the *menus
plaisirs*° of the circulating library and the Theatre; and
this was no trifling incentive to labour. When actually
5 at the oar, no man could pull it harder than I; and I
remember writing upwards of 120 folio pages with no
interval either for food or rest. Again, the hours of attendance on the office were lightened by the power of
choosing my own books, and reading them in my own way,
10 which often consisted in beginning at the middle or the
end of a volume. A deceased friend, who was a fellow-
apprentice with me, used often to express his surprise
that, after such a hop-step-and-jump perusal, I knew
as much of the book as he had been able to acquire
15 from reading it in the usual manner. My desk usually
contained a store of most miscellaneous volumes, especially works of fiction of every kind, which were my supreme delight. I might except novels, unless those of the
better and higher class; for though I read many of them,
20 yet it was with more selection than might have been expected. The whole Jemmy and Jenny Jessamy° tribe I
abhorred; and it required the art of Burney,° or the feeling
of Mackenzie,° to fix my attention upon a domestic tale.
But all that was adventurous and romantic I devoured
25 without much discrimination, and I really believe I have
read as much nonsense of this class as any man now living.
Everything which touched on knight-errantry was particularly acceptable to me, and I soon attempted to imitate
what I so greatly admired. My efforts, however, were in
30 the manner of the tale-teller, not of the bard.
　My greatest intimate, from the days of my school-tide,
was Mr. John Irving, now a Writer to the Signet. We
lived near each other, and by joint agreement were wont,

each of us, to compose a romance for the other's amusement. These legends, in which the martial and the miraculous always predominated, we rehearsed to each other during our walks, which were usually directed to the most solitary spots about Arthur's Seat and Salisbury Crags. 5 We naturally sought seclusion, for we were conscious no small degree of ridicule would have attended our amusement, if the nature of it had become known. Whole holidays were spent in this singular pastime, which continued for two or three years, and had, I believe, no small effect 10 in directing the turn of my imagination to the chivalrous and romantic in poetry and prose.

Meanwhile, the translations of Mr. Hoole having made me acquainted with Tasso and Ariosto, I learned from his notes on the latter, that the Italian language contained a 15 fund of romantic lore. A part of my earnings was dedicated to an Italian class which I attended twice a-week, and rapidly acquired some proficiency. I had previously renewed and extended my knowledge of the French language, from the same principle of romantic research. 20 Tressan's romances, the Bibliothèque Bleue, and Bibliothèque de Romans, were already familiar to me; and I now acquired similar intimacy with the works of Dante, Boiardo, Pulci, and other eminent Italian authors. I fastened also, like a tiger, upon every collection of old 25 songs or romances which chance threw in my way, or which my scrutiny was able to discover on the dusty shelves of James Sibbald's circulating library in the Parliament Square. This collection, now dismantled and dispersed, contained at that time many rare and curious 30 works, seldom found in such a collection. Mr. Sibbald himself, a man of rough manners but of some taste and judgment, cultivated music and poetry, and in his shop

I had a distant view of some literary characters, besides
the privilege of ransacking the stores of old French and
Italian books, which were in little demand among the bulk
of his subscribers.   Here I saw the unfortunate Andrew
5 Macdonald,° author of Vimonda; and here, too, I saw at
a distance, the boast of Scotland, Robert Burns.

My frame gradually became hardened with my constitution, and being both tall and muscular, I was rather
disfigured than disabled by my lameness.   This personal
10 disadvantage did not prevent me from taking much
exercise on horseback, and making long journeys on foot,
in the course of which I often walked from twenty to thirty
miles a day.   A distinct instance occurs to me.   I remember walking with poor James Ramsay, my fellow-
15 apprentice, now no more, and two other friends, to breakfast at Prestonpans.   We spent the forenoon in visiting
the ruins at Seton and the field of battle at Preston° —
dined at Prestonpans on *tiled haddocks*° very sumptuously
— drank half a bottle of port each, and returned in the
20 evening.   This could not be less than thirty miles, nor do
I remember being at all fatigued upon the occasion.

These excursions on foot or horseback formed by far
my most favourite amusement.   I have all my life delighted in travelling, though I have never enjoyed that
25 pleasure upon a large scale.   It was a propensity which I
sometimes indulged so unduly as to alarm and vex my
parents.   Wood, water, wilderness itself, had an inex-
pressible charm for me, and I had a dreamy way of going
much further than I intended, so that unconsciously my
30 return was protracted, and my parents had sometimes
serious cause of uneasiness.   For example, I once set
out with Mr. George Abercromby (the son of the immortal
General°), Mr. William Clerk, and some others, to fish

in the lake above Howgate, and the stream which descends from it into the Esk. We breakfasted at Howgate, and fished the whole day; and while we were on our return next morning, I was easily seduced by William Clerk, then a great intimate, to visit Pennycuik-House, the seat of his family. Here he and John Irving, and I for their sake, were overwhelmed with kindness by the late Sir John Clerk and his lady, the present Dowager Lady Clerk. The pleasure of looking at fine pictures, the beauty of the place, and the flattering hospitality of the owners, drowned all recollection of home for a day or two. Meanwhile our companions, who had walked on without being aware of our digression, returned to Edinburgh without us, and excited no small alarm in my father's household. At length, however, they became accustomed to my escapades. My father used to protest to me on such occasions that he thought I was born to be a strolling pedlar; and though the prediction was intended to mortify my conceit, I am not sure that I altogether disliked it. I was now familiar with Shakspeare, and thought of Autolycus's° song —

> "Jog on, jog on, the foot-path way,
>   And merrily hent the stile-a;
> A merry heart goes all the day,
>   Your sad tires in a mile-a."

My principal object in these excursions was the pleasure of seeing romantic scenery, or what afforded me at least equal pleasure, the places which had been distinguished by remarkable historical events. The delight with which I regarded the former, of course had general approbation, but I often found it difficult to procure sympathy with the interest I felt in the latter. Yet to me, the wandering

over the field of Bannockburn° was the source of more
exquisite pleasure than gazing upon the celebrated landscape from the battlements of Stirling castle. I do not
by any means infer that I was dead to the feeling of pic-
5 turesque scenery; on the contrary, few delighted more
in its general effect. But I was unable with the eye of
a painter to dissect the various parts of the scene, to comprehend how the one bore upon the other, to estimate the
effect which various features of the view had in producing
10 its leading and general effect. I have never, indeed, been
capable of doing this with precision or nicety, though my
latter studies have led me to amend and arrange my
original ideas upon the subject. Even the humble ambition, which I long cherished, of making sketches of
15 those places which interested me, from a defect of eye
or of hand was totally ineffectual. After long study and
many efforts, I was unable to apply the elements of per-
spective or of shade to the scene before me, and was
obliged to relinquish in despair an art which I was most
20 anxious to practise. But shew me an old castle or a
field of battle, and I was at home at once, filled it with
its combatants in their proper costume, and overwhelmed
my hearers by the enthusiasm of my description. In
crossing Magus Moor, near St. Andrews, the spirit moved
25 me to give a picture of the assassination of the Archbishop
of St. Andrews to some fellow-travellers with whom I was
accidentally associated, and one of them, though well
acquainted with the story, protested my narrative had
frightened away his night's sleep. I mention this to shew
30 the distinction between a sense of the picturesque in
action and in scenery. If I have since been able in poetry
to trace with some success the principles of the latter,
it has always been with reference to its general and lead-

ing features, or under some alliance with moral feeling;
and even this proficiency has cost me study. — Meanwhile I endeavoured to make amends for my ignorance
of drawing, by adopting a sort of technical memory
respecting the scenes I visited. Wherever I went I cut 5
a piece of a branch from a tree — these constituted what
I called my log-book; and I intended to have a set of
chessmen out of them, each having reference to the place
where it was cut — as the kings from Falkland° and Holy-
Rood°; the queens from Queen Mary's yew tree at Crooks- 10
ton°; the bishops from abbeys or episcopal palaces; the
knights from baronial residences; the rooks from royal
fortresses; and the pawns generally from places worthy
of historical note. But this whimsical design I never
carried into execution. 15

With music it was even worse than with painting. My
mother was anxious we should at least learn Psalmody,
but the incurable defects of my voice and ear soon drove
my teacher to despair. It is only by long practice that I
have acquired the power of selecting or distinguishing 20
melodies; and although now few things delight or affect
me more than a simple tune sung with feeling, yet I am
sensible that even this pitch of musical taste has only
been gained by attention and habit, and, as it were, by
my feeling of the words being associated with the tune. 25
I have therefore been usually unsuccessful in composing
words to a tune, although my friend Dr. Clarke, and other
musical composers, have sometimes been able to make a
happy union between their music and my poetry.

In other points, however, I began to make some amends 30
for the irregularity of my education. It is well known
that in Edinburgh one great spur to emulation among
youthful students is in those associations called *literary*

societies, formed not only for the purpose of debate, but of composition. I am particularly obliged to this sort of club for introducing me about my seventeenth year into the society which at one time I had entirely dropped;
5 for, from the time of my illness at college, I had had little or no intercourse with any of my class-companions, one or two only excepted. Now, however, about 1788, I began to feel and take my ground in society. A ready wit, a good deal of enthusiasm, and a perception that soon
10 ripened into tact and observation of character, rendered me an acceptable companion to many young men whose acquisitions in philosophy and science were infinitely superior to any thing I could boast.

Looking back on these times, I cannot applaud in all
15 respects the way in which our days were spent. There was too much idleness, and sometimes too much conviviality: but our hearts were warm, our minds honourably bent on knowledge and literary distinction; and if I, certainly the least informed of the party, may be permitted
20 to bear witness, we were not without the fair and creditable means of attaining the distinction to which we aspired. In this society I was naturally led to correct my former useless course of reading; for — feeling myself greatly inferior to my companions in metaphysical philosophy
25 and other branches of regular study — I laboured, not without some success, to acquire at least such a portion of knowledge as might enable me to maintain my rank in conversation. In this I succeeded pretty well; but unfortunately then, as often since through my life, I incurred
30 the deserved ridicule of my friends from the superficial nature of my acquisitions, which being, in the mercantile phrase, *got up* for society, very often proved flimsy in the texture; and thus the gifts of an uncommonly retentive

memory and acute powers of perception were sometimes detrimental to their possessor, by encouraging him to a presumptuous reliance upon them.

Amidst these studies, and in this society, the time of my apprenticeship elapsed; and in 1790, or thereabouts, it became necessary that I should seriously consider to which department of the law I was to attach myself. My father behaved with the most parental kindness. He offered, if I preferred his own profession, immediately to take me into partnership with him, which, though his business was much diminished, still afforded me an immediate prospect of a handsome independence. But he did not disguise his wish that I should relinquish this situation to my younger brother, and embrace the more ambitious profession of the bar. I had little hesitation in making my choice — for I was never very fond of money; and in no other particular do the professions admit of a comparison. The bar, though I was conscious of my deficiencies as a public speaker, was the line of ambition and liberty; it was that also for which most of my contemporary friends were destined. And, lastly, although I would willingly have relieved my father of the labours of his business, yet I saw plainly we could not have agreed on some particulars if we had attempted to conduct it together, and that I should disappoint his expectations if I did not turn to the bar. So to that object my studies were directed with great ardour and perseverance during the years 1789, 1790, 1791, 1792.

This course of study enabled *me* to pass with credit the usual trials, which, by the regulations of the Faculty of Advocates, must be undergone by every candidate for admission into their body. My friend William Clerk and I passed these ordeals on the same days — namely, the

Civil Law° trial on the [30th June 1791], and the Scots
Law trial on the [6th July 1792]. On the [11th July
1792], we both assumed the gown with all its duties and
honours.

5   My progress in life during these two or three years had
been gradually enlarging my acquaintance, and facilitating
my entrance into good company. My father and mother,
already advanced in life, saw little society at home, excepting that of near relations, or upon particular occasions,
10 so that I was left to form connexions in a great measure
for myself. It is not difficult for a youth with a real desire
to please and be pleased, to make his way into good society
in Edinburgh — or indeed anywhere; and my family
connexions, if they did not greatly further, had nothing to
15 embarrass my progress. I was a gentleman, and so
welcome anywhere, if so be I could behave myself, as
Tony Lumpkin° says, "in a concatenation accordingly."

*   *   *   *   *   *   *

CHAPTER II

Call to the Bar — Early Friendships and Pursuits — Disappointment in Love — Excursions to the Highlands and Border — Publication of Ballads after Bürger — Light-Horse Volunteers — 1792-1797.

As may be said, I believe, with perfect truth of every really great man, Scott was self-educated in every branch of knowledge which he ever turned to account in the works of his genius — and he has himself told us that his real studies were those lonely and desultory ones of which 5 he has given a copy in the first chapter of Waverley, where the hero is represented as "driving through the sea of books, like a vessel without pilot or rudder;" that is to say, obeying nothing but the strong breath of native inclination. The *literary* details of that chapter may all 10 be considered as autobiographical.

In all the studies of the two or three years preceding his call to the bar, his chief associate was William Clerk; and, indeed, of all the connections he formed in life, I now doubt if there was one to whom he owed more. Yet 15 both in his adoption, soon after that friendship began, of a somewhat superior tone of manners and habits generally, and in his ultimate decision for the bar, as well as in his strenuous preparation during a considerable space of time for that career, there is little question that another 20 influence must have powerfully co-operated. His friends, I have heard more than one of them confess, used often to rally him on the coldness of his nature. By degrees they discovered that he had, from almost the dawn of the

passions, cherished a secret attachment, which continued,
through all the most perilous stage of life, to act as a
romantic charm in safeguard of virtue. This was the
early and innocent affection to which we owe the tender-
5 est pages, not only of Redgauntlet, but of the Lay of
the Last Minstrel, and of Rokeby. In all of these
works the heroine has certain distinctive features, drawn
from one and the same haunting dream of his manly
adolescence.

10 It was about 1790, according to Mr. William Clerk,
that Scott was observed to lay aside that carelessness, not
to say slovenliness, as to dress, which used to furnish
matter for joking at the beginning of their acquaintance.
He now did himself more justice in these little matters,
15 became fond of mixing in general female society, and, as
his friend expresses it, "began to set up for a squire of
dames."

His personal appearance at this time was not unengaging.
A lady of high rank, who well remembers him in the Old
20 Assembly Rooms, says, "Young Walter Scott was a comely
creature." [1] He had outgrown the sallowness of early ill
health, and had a fresh brilliant complexion. His eyes
were clear, open, and well set, with a changeful radiance,
to which teeth of the most perfect regularity and whiteness
25 lent their assistance, while the noble expanse and elevation
of the brow gave to the whole aspect a dignity far above
the charm of mere features. His smile was always delightful; and I can easily fancy the peculiar intermixture
of tenderness and gravity, with playful innocent hilarity
30 and humour in the expression, as being well calculated
to fix a fair lady's eye. His figure, excepting the blemish

---

[1] The late Duchess Countess of Sutherland.

in one limb, must in those days have been eminently handsome; tall, much above the usual standard, it was cast in the very mould of a young Hercules°; the head set on with singular grace, the throat and chest after the truest model of the antique, the hands delicately finished; 5 the whole outline that of extraordinary vigour, without as yet a touch of clumsiness. When he had acquired a little facility of manner, his conversation must have been such as could have dispensed with any exterior advantages, and certainly brought swift forgiveness for the one unkind- 10 ness of nature. I have heard him, in talking of this part of his life, say, with an arch simplicity of look and tone, which those who were familiar with him can fill in for themselves — "It was a proud night with me when I first found that a pretty young woman could think it 15 worth her while to sit and talk with me, hour after hour, in a corner of the ball-room, while all the world were capering in our view."

I believe, however, that the "pretty young woman" here specially alluded to, had occupied his attention before 20 he ever appeared in the Edinburgh Assembly Rooms, or any of his friends took note of him as "setting up for a squire of dames." I have been told that their acquaintance began in the Greyfriars' churchyard, where rain beginning to fall one Sunday as the congregation were 25 dispersing, Scott happened to offer his umbrella, and the tender being accepted, so escorted *the lady of the green mantle* to her residence, which proved to be at no great distance from his own. To return from church together had, it seems, grown into something like a custom before 30 they met in society, Mrs. Scott being of the party.° It then appeared that she and the lady's mother had been companions in their youth, though, both living secludedly,

they had scarcely seen each other for many years; and the
two matrons now renewed their former intercourse.
But no acquaintance appears to have existed between the
fathers of the young people, until things had advanced
5 in appearance farther than met the approbation of the
good Clerk to the Signet.

Being aware that the young lady — Margaret, daughter
of Sir John and Lady Jane Stuart Belches of Invermay,
had prospects of fortune far above his son's, Mr. Scott
10 conceived it his duty to give her parents warning that he
observed a degree of intimacy which, if allowed to go on,
might involve the parties in pain and disappointment.
He had heard his son talk of a contemplated excursion
to the part of the country in which his neighbour's estates
15 lay, and not doubting that Walter's real object was different
from that which he announced, introduced himself with a
frank statement that he wished no such affair to proceed,
without the express sanction of those most interested in
the happiness of persons as yet too young to calculate
20 consequences for themselves. — The northern Baronet
had heard nothing of the young apprentice's intended
excursion, and appeared to treat the whole business very
lightly. He thanked Mr. Scott for his scrupulous attention — but added, that he believed he was mistaken;
25 and this paternal interference, which Walter did not hear
of till long afterwards, produced no change in his relations
with the object of his growing attachment.

I have neither the power nor the wish to give in detail
the sequel of this story. It is sufficient to say, at present,
30 that after he had through several years nourished the
dream of an ultimate union with this lady, his hopes
terminated in her being married to the late Sir William
Forbes, of Pitsligo, Baronet, a gentleman of the highest

character, to whom some affectionate allusions occur in one of the greatest of his works, and who lived to act the part of a most generous friend to his early rival throughout the anxieties and distresses of 1826 and 1827.

I venture to recall here to the reader's memory the open- 5 ing of the twelfth chapter of Peveril of the Peak, written twenty-six years after this youthful disappointment: — "The period at which love is formed for the first time, and felt most strongly, is seldom that at which there is much prospect of its being brought to a happy issue. The state 10 of artificial society opposes many complicated obstructions to early marriages ; and the chance is very great that such obstacles prove insurmountable. In fine, there are few men who do not look back in secret to some period of their youth, at which a sincere and early affection was 15 repulsed, or betrayed, or became abortive from opposing circumstances. It is these little passages of secret history which leave a tinge of romance in every bosom, scarce permitting us, even in the most busy or the most advanced period of life, to listen with total indifference to a tale of 20 true love."

Shortly after his admission to the bar, Scott made an expedition of great importance to the history of his life. While attending the Michaelmas° head-court at Jedburgh, he was introduced to Mr. Robert Shortreed, who spent the 25 greater part of his life in the enjoyment of much respect as Sheriff-substitute of Roxburghshire. Scott expressed his wish to visit the then wild and inaccessible district of Liddesdale,° particularly with a view to examine the ruins of the famous castle of Hermitage, and to pick up 30 some of the ancient *riding ballads,*° said to be still preserved among the descendants of the moss-troopers° who had followed the banner of the Douglasses,° when

lords of that grim and remote fastness; and his new acquaintance offered to be his guide.

During seven successive years he made a *raid*, as he
called it, into Liddesdale, in company with Mr. Short-
5 reed; exploring every rivulet to its source, and every
ruined *peel* from foundation to battlement. At this
time no wheeled carriage had ever been seen in the district — the first, indeed, that ever appeared there was a
gig, driven by Scott himself for a part of his way, when on
10 the last of these seven excursions. There was no inn nor
public-house of any kind in the whole valley; the travellers passed from the shepherd's hut to the minister's
manse, and again from the cheerful hospitality of the
manse to the rough and jolly welcome of the homestead;
15 gathering, wherever they went, songs and tunes, and
occasionally more tangible relics of antiquity — even such
"a rowth of auld nicknackets" as Burns ascribes to Captain Grose. To these rambles Scott owed much of the
materials of his Minstrelsy of the Border; and not less
20 of that intimate acquaintance with the living manners of
these unsophisticated regions, which constitutes the
chief charm of one of the most charming of his prose works.
But how soon he had any definite object before him in his
researches, seems very doubtful. "He was *makin' him-*
25 *sell* a' the time," said Mr. Shortreed; "but he didna ken
maybe what he was about till years had passed: At first
he thought o' little, I dare say, but the queerness and the
fun."

"In those days," says the Memorandum before me,
30 "advocates were not so plenty — at least about Liddesdale;" and the worthy Sheriff-substitute goes on to
describe the sort of bustle, not unmixed with alarm, produced at the first farm-house they visited (Willie Elliot's

at Millburnholm), when the honest man was informed of
the quality of one of his guests. When they dismounted,
accordingly, he received the stranger with great ceremony, and insisted upon himself leading his horse to the
stable. Shortreed accompanied Willie, however, and the
latter, after taking a deliberate peep at Scott, "out by
the edge of the door-cheek," whispered, "Weel, Robin,
I say, de'il hae me if I's be a bit feared for him now; he's
just a chield like ourselves, I think." Half-a-dozen
dogs of all degrees had already gathered round "the
advocate," and his way of returning their compliments
had set Willie at his ease.

They dined at Millburnholm, and after having lingered
over Willie Elliot's punch-bowl, until, in Mr. Shortreed's
phrase, they were "half glowrin," mounted their steeds
again, and proceeded to Dr. Elliot's at Cleughhead, where
("for," says my Memorandum, "folk were na very nice
in those days") the two travellers slept in one bed — as,
indeed, seems to have been the case throughout most of
their excursions in this district. Dr. Elliot had already
a MS. collection of ballads; but he now exerted himself,
for several years, with redoubled diligence, in seeking out
the living depositaries of such lore among the darker
recesses of the mountains. "The Doctor," says Mr.
Shortreed, "would have gane through fire and water for
Sir Walter, when he ance kenned him." "Eh me!"
says Shortreed, "sic an endless fund o' humour and drollery as he then had wi' him! Never ten yards but we
were either laughing or roaring and singing. Wherever
we stopped, how brawlie he suited himsel' to everybody!
He ay did as the lave did; never made himsel' the great
man, or took ony airs in the company."

"It was in that same season, I think," says Mr. Short-

reed, "that Sir Walter got from Dr. Elliot the large old
border war-horn, which ye may still see hanging in the
armoury at Abbotsford. How *great* he was when he was
made master o' *that !* I believe it had been found in Her-
5 mitage Castle — and one of the Doctor's servants had
used it many a day as a grease-horn for his scythe,
before they discovered its history. When cleaned out,
it was never a hair the worse — the original chain, hoop,
and mouth-piece of steel, were all entire, just as you now
10 see them. Sir Walter carried it home all the way from
Liddesdale to Jedburgh, slung about his neck like Johnny
Gilpin's bottle, while I was intrusted with an ancient
bridle-bit, which we had likewise picked up. O what
pleasant days ! And then a' the nonsense we had cost
15 us naething. We never put hand in pocket for a week
on end. Toll-bars there were nane — and indeed I think
our haill charges were a feed o' corn to our horses in the
gangin' and comin' at Riccartoun mill."

In November 1792, Scott and Clerk began their regular
20 attendance at the Parliament House,° and Scott, to use
Mr. Clerk's words, "by and by crept into a tolerable share
of such business as may be expected from a writer's connexion." By this we are to understand that he was
employed from time to time by his father, and probably
25 a few other solicitors, in that dreary every-day taskwork,
chiefly of long written *informations*, and other papers
for the Court, on which young counsellors of the Scotch
Bar were then expected to bestow a great deal of trouble
for very scanty pecuniary remuneration, and with scarcely
30 a chance of finding reserved for their hands any matter
that could elicit the display of superior knowledge
or understanding.

But he soon became as famous for his powers of story-

telling among the lawyers of the Outer-House,° as he had
been among the companions of his High-School days. The
place where these idlers mostly congregated was called,
it seems, by a name which sufficiently marks the date —
it was *the Mountain.*°   Mr. Clerk remembers complaining 5
one morning on finding the group convulsed with laughter, that *Duns Scotus* had been forestalling him in a good
story, which he had communicated privately the day
before — adding, moreover, that his friend had not only
stolen, but disguised it. "Why," answered he, skilfully 10
waiving the main charge, "this is always the way with
the Baronet.[1] He is continually saying that I change
his stories, whereas in fact I only put a cocked hat on their
heads, and stick a cane into their hands — to make them
fit for going into company."   15

Some interest had been excited in Edinburgh as to the
rising literature of Germany, by an essay of Mackenzie's
in 1778, and a subsequent version of The Robbers, by Mr.
Tytler (Lord Woodhouselee). About Christmas 1792,
a German class was formed under a Dr. Willick, which 20
included Scott, Clerk, Thomson, and Erskine; all of
whom soon qualified themselves to taste the beauties of
Schiller and Goethe in the original. This class contributed greatly to Scott's familiarity with Erskine; a familiarity which grew into one of the warmest and closest 25
of his friendships.   Nor can it be doubted that he exercised, at the active period we have now reached, a very
important influence on his friend's literary tastes, and
especially on his German studies. From the beginning,

[1] *Duns Scotus*° was an old college-club nickname for
Walter Scott, a tribute to his love of antiquities. Clerk
was with the same set *the Baronet*, as belonging to the
family of the Baronets of Pennycuick.

Scott had in Erskine a monitor who, entering most warmly
into his taste for national lore — the life of the past —
and the bold and picturesque style of the original English
school — was constantly urging the advantages to be
5 derived from combining with its varied and masculine
breadth of delineation such attention to the minor graces
of arrangement and diction as might conciliate the fastid-
iousness of modern taste.

If the preceding autumn forms a remarkable point in
10 his history, as first introducing him to the manners of
the wilder Border country, the summer which followed
left traces of equal importance. He then visited some of
the finest districts of Stirlingshire and Perthshire; and not
in the precursory manner of his more boyish expeditions
15 but taking up his residence for a week or ten days in succession at the family residences of several of his young
allies of *The Mountain*, and from thence familiarizing
himself at leisure with the country and the people round
about. In this way he lingered some time at Tullibody,
20 the seat of the father of Sir Ralph Abercromby, and
grandfather of his friend George Abercromby; and heard
from the old gentleman's own lips the narrative of a journey which he had been obliged to make to the retreat
of Rob Roy. The venerable laird told how he was re-
25 ceived by the cateran "with much courtesy," in a cavern
exactly such as that of *Bean Lean*°; dined on collops cut
from some of his own cattle, which he recognised hanging
by their heels from the rocky roof beyond; and returned
in all safety, after concluding a bargain of *black-mail* —
30 in virtue of which annual payment, Rob Roy guaranteed
the future security of his herds against, not his own fol-
lowers merely, but all freebooters whatever. Scott next
visited his friend Edmonstone, at Newton, a beautiful

seat close to the ruins of the once magnificent Castle of Doune, and heard another aged gentleman's vivid recollections of all that happened there when John Home, the author of Douglas, and other Hanoverian prisoners, escaped from the Highland garrison in 1745. Proceeding [5] towards the sources of the Teith, he was received for the first time under a roof which, in subsequent years, he regularly revisited, that of another of his associates, Buchanan, the young Laird of Cambusmore. It was thus that the scenery of Loch Katrine came to be so associated with [10] "the recollection of many a dear friend and merry expedition of former days," that to compose the Lady of the Lake was "a labour of love, and no less so to recall the manners and incidents introduced." [1] It was starting from the same house, when the poem itself had made some [15] progress, that he put to the test the practicability of riding from the banks of Loch Vennachar to the Castle of Stirling within the brief space which he had assigned to Fitz-James's Grey Bayard, after the duel with Roderick Dhu; and the principal land-marks in the description of that [20] fiery progress are so many hospitable mansions, all familiar to him at the same period : — Blair-drummond, the residence of Lord Kaimes; Ochtertyre, that of John Ramsay, the scholar and antiquary (now best remembered for his kind and sagacious advice to Burns ;) and "the lofty [25] brow of ancient Kier," the fine seat of the chief family of the name of Stirling; from which, to say nothing of remoter objects, the prospect has on one hand the rock of "Snowdon," and in front the field of Bannockburn.

Another resting place was Craighall, in Perthshire, the [30] seat of the Rattrays, a family related to Mr. Clerk, who

[1] Introduction to *The Lady of the Lake.*

accompanied him. From the position of this striking
place, as Mr. Clerk at once perceived, and as the author
afterwards confessed to him, that of *Tully-Veolan* was
faithfully copied; though in the description of the house
5 itself, and its gardens, many features were adopted from
Bruntsfield and Ravelstone. Mr. Clerk told me that he
went through the first chapters of Waverley without more
than a vague suspicion of the new novelist; but that when
he read the arrival at Tully-Veolan, his suspicion was
10 converted into certainty, and he handed the book to a
common friend of his and the author's, saying, "This is
Scott's — and I'll lay a bet you'll find such and such
things in the next chapter." I hope to be forgiven for
mentioning *the* circumstance that flashed conviction.
15 In the course of a ride from Craighall, they had both
become considerably fagged and heated, and Clerk,
seeing the smoke of a *clachan* a little way before them,
ejaculated — "How agreeable if we should here fall in
with one of those signposts where a red lion predominates
20 over a punch-bowl!" The phrase happened to tickle
Scott's fancy — he often introduced it on similar occasions afterwards — and at the distance of twenty years
Mr. Clerk was at no loss to recognise an old acquaintance
in the "huge bear" which "predominates" over the stone
25 basin in the courtyard of Baron Bradwardine.

I believe the longest stay was at Meigle in Forfarshire,
the seat of Patrick Murray of Simprim, whose passion for
antiquities, especially military antiquities, had peculiarly
endeared him both to Scott and Clerk. Here Adam
30 Fergusson, too, was of the party; and I have often heard
them each and all dwell on the thousand scenes of adventure and merriment which diversified that visit. In the
village churchyard, close beneath Mr. Murray's gardens,

tradition still points out the tomb of Queen Guenever°; and the whole district abounds in objects of historical interest. Amidst them they spent their wandering days, while their evenings passed in the joyous festivity of a wealthy young bachelor's establishment, or sometimes 5 under the roofs of neighbours less refined than their host, the *Balmawhapples*° of the Braes of Angus. From Meigle they made a trip to Dunottar Castle, the ruins of the huge old fortress of the Earls Marischall, and it was in the churchyard of that place that Scott then saw for the 10 first and last time Peter Paterson, the living *Old Mortality*.

If his father had some reason to complain of want of ardour as to the weightier matters of the law, it probably gave him little consolation to hear, in June 1795, of his appointment to be one of the curators of the Advocates' 15 Library, an office always reserved for those members of the Faculty who have the reputation of superior zeal in literary affairs. From the first assumption of the gown, he had been accustomed to spend many of his hours in the low gloomy vaults under the Parliament House, which 20 then formed the only receptacle for their literary and antiquarian collections. This habit, it may be supposed, grew by what it fed on. MSS. can only be consulted within the library, and his highland and border raids were constantly suggesting inquiries as to ancient local history and 25 legends, which could nowhere else have been pursued with equal advantage. He became an adept in the deciphering of old deeds; and whoever examines the rich treasure of the MacFarlan MSS., and others serviceable for the illustration of Scotch topography and genealogy, will, 30 I am told, soon become familiar with the marks of his early pencil.

After his early disappointment in love, Scott seems to

have turned with renewed ardour to his literary pursuits;
and in that same October, 1796, he was "prevailed on,"
as he playfully expresses it, "by the *request of friends*, to
indulge his own vanity, by publishing the translation of
5 Lenore, with that of the Wild Huntsman, also from Bürger, in a thin quarto." He had owed his copy of Bürger
to a young gentlewoman of high German blood, who in
1795 became the wife of his friend and chief Hugh Scott
of Harden. The young kinsman was introduced to her
10 soon after her arrival at Mertoun, and his attachment to
German studies excited her attention and interest. I
have often heard him say, that among those many "obligations of a distant date which remained impressed on his
memory, after a life spent in a constant interchange of
15 friendship and kindness," he counted not as the least the
lady's frankness in correcting his Scotticisms, and more
especially his Scottish *rhymes*.

"When I first saw Sir Walter," she writes to me, "he
was about four or five-and-twenty, but looked much
20 younger. He seemed bashful and awkward; but there
were from the first such gleams of superior sense and
spirit in his conversation, that I was hardly surprised
when, after our acquaintance had ripened a little, I felt
myself to be talking with a man of genius. He was most
25 modest about himself, and shewed his little pieces apparently without any consciousness that they could possess
any claim on particular attention. Nothing so easy and
good-humoured as the way in which he received any
hints I might offer, when he seemed to be tampering with
30 the King's English. I remember particularly how he
laughed at himself, when I made him take notice that
'the little two dogs,' in some of his lines, did not please
an English ear accustomed to 'the two little dogs.'"

In his German studies, Scott acquired, about this time, another assistant in Mr. Skene of Rubislaw — a gentleman considerably his junior, who had just returned to Scotland from a residence of several years in Saxony. Their fondness for the same literature, with Scott's eager-ness to profit by his new acquaintance's superior attainment in it, opened an intercourse which general similarity of tastes, and I venture to add, in many of the most important features of character, soon ripened into the familiarity of a tender friendship — "An intimacy," Mr. Skene says, in a paper before me, "of which I shall ever think with so much pride — a friendship so pure and cordial as to have been able to withstand all the vicissitudes of nearly forty years, without ever having sustained even a casual chill from unkind thought or word." Mr. Skene adds — "During the whole progress of his varied life, to that eminent station which he could not but feel he at length held in the estimation, not of his countrymen alone, but of the whole world, I never could perceive the slightest shade of variance from that simplicity of character with which he impressed me on the first hour of our meeting."

Among the common tastes which served to knit these friends together, was their love of horsemanship, in which, as in all other manly exercises, Skene highly excelled; and the fears of a French invasion becoming every day more serious, their thoughts were turned with corresponding zeal to the project of mounted volunteers. "The London Light-horse had set the example," says Mr. Skene; "but in truth it was to Scott's ardour that this force in the North owed its origin. Unable, by reason of his lameness, to serve amongst his friends on foot, he had nothing for it but to rouse the spirit of the moss-

trooper, with which he readily inspired all who possessed
the means of substituting the sabre for the musket." On
the 14th February 1797, these friends and many more met
and drew up an offer to serve as a body of volunteer
5 cavalry in Scotland; which was accepted by Government.

"The part of quartermaster," says Mr. Skene, "was pur-
posely selected for him, that he might be spared the rough
usage of the ranks; but, notwithstanding his infirmity,
he had a remarkably firm seat on horseback, and in all
10 situations a fearless one: no fatigue ever seemed too
much for him, and his zeal and animation served to sustain the enthusiasm of the whole corps, while his ready
'mot à rire' kept up, in all, a degree of good-humour and
relish for the service, without which, the toil and privations
15 of long *daily* drills would not easily have been submitted
to by such a body of gentlemen. At every interval
of exercise, the order, *sit at ease*, was the signal for the
quartermaster to lead the squadron to merriment; every
eye was intuitively turned on 'Earl Walter,' as he was
20 familiarly called by his associates of that date, and his
ready joke seldom failed to raise the ready laugh. He
took his full share in all the labours and duties of the corps,
had the highest pride in its progress and proficiency, and
was such a trooper himself, as only a very powerful frame
25 of body and the warmest zeal in the cause could have
enabled any one to be. But his habitual good-humour
was the great charm, and at the daily mess (for we all
dined together when in quarters) that reigned supreme."
Earl Walter's first charger, by the way, was a tall and
30 powerful animal, named *Lenore.*° These daily drills
appear to have been persisted in during the spring and
summer of 1797; the corps spending moreover some
weeks in quarters at Musselburgh. The majority of the

troop having professional duties to attend to, the ordinary
hour for drill was five in the morning; and when we reflect,
that after some hours of hard work in this way, Scott
had to produce himself regularly in the Parliament House
with gown and wig, for the space of four or five hours at 5
least, while his chamber practice, though still humble,
was on the increase — and that he had found a plentiful
source of new social engagements in his troop connexions —
it certainly could have excited no surprise had his literary
studies been found suffering total intermission during this 10
busy period. That such was not the case, however, his
correspondence and note-books afford ample evidence.
His *fee-book* shews that he made by his first year's practice
L.24, 3s.; by the second, L.57, 15s.; by the third, L.84,
4s.; by the fourth, L.90; and in his fifth year at the Bar — 15
that is, from November 1796 to July 1797 — L.144, 10s.,
of which L.50 were fees from his father's chamber. He had
no turn, at this time of his life, for early rising; so that the
regular attendance at the morning drills was of itself a
strong evidence of his military zeal; but he must have, 20
in spite of them, and of all other circumstances, persisted
in what was the usual custom of all his earlier life, namely,
the devotion of the best hours of the night to solitary
study. In general, both as a young man, and in more
advanced age, his constitution required a good allowance 25
of sleep, and he, on principle, indulged in it, saying, "he
was but half a man if he had not full seven hours of utter
unconsciousness;" but his whole mind and temperament
were, at this period, in a state of most fervent exaltation,
and spirit triumphed over matter. 30

E

CHAPTER III

Tour to the English Lakes — Miss Carpenter — Marriage — Lasswade Cottage — Original Ballads — James Ballantyne — Sheriffship of Selkirk — Publication of the Minstrelsy of the Border — First Draft of The Lay of the Last Minstrel — 1797–1803.

AFTER the rising of the Court of Session in July 1797, Scott set out on a tour to the English lakes, accompanied by his brother John and Adam Fergusson. Their first stage was Halyards in Tweeddale, then inhabited by his 5 friend's father, the philosopher and historian; and they stayed there for a day or two, in the course of which he had his first and only interview with David Ritchie, the original of his Black Dwarf. Proceeding southwards, the tourists visited Carlisle, Penrith, — the vale of the Eamont, includ-10 ing Mayburgh and Brougham Castle, — Ulswater and Windermere; and at length fixed their head-quarters at the then peaceful and sequestered little watering place of Gilsland, making excursions from thence to the various scenes of romantic interest which are commemorated in 15 The Bridal of Triermain, and otherwise leading very much the sort of life depicted among the loungers of St. Ronan's Well.

Riding one day with Fergusson, they met, some miles from their quarters, a young lady taking the air on horse-20 back, whom neither of them had previously remarked, and whose appearance instantly struck both so much, that they kept her in view until they had satisfied them-

50

selves that she also was one of the party at Gilsland. The
same evening there was a ball, at which Captain Scott
produced himself in his regimentals, and Fergusson also
thought proper to be equipped in the uniform of the Edinburgh Volunteers. There was no little rivalry among the 5
young travellers as to who should first get presented to
the unknown beauty of the morning's ride; but though
both the gentlemen in scarlet had the advantage of being
dancing partners, their friend succeeded in handing the
fair stranger to supper — and such was his first introduc- 10
tion to Charlotte Margaret Carpenter. A lovelier vision,
as all who remember her in the bloom of her days have
assured me, could hardly have been imagined; and from
that hour the fate of the young poet was fixed.

She was the daughter of Jean Charpentier, of Lyons, a 15
devoted royalist, who held an office under Government,
and Charlotte Volere, his wife. She and her only brother,
Charles Charpentier, had been educated in the Protestant
religion of their mother; and when their father died,
which occurred in the beginning of the Revolution, Ma- 20
dame Charpentier made her escape with her children first
to Paris, and then to England.

Scott's father was now in a very feeble state of health,
which accounts for his first announcement of this affair
being made in a letter to his mother: "My dear Mother, — 25
I should very ill deserve the care and affection with which
you have ever regarded me, were I to neglect my duty so
far as to omit consulting my father and you in the most
important step which I can possibly take in life, and upon
the success of which my future happiness must depend. 30
It is with pleasure I think that I can avail myself of your
advice and instructions in an affair of so great importance
as that which I have at present on my hands. You will

probably guess from this preamble, that I am engaged in
a matrimonial plan, which is really the case. You will
not expect from me a description of her person — for
which I refer you to my brother, as also for a fuller account
5 of all the circumstances attending the business than can
be comprised in the compass of a letter. Without flying
into raptures, for I must assure you that my judgment as
well as my affections are consulted upon this occasion —
without flying into raptures, then, I may safely assure you,
10 that her temper is sweet and cheerful, her understanding
good, and, what I know will give you pleasure, her principles of religion very serious. I have been very explicit
with her upon the nature of my expectations, and she
thinks she can accommodate herself to the situation which
15 I should wish her to hold in society as my wife, which,
you will easily comprehend, I mean should neither be
extravagant nor degrading. Her fortune, though partly
dependent upon her brother, who is high in office at
Madras, is very considerable — at present L.500 a-year.
20 This, however, we must, in some degree, regard as precarious — I mean to the full extent ; and indeed, when you
know her, you will not be surprised that I regard this
circumstance chiefly because it removes those prudential
considerations which would otherwise render our union
25 impossible for the present. Betwixt her income and my
own professional exertions, I have little doubt we will be
enabled to hold the rank in society which my family and
situation entitle me to fill. Write to me very fully upon
this important subject — send me your opinion, your
30 advice, and, above all, your blessing."

Scott was married at Carlisle during the Christmas
recess, and carried his bride to a lodging in George
Street, Edinburgh ; a house which he had taken, not being

quite prepared for her reception. The first fortnight was, I believe, sufficient to convince her husband's family that, however rashly he had formed the connexion, she had the sterling qualities of a wife. Notwithstanding some little leaning to the pomps and vanities of the world, she had 5 made up her mind to find her happiness in better things; and so long as their circumstances continued narrow, no woman could have conformed herself to them with more of good feeling and good sense.

In the summer of 1798 Scott hired a cottage at Lass- 10 wade, on the Esk, about six miles from Edinburgh. It is a small house, but with one room of good dimensions, which Mrs. Scott's taste set off to advantage at very humble cost — a paddock or two — and a garden (commanding a most beautiful view) in which Scott delighted to 15 train his flowers and creepers. Never, I have heard him say, was he prouder of his handiwork than when he had completed the fashioning of a rustic archway, now overgrown with hoary ivy, by way of ornament to the entrance from the Edinburgh road. In this retreat they spent some 20 happy summers, receiving the visits of their few chosen friends from the neighbouring city, and wandering at will amidst some of the most romantic scenery that Scotland can boast — Scott's dearest haunt in the days of his boyish ramblings. It was here, that when his warm heart 25 was beating with young and happy love, and his whole mind and spirit were nerved by new motives for exertion — it was here, that in the ripened glow of manhood he seems to have first felt something of his real strength, and poured himself out in those splendid original ballads which were 30 at once to fix his name.

In March 1799, he carried his wife to London, this being the first time that he had seen the metropolis since

the days of his infancy.   His great anxiety was to examine
the antiquities of the Tower and Westminster Abbey,
and to make some researches among the MSS. of the
British Museum.   His return to Edinburgh was accel-
5 erated by the tidings of his father's death.   This worthy
man had had a succession of paralytic attacks, under which,
mind as well as body had by degrees been laid quite pros-
trate.

Mr. Thomas Scott continued to manage his father's
10 business.   He married early; he was in his circle of society
extremely popular; and his prospects seemed fair in all
things.   The property left by the old gentleman was less
than had been expected, but sufficient to make ample
provision for his widow, and a not inconsiderable addition
15 to the resources of those among whom the remainder was
divided.

The summer after his father's death produced what
Scott justly calls his "first serious attempts in verse";
and of these, the earliest appears to have been the Glen-
20 finlas.   The next of these compositions was, I believe,
the Eve of St. John, in which Scott re-peoples the tower of
Smailholm, the awe-inspiring haunt of his infancy; and
here he touches, for the first time, the one superstition
which can still be appealed to with full and perfect effect;
25 the only one which lingers in minds long since weaned from
all sympathy with the machinery of witches and goblins.
And surely this mystery was never touched with more
thrilling skill than in that noble ballad.   It is the first
of his original pieces, too, in which he uses the measure
30 of his own favourite Minstrels; a measure which the
monotony of mediocrity had long and successfully been
labouring to degrade, but in itself adequate to the expression of the highest thoughts, as well as the gentlest emo-

tions; and capable, in fit hands, of as rich a variety of
music as any other of modern times. This was written
at Mertoun-house in the autumn of 1799. Some dilap-
idations had taken place in the tower of Smailholm, and
Harden, being informed of the fact, and entreated with 5
needless earnestness by his kinsman to arrest the hand of
the spoiler, requested playfully a ballad, of which Smailholm should be the scene, as the price of his assent.

Then came The Grey Brother, founded on another
superstition, which seems to have been almost as ancient 10
as the belief in ghosts; namely, that the holiest service of
the altar cannot go on in the presence of an unclean person — a heinous sinner unconfessed and unabsolved.

Having again given a week to Liddesdale, in company
with Mr. Shortreed, he spent a few days at Rosebank, 15
and was preparing to return to Edinburgh for the winter,
when he received a visit which had consequences of importance.

In the early days of Lancelot Whale, he had had for a
classfellow Mr. James. Ballantyne, the eldest son of a 20
decent shopkeeper in Kelso, and their acquaintance had
never been altogether broken off, as Scott's visits to Rosebank were frequent, and the other had resided for a time
in Edinburgh, when pursuing his education with a view
to the profession of a solicitor. Mr. Ballantyne had not 25
been successful in his attempts to establish himself in that
branch of the law, and was now the printer and editor of
a weekly newspaper in his native town. He called at Rosebank one morning, and requested his old acquaintance to
supply a few paragraphs on some legal question of the day 30
for his *Kelso Mail*. Scott complied; and carried his
article himself to the printing-office. At parting, Scott
threw out a casual observation, that he wondered his old

friend did not try to get some little booksellers' work, "to keep his types in play during the rest of the week." Ballantyne answered, that such an idea had not before occurred to him — that he had no acquaintance with the Edinburgh "trade"; but, if he had, his types were good, and he thought he could afford to work more cheaply than town-printers. Scott, "with his good humoured smile," said, — "You had better try what you can do. You have been praising my little ballads; suppose you print off a dozen copies or so of as many as will make a pamphlet, sufficient to let my Edinburgh acquaintances judge of your skill for themselves." Ballantyne assented; and I believe exactly twelve copies of William and Ellen, The Fire-King, The Chase, and a few more of those pieces, were thrown off accordingly. This first specimen of a press, afterwards so celebrated, pleased Scott; and he said to Ballantyne — "I have been for years collecting old Border ballads, and I think I could, with little trouble, put together such a selection from them as might make a neat little volume, to sell for four or five shillings. I will talk to some of the booksellers about it when I get to Edinburgh, and if the thing goes on, you shall be the printer." Ballantyne highly relished the proposal; and the result of this little experiment changed wholly the course of his worldly fortunes, as well as of his friend's.

Shortly after the commencement of the Winter Session, the office of Sheriff-depute of Selkirkshire became vacant by the death of an early ally of Scott's, Andrew Plummer of Middlestead, a scholar and antiquary, who had entered with zeal into his ballad researches, and whose name occurs accordingly more than once in the notes to the Border Minstrelsy. Perhaps the community of their tastes may have had some part in suggesting to the Duke of Buccleuch, that Scott might fitly succeed Mr. Plummer in the magistrature. Be that as it might, his Grace's influence was used with Mr. Henry Dundas (afterwards Viscount Melville) who in those days had the general control of the Crown patronage in Scotland, and was prepared to look 5 favourably on Scott's pretensions to some office of this description.

His appointment to the *Sheriffship* bears date 16th December 1799. It secured him an annual salary of L. 300; an addition to his resources which at once relieved 10 his mind from whatever degree of anxiety he might have felt in considering the prospect of an increasing family, along with the ever precarious chances of a profession, in the daily drudgery of which it is impossible to suppose that he ever could have found much pleasure. The duties of 15 the office were far from heavy; the territory, small, peaceful, and pastoral, was in great part the property of the Duke of Buccleuch; and he turned with redoubled zeal to his project of editing the ballads, many of the best of which belonged to this very district of his favourite Border 20 — those "tales" which, as the Dedication of the Minstrelsy expresses it, had "in elder times celebrated the prowess and cheered the halls" of his noble patron's ancestors.

During the years 1800 and 1801, the Minstrelsy formed its editor's chief occupation — a labour of love truly, if ever 25 such there was; but neither this nor his sheriffship interfered with his regular attendance at the Bar, the abandonment of which was all this while as far as it ever had been from his imagination, or that of any of his friends. He continued to have his summer headquarters at Lasswade. 30 His means of hospitality were now much enlarged, and the cottage on a Saturday and Sunday at least, was seldom without visitors.

Volumes I. and II. of the Minstrelsy appeared in January 1802, from the respectable house of Cadell and Davies in the Strand; and these may be said to have first introduced Scott as an original writer to the English public.   In his
5 Remarks on the imitation of Popular Poetry, he says : — "When the book came out, the imprint, Kelso, was read with wonder by amateurs of typography, who had never heard of such a place, and were astonished at the example to handsome printing which so obscure a town had pro-
10 duced."   The edition was exhausted in the course of the year, and the terms of publication having been that Scott should have half the clear profits, his share was exactly L.78, 10s. — a sum which certainly could not have repaid him for the actual expenditure incurred in the collection
15 of his materials.

The reception of the first volumes elated naturally their printer, who went up to London to cultivate acquaintance with publishers, and on his return writes thus to his employer : — "I shall ever think the printing the Scottish
20 Minstrelsy one of the most fortunate circumstances of my life.   I have gained, not lost by it, in a pecuniary light; and the prospects it has been the means of opening to me, may advantageously influence my future destiny. I can never be sufficiently grateful for the interest you un-
25 ceasingly take in my welfare.   One thing is clear — that Kelso cannot be my abiding place for aye."   The great bookseller, Longman, repaired to Scotland soon after this, and made an offer for the copyright of the Minstrelsy, the third volume included.   This was accepted.

30   Shortly after this, in a letter to Ellis,° Scott mentions, among other things to be included in the third volume of the Minstrelsy, "a long poem" from his own pen — "a kind of romance of Border chivalry, in a light-horseman

sort of stanza." This refers to the first draft of The
Lay of the Last Minstrel; and the author's description of
it as being "in a light-horseman sort of stanza," was probably suggested by the circumstances under which the
greater part of that draft had been accomplished. He 5
has told us, in his Introduction of 1830, that the poem
originated in a request of the young and lovely Countess of
Dalkeith, that he would write a ballad on the legend of
Gilpin Horner: that he began it at Lasswade, and read
the opening stanzas, as soon as they were written, to 10
Erskine and Cranstoun : that their reception of these was
apparently so cold as to disgust him with what he had
done; but that finding, a few days afterwards, that the
verses had nevertheless excited their curiosity, and haunted
their memory, he was encouraged to resume the under- 15
taking. The scene and date of this resumption I owe to
the recollection of the then Cornet of the Light-horse.
While the troop were on permanent duty at Musselburgh, in the autumnal recess of 1802, the Quarter-Master,
during a charge on Portobello sands, received a kick of a 20
horse, which confined him for three days to his lodgings.
Mr. Skene found him busy with his pen; and he produced
before these three days expired the first canto of the Lay,
very nearly, if his friend's memory may be trusted, in the
state in which it was ultimately published. That the 25
whole poem was sketched and filled in with extraordinary
rapidity, there can be no difficulty in believing. He himself says (in the Introduction of 1830), that after he had
once got fairly into the vein, it proceeded at the rate of
about a canto in a week. The Lay, however, soon out- 30
grew the dimensions which he had originally contemplated;
the design of including it in the third volume of the Minstrelsy was of course abandoned; and it did not appear

until nearly three years after that fortunate mishap on the beach of Portobello.

He thus writes to Ballantyne, on the 21st April 1803: — "I have to thank you for the accuracy with which the 5 Minstrelsy is thrown off. Longman and Rees are delighted with the printing. I mean this note to be added, by way of advertisement : — 'In the press, and will speedily be published, the Lay of the Last Minstrel, by Walter Scott, Esq., Editor of the Minstrelsy of the Scottish Bor- 10 der. Also Sir Tristrem, a Metrical Romance, by Thomas of Ercildoune, called the Rhymer, edited from an ancient MS., with an Introduction and Notes, by Walter Scott, Esq.' Will you cause such a thing to be appended in your own way and fashion ? "

15   The letter is addressed to "Mr. James Ballantyne, printer, Abbey-hill, Edinburgh"; which shews, that before the third volume of the Minstrelsy passed through the press, the migration recommended two years earlier had at length taken place. "It was about the end of 1802," 20 says Ballantyne, "that I closed with a plan so congenial to my wishes. I removed, bag and baggage, to Edinburgh, finding accommodation for two presses, and a proof one, in the precincts of Holyrood-house, then deriving new lustre and interest from the recent arrival of the royal 25 exiles of France. In these obscure premises some of the most beautiful productions of what we called *The Border Press* were printed." The Memorandum states, that Scott having renewed his hint as to pecuniary assistance, as soon as the printer found his finances straitened 30 "a liberal loan was advanced accordingly."

Scott speaks, in an Essay of his closing years, as if the first reception of the Minstrelsy on the south of the Tweed had been cold. "The curiosity of the English," he says, "was not much awakened by poems in the rude garb of antiquity, accompanied with notes referring to the obscure feuds of barbarous clans, of whose very names civilized history was ignorant." In writing those beautiful Introductions of 1830, however, he seems to have trusted 5 entirely to his recollection of days long gone by, and he has accordingly let fall many statements which we must take with some allowance. His impressions as to the reception of the Minstrelsy were different, when writing to his brother-in-law, Charles Carpenter, on the 3d March 1803, 10 he said — "I have contrived to turn a very slender portion of literary talents to some account, by a publication of the poetical antiquities of the Border, where the old people had preserved many ballads descriptive of the manners of the country during the wars with England. 15 This trifling collection was so well received by a *discerning public*, that, after receiving about L.100 profit for the first edition, which my vanity cannot omit informing you went off in six months, I have sold the copyright for L. 500 more." Had the sale of the original edition been chiefly Scotch, I 20 doubt whether Messrs. Longman would have so readily offered L. 500, in those days of the trade a large sum, for the second. Scott had become habituated, long before 1830, to a scale of bookselling transactions, measured by which the largest editions and copy-monies of his own 25 early days appeared insignificant; but the evidence seems complete that he was well contented at the time.

One of the critics of that day said that the book contained "the elements of a hundred historical romances"; — and this critic was a prophetic one. No person who 30 has not 'gone through its volumes for the express purpose of comparing their contents with his great original works, can have formed a conception of the endless variety of incidents and images now expanded and emblazoned by his mature art. The taste and fancy of Scott appear to have been formed as early as his moral character; and he had, before he passed the threshold of authorship, assembled about him, in the uncalculating delight of native enthusiasm, almost all the materials on which his genius was destined to be employed for the gratification and instruction of the world.

CHAPTER IV

Wordsworth — Hogg — Sir Tristrem — Removal to Ashestiel — Publication of The Lay of the Last Minstrel —
Partnership with James Ballantyne — Opening Chapters of Waverley — Visit to London — Appointment as
Clerk of Session — 1804–1806.

DURING the summer of 1803, his chief literary work
was on the *Sir Tristrem*, but the Lay of the Last Minstrel
made progress at intervals — mostly, it would seem, when
he was in quarters with his troop of horse, and necessarily without his books of reference. It was in that 5
autumn that Scott first saw Wordsworth.° Their common acquaintance, Stoddart,° had so often talked of them
to each other, that they met as if they had not been
strangers; and they parted friends.

Mr. and Miss Wordsworth had just completed their 10
tour in the Highlands, of which so many incidents have
since been immortalized, both in the poet's verse and in
the hardly less poetical prose of his sister's Diary. On the
morning of the 17th of September, having left their carriage at Roslin, they walked down the valley to Lasswade 15
and arrived there before Mr. and Mrs. Scott had risen,
"We were received," Mr. Wordsworth has told me, "with
that frank cordiality which, under whatever circumstances
I afterwards met him, always marked his manners; and,
indeed, I found him then in every respect — except, per- 20
haps, that his animal spirits were somewhat higher —
precisely the same man that you knew him in later life.

"Sir Tristrem" was at length published on the 2d of May 1804, by Constable, who, however, expected so little popularity for the work, that the edition consisted only of 150 copies. These were sold at a high price (two 5 guineas), otherwise they would not have been enough to cover the expenses of paper and printing. Mr. Ellis and other friends were much dissatisfied with these arrangements; but I doubt not that Constable was a better judge than any of them.

10   In the course of the preceding summer, the Lord-Lieutenant of Selkirkshire complained of Scott's military zeal as interfering sometimes with the discharge of his shrieval functions, and took occasion to remind him, that the law, requiring every Sheriff to reside at least four months in the 15 year within his own jurisdiction, had not hitherto been complied with. On the 4th May, two days after the Tristrem had been published, Scott says to Ellis, who was meditating a northern tour — "I have been engaged in travelling backwards and forwards to Selkirkshire upon 20 little pieces of business, just important enough to prevent my doing anything to purpose. One great matter, however, I have achieved, which is, procuring myself a place of residence, which will save me these teasing migrations in future, so that though I part with my sweet little cot- 25 tage on the banks of the Esk, you will find me this summer in the very centre of the ancient Reged° in a decent farmhouse overhanging the Tweed and situated in a wild pastoral country."

On the 10th of June 1804, died, at his seat of Rosebank, 30 Captain Robert Scott, the affectionate uncle whose name has often occurred in this narrative. "He was," says his nephew to Ellis, on the 18th, "a man of universal benevolence and great kindness towards his friends, and to me individually. He has distinguished me by leaving me a beautiful little villa on the banks of the Tweed, with every possible convenience annexed to it, and about thirty acres of the finest land in Scotland. Notwithstanding, however, the temptation that this bequest offers, I con- 5 tinue to pursue my Reged plan, and expect to be settled at Ashestiel in the course of a month. Rosebank is situated so near the village of Kelso, as hardly to be sufficiently a country residence; besides, it is hemmed in by hedges and ditches, not to mention Dukes and Lady Dowagers, 10 which are bad things for little people. It is expected to sell to great advantage. I shall buy a mountain farm with the purchase-money, and be quite the Laird of the Cairn and the Scaur."

Scott sold Rosebank in the course of the year for L.5000. 15 This bequest made an important change in his pecuniary position, and influenced accordingly the arrangements of his future life. Independently of practice at the Bar, and of literary profits, he was now, with his little patrimony, his Sheriffship, and about L.200 per annum arising from 20 the stock ultimately settled on his wife, in possession of a fixed revenue of nearly L.1000 a-year.

When he first examined Ashestiel, with a view to being his cousin's tenant, he thought of taking home James Hogg° to superintend the sheep-farm, and keep watch over 25 the house also during the winter. I am not able to tell exactly in what manner this proposal fell to the ground; but in truth the Sheriff had hardly been a week in possession of his new domains, before he made acquaintance with a character much better suited to his purpose than 30 James Hogg ever could have been. I mean honest Thomas Purdie, his faithful servant — his affectionately devoted humble friend from this time until death parted them.

F

Tom was first brought before him, in his capacity of Sheriff, on a charge of poaching, when the poor fellow gave such a touching account of his circumstances, — a wife, and I know not how many children, depending on his exertions
5 — work scarce and grouse abundant, — and all this with a mixture of odd sly humour, — that the Sheriff's heart was moved. Tom escaped the penalty of the law — was taken into employment as shepherd, and shewed such zeal, activity, and shrewdness in that capacity, that Scott
10 never had any occasion to repent of the step he soon afterwards took, in promoting him to the position which had been originally offered to James Hogg.

It was also about the same time that he took into his service as coachman Peter Mathieson, brother-in-law to
15 Thomas Purdie, another faithful servant, who never afterwards left him, and still (1848) survives his kind master. Scott's awkward management of the little phaeton had exposed his wife to more than one perilous overturn, before he agreed to set up a close carriage, and call in the assist-
20 ance of this steady charioteer.

To return to the Lay of the Last Minstrel: Scott wrote Ellis, August 21 — "I wish very much I could have sent you the Lay while in MS., to have had the advantage of your opinion and corrections. But Ballantyne galled
25 my kibes° so severely during an unusual fit of activity, that I gave him the whole story in a sort of pet both with him and with it."

There is a circumstance which must already have struck such of my readers as knew the author in his latter days,
30 namely, the readiness with which he seems to have communicated this poem, in its progress, not only to his own familiar friends, but to new and casual acquaintances. We shall find him following the same course with his Marmion

— but not, I think, with any of his subsequent works.
His determination to consult the movements of his own
mind alone in the conduct of his pieces, was probably taken
before he began the Lay; and he soon resolved to trust
for the detection of minor inaccuracies to two persons only 5
— James Ballantyne and William Erskine. The printer
was himself a man of considerable literary talents : his own
style had the incurable faults of pomposity and affectation ;
but his eye for more venial errors in the writings of others
was quick, and, though his personal address was apt to give 10
a stranger the impression of insincerity, he was in reality
an honest man, and conveyed his mind on such matters
with equal candour and delicacy during the whole of Scott's
brilliant career. In the vast majority of instances he
found his friend acquiesce at once in the propriety of his 15
suggestions ; nay, there certainly were cases, though rare,
in which his advice to alter things of much more consequence than a word or a rhyme, was frankly tendered, and
on deliberation adopted by Scott. Mr. Erskine was the
referee whenever the poet hesitated about taking the hints 20
of the zealous typographer; and his refined taste and
gentle manners rendered his critical alliance highly valuable. With two such faithful friends within his reach,
the author of the Lay might safely dispense with sending
his MS. to be revised even by George Ellis. 25
  In the first week of January 1805, "The Lay" was published; and its success at once decided that literature
should form the main business of Scott's life. I shall not
mock the reader with many words as to the merits of a
poem which has now kept its place for nearly half a cen- 30
tury; but one or two additional remarks on the history of
the composition may be pardoned.
  It is curious to trace the small beginnings and gradual

development of his design. The lovely Countess of Dalkeith hears a wild rude legend of Border *diablerie*, and
sportively asks him to make it the subject of a ballad.
A single scene of feudal festivity in the hall of Branksome,
5 disturbed by some pranks of a nondescript goblin, was probably all that he contemplated; but his accidental confinement in the midst of a volunteer camp gave him leisure
to meditate his theme to the sound of the bugle; — and
suddenly there flashes on him the idea of extending his
10 simple outline, so as to embrace a vivid panorama of that
old Border life of war and tumult, and all earnest passions,
with which his researches on the "Minstrelsy" had by degrees fed his imagination, until even the minutest feature
had been taken home and realized with unconscious in-
15 tenseness of sympathy; so that he had won for himself in
the past, another world, hardly less complete or familiar
than the present. Erskine or Cranstoun suggests that he
would do well to divide the poem into cantos, and prefix
to each of them a motto explanatory of the action, after
20 the fashion of Spenser in the Faery Queen. He pauses for
a moment — and the happiest conception of the framework
of a picturesque narrative that ever occurred to any poet —
one that Homer might have envied — the creation of the
ancient harper, starts to life. By such steps did the Lay
25 of the Last Minstrel grow out of the Minstrelsy of the
Scottish Border.

"It would be great affectation," says the Introduction
of 1830, "not to own that the author expected some success from the Lay of the Last Minstrel. The attempt
30 to return to a more simple and natural poetry was likely to
be welcomed, at a time when the public had become tired
of heroic hexameters, with all the buckram and binding
that belong to them in modern days. But whatever might

have been his expectations, whether moderate or unreasonable, the result left them far behind; for among those who smiled on the adventurous minstrel were numbered the great names of William Pitt and Charles Fox. Neither was the extent of the sale inferior to the character of the judges who received the poem with approbation. Upwards of 30,000 copies were disposed of by the trade; and the author had to perform a task difficult to human vanity, when called upon to make the necessary deductions from his own merits, in a calm attempt to account for its popularity."

The publishers of the first edition were Longman and Co. of London, and Archibald Constable and Co. of Edinburgh; which last house, however, had but a small share in the adventure. The profits were to be divided equally between the author and his publishers; and Scott's moiety was £169, 6s. Messrs. Longman, when a second edition was called for, offered £500 for the copyright; this was accepted; but they afterwards, as the Introduction says, "added £100 in their own unsolicited kindness. It was handsomely given, to supply the loss of a fine horse which broke down suddenly while the author was riding with one of the worthy publishers." The author's whole share, then, in the profits of the Lay, came to £769, 6s.

Mr. Ballantyne, in his Memorandum, says, that very shortly after the publication of the Lay, he found himself obliged to apply to Mr. Scott for an advance of money; his own capital being inadequate for the business which had been accumulated on his press, in consequence of the reputation it had acquired for beauty and correctness of execution. Already, as we have seen, the printer had received "a liberal loan;" — "and now," says he, "being compelled, maugre all delicacy, to renew my application,

he candidly answered that he was not quite sure that it
would be prudent for him to comply, but in order to evince
his entire confidence in me, he was willing to make a suitable advance to be admitted as a third-sharer of my
5 business." No trace has been discovered of any examination into the state of the business, on the part of Scott,
at this time. However, he now embarked in Ballantyne's
concern almost the whole of the capital which he had a few
months before designed to invest in the purchase of
10 Broadmeadows. *Dis aliter visum.*°

We have seen that, before he formed his contract with
Ballantyne, he was in possession of such a fixed income as
might have satisfied all his desires, had he not found his
family increasing rapidly about him. Even as that was,
15 with nearly if not quite £1000 per annum, he might perhaps have retired not only from the Bar, but from Edinburgh, and settled entirely at Ashestiel or Broadmeadows,
without encountering what any man of his station and
habits ought to have considered as an imprudent risk. He
20 had, however, no wish to cut himself off from the busy and
intelligent society to which he had been hitherto accustomed; and resolved not to leave the Bar until he should
have at least used his best efforts for obtaining, in addition
to his Shrievalty, one of those Clerkships of the Supreme
25 Court which are usually considered as honourable retire-
ments for advocates who, at a certain standing, give up all
hopes of reaching the Bench. "I determined," he says,
"that literature should be my staff but not my crutch,
and that the profits of my literary labour, however con-
30 venient otherwise, should not, if I could help it, become
necessary to my ordinary expenses. Upon such a post
an author might hope to retreat, without any perceptible
alteration of circumstances, whenever the time should

arrive that the public grew weary of his endeavours to please, or he himself should tire of the pen. I possessed so many friends capable of assisting me in this object of ambition, that I could hardly overrate my own prospects of obtaining the preferment to which I limited my wishes; 5 and, in fact, I obtained, in no long period, the reversion of a situation which completely met them."

The forming of this commercial tie was one of the most important steps in Scott's life. He continued bound by it during twenty years, and its influence on his literary 10 exertions and his worldly fortunes was productive of much good and not a little evil. Its effects were in truth so mixed and balanced during the vicissitudes of a long and vigorous career, that I at this moment doubt whether it ought, on the whole, to be considered with more of satis- 15 faction or of regret.

With what zeal he proceeded in advancing the views of the new copartnership, his correspondence bears ample evidence. The brilliant and captivating genius, now acknowledged universally, was soon discovered by the lead- 20 ing booksellers of the time to be united with such abundance of matured information in many departments, and, above all, with such indefatigable habits, as to mark him out for the most valuable workman they could engage for the furtherance of their schemes. He had, long before 25 this, cast a shrewd and penetrating eye over the field of literary enterprise, and developed in his own mind the outlines of many extensive plans, which wanted nothing but the command of a sufficient body of able subalterns to be carried into execution with splendid success. Such of 30 these as he grappled with in his own person were, with rare exceptions, carried to a triumphant conclusion; but the alliance with Ballantyne soon infected him with the

proverbial rashness of mere mercantile adventure — while,
at the same time, his generous feelings for other men of
letters, and his characteristic propensity to overrate their
talents, combined to hurry him and his friends into a
5 multitude of arrangements, the results of which were often
extremely embarrassing, and ultimately, in the aggregate,
all but disastrous.   It is an old saying, that wherever there
is a secret there must be something wrong; and dearly did
he pay the penalty for the mystery in which he had chosen
10 to involve this transaction.   It was his rule, from the beginning, that whatever he wrote or edited must be printed
at that press; and had he catered for it only as author and
sole editor, all had been well; but had the booksellers known
his direct pecuniary interest in keeping up and extend-
15 ing the occupation of those types, they would have taken
into account his lively imagination and sanguine temperament, as well as his taste and judgment, and considered, far more deliberately than they too often did, his
multifarious recommendations of new literary schemes,
20 coupled though these were with some dim understanding
that, if the Ballantyne press were employed, his own literary skill would be at his friend's disposal for the general
superintendence of the undertaking.   On the other hand,
Scott's suggestions were, in many cases, perhaps in the
25 majority of them, conveyed through Ballantyne, whose
habitual deference to his opinion induced him to advocate
them with enthusiastic zeal; and the printer, who had thus
pledged his personal authority for the merits of the proposed scheme, must have felt himself committed to the
30 bookseller, and could hardly refuse with decency to take a
certain share of the pecuniary risk, by allowing the time
and method of his own payment to be regulated according
to the employer's convenience.   Hence, by degrees, was

woven a web of entanglement from which neither Ballantyne nor his adviser had any means of escape, except only in that indomitable spirit, the mainspring of personal industry altogether unparalleled, to which, thus set in motion, the world owes its most gigantic monument of literary genius. 5

The General Preface to his Novels informs us, that "about 1805" he wrote the opening chapters of Waverley; and the second title, *'Tis Sixty Years Since,* selected, as he says, "that the actual date of publication 10 might correspond with the period in which the scene was laid," leaves no doubt that he had begun the work so early in 1805 as to contemplate publishing it before Christmas. He adds, in the same page, that he was induced, by the favourable reception of the Lady of the Lake, to think 15 of giving some of his recollections of Highland Scenery and customs in prose; but this is only one instance of the inaccuracy as to matters of date which pervades all those delightful Prefaces. The Lady of the Lake was not published until five years after the first chapters of Waverley 20 were written; its success, therefore, could have had no share in suggesting the original design of a Highland novel, though no doubt it principally influenced him to take up that design after it had been long suspended, and almost forgotten. 25

"Having proceeded," he says, "as far as I think the seventh chapter, I shewed my work to a critical friend, whose opinion was unfavourable; and having then some poetical reputation, I was unwilling to risk the loss of it by attempting a new style of composition. I, therefore, then 30 threw aside the work I had commenced, without either reluctance or remonstrance. I ought to add, that though my ingenuous friend's sentence was afterwards reversed, on

an appeal to the public, it cannot be considered as any
imputation on his good taste; for the specimen subjected
to his criticism did not extend beyond the departure of the
hero for Scotland, and consequently had not entered upon
5 the part of the story which was finally found most interesting." It is, I think, evident from a letter of 1810, that
the first critic of the opening chapters of Waverley was
William Erskine.

Meanwhile, Ashestiel, in place of being less resorted to
10 by literary strangers than Lasswade cottage had been,
shared abundantly in the fresh attractions of the Lay, and
"booksellers in the plural number" were preceded and
followed by an endless variety of tourists, whose main
temptation from the south had been the hope of seeing
15 the Borders in company with their Minstrel. One of this
year's guests was Mr. Southey° — their first meeting, the
commencement of much kind intercourse.

Mr. Skene soon discovered a change which had recently
been made in his friend's distribution of his time. Pre-
20 viously it had been his custom, whenever professional business or social engagements occupied the middle part of
his day, to seize some hours for study after he was supposed to have retired to bed. His physician suggested
that this was very likely to aggravate his nervous head-
25 aches, the only malady he was subject to in the prime of
his manhood; and, contemplating with steady eye a
course not only of unremitting but of increasing industry,
he resolved to reverse his plan. In short he had now
adopted the habits in which, with slender variation, he
30 ever after persevered when in the country. He rose by
five o'clock, lit his fire when the season required one, and
shaved and dressed with great deliberation — for he was
a very martinet as to all but the mere coxcombries of the

toilet, not abhorring effeminate dandyism itself so cordially as the slightest approach to personal slovenliness, or even those "bed-gown and slipper tricks," as he called them, in which literary men are so apt to indulge. Clad in his shooting-jacket, or whatever dress he meant to use till 5 dinner time, he was seated at his desk by six o'clock, all his papers arranged before him in the most accurate order, and his books of reference marshalled around him on the floor, while at least one favourite dog lay watching his eye, just beyond the line of circumvallation. Thus, by the 10 time the family assembled for breakfast between nine and ten, he had done enough (in his own language) *"to break the neck of the day's work."* After breakfast, a couple of hours more were given to his solitary tasks, and by noon he was, as he used to say, "his own man." When the 15 weather was bad, he would labour incessantly all the morning; but the general rule was to be out and on horse-back by one o'clock at the latest; while, if any more dis-tant excursion had been proposed over night, he was ready to start on it by ten; his occasional rainy days of unin- 20 termitted study forming, as he said, a fund in his favour, out of which he was entitled to draw for accommodation whenever the sun shone with special brightness.

It was another rule, that every letter he received should be answered that same day. Nothing else could have en- 25 abled him to keep abreast with the flood of communica-tions that in the sequel put his good nature to the severest test — but already the demands on him in this way also were numerous; and he included attention to them among the necessary business which must be dispatched before 30 he had a right to close his writing-box, or as he phrased it, "to say, *out damned spot,*° and be a gentleman." In turning over his enormous mass of correspondence, I have

almost invariably found some indication that, when a
letter had remained more than a day or two unanswered,
it was because he found occasion for inquiry.

I ought not to omit, that in those days Scott was far too
5 zealous a dragoon not to take a principal share in the
stable duty.   Before beginning his desk-work in the morning, he uniformly visited his favourite steed, and neither
Captain nor *Lieutenant* nor *Brown Adam* (so called after
one of the heroes of the Minstrelsy), liked to be fed except
10 by him.   The latter charger was indeed altogether in-
tractable in other hands, though in his the most submissive
of faithful allies.   The moment he was bridled and sad-
dled, it was the custom to open the stable door as a signal
that his master expected him, when he immediately trotted
15 to the side of the *leaping-on-stone*, of which Scott from his
lameness found it convenient to make use, and stood there,
silent and motionless as a rock, until he was fairly in his
seat, after which he displayed his joy by neighing tri-
umphantly through a brilliant succession of curvettings.
20 Brown Adam never suffered himself to be backed but by
his master.   He broke, I believe, one groom's arm and another's leg in the rash attempt to tamper with his dignity.

Camp was at this time the constant parlour dog.   He
was very handsome, very intelligent, and naturally very
25 fierce, but gentle as a lamb among the children.   As for
a brace of lighter pets, styled Douglas and Percy, he kept
one window of his study open, whatever might be the state
of the weather, that they might leap out and in as the fancy
moved them.   He always talked to Camp as if he under-
30 stood what was said — and the animal certainly did understand not a little of it; in particular, it seemed as if he
perfectly comprehended on all occasions that his master
considered him as a sensible and steady friend — the

greyhounds as volatile young creatures whose freaks must be borne with.

"Every day," says Mr. Skene, "we had some hours of coursing with the greyhounds, or riding at random over the hills, or of spearing salmon in the Tweed by sunlight: 5 which last sport, moreover, we often renewed at night by the help of torches. This amusement of *burning the water*, as it is called, was not without some hazard; for the large salmon generally lie in the pools, the depths of which it is not easy to estimate with precision by torchlight, — so that 10 not unfrequently, when the sportsman makes a determined thrust at a fish apparently within reach, his eye has grossly deceived him, and instead of the point of the weapon encountering the prey, he finds himself launched with corresponding vehemence heels over head into the pool, both 15 spear and salmon gone, the torch thrown out by the concussion of the boat, and quenched in the stream, while the boat itself has of course receded to some distance. I remember the first time I accompanied our friend, he went right over the gunwale in this manner, and had I not 20 accidentally been at his side, and made a successful grasp at the skirt of his jacket as he plunged overboard, he must at least have had an awkward dive for it. Such are the contingencies of *burning the water*. The pleasures consist in being penetrated with cold and wet, having your shins 25 broken against the stones in the dark, and perhaps mastering one fish out of every twenty you take aim at."

About this time Mr. and Mrs. Scott made a short excursion to the Lakes of Cumberland and Westmoreland, and visited some of their finest scenery, in company with Mr. 30 Wordsworth. I have found no written narrative of this little tour, but I have often heard Scott speak with enthusiastic delight of the reception he met with in the

humble cottage which his brother poet then inhabited on
the banks of Grasmere; and at least one of the days they
spent together was destined to furnish a theme for the verse
of each, namely, that which they gave to the ascent of
5 Helvellyn. This day they were accompanied by an
illustrious philosopher, who was also a true poet — and
might have been one of the greatest of poets had he chosen;
and I have heard Mr. Wordsworth say, that it would be
difficult to express the feelings with which he, who so often
10 had climbed Helvellyn alone, found himself standing on
its summit with two such men as Scott and Davy.°

Meantime, the affair of the Clerkship, opened nine or
ten months before, had not been neglected by the friends
on whose counsel and assistance Scott had relied. George
15 Home of Wedderburn, an old friend of his family, had now
held a Clerkship for upwards of thirty years. In those
days there was no system of retiring pensions for the worn-
out functionary of this class, and the usual method was,
either that he should resign in favour of a successor who
20 advanced a sum of money according to the circumstances
of his age and health, or for a coadjutor to be associated
with him in his patent, who undertook the duty on condition of a division of salary. Scott offered to relieve Mr.
Home of all the labours of his office, and to allow him,
25 nevertheless, to retain its emoluments entire; and the
aged clerk of course joined his exertions to procure a con-
joint-patent on these very advantageous terms.

The Court of Session sat, in his time, from the 12th of
May to the 12th of July, and again from the 12th of No-
30 vember, with a short interval at Christmas, to the 12th of
March. The Judges of the Inner Court took their places
on the Bench, every morning not later than ten o'clock,
and remained according to the amount of business ready

for despatch, but seldom for less than four or more than six hours daily; during which space the Principal Clerks continued seated at a table below the Bench, to watch the progress of the suits, and record the decisions — the cases of all classes being equally apportioned among their num- 5 ber. The Court of Session, however, does not sit on Monday, that day being reserved for the criminal business of the High Court of Justiciary, and there is also another blank day every other week, — the *Teind ° Wednesday*, as it is called, when the Judges are assembled for the hearing 10 of tithe questions, which belong to a separate jurisdiction, of comparatively modern creation, and having its own separate establishment of officers. On the whole, then, Scott's attendance in Court may be taken to have amounted, on the average, to from four to six hours daily 15 during rather less than six months out of the twelve.

Not a little of the Clerk's business in Court is merely formal, and indeed mechanical; but there are few days in which he is not called upon for the exertion of his higher faculties, in reducing the decisions of the Bench, orally 20 pronounced, to technical shape; which, in a new, complex, or difficult case, cannot be satisfactorily done without close attention to all the previous proceedings and written documents, an accurate understanding of the principles or precedents on which it has been determined, and a 25 thorough command of the whole vocabulary of legal forms. Dull or indolent men, promoted through the mere wantonness of political patronage, might, no doubt, contrive to devolve the harder part of their duty upon humbler assistants; but in general, the office had been held by gentle- 30 men of high character and attainments; and more than one among Scott's own colleagues enjoyed the reputation of legal science that would have done honour to the Bench.

Such men, of course, prided themselves on doing well whatever it was their proper function to do; and it was by their example, not that of the drones who condescended to lean upon unseen and irresponsible inferiors, that Scott 5 uniformly modelled his own conduct as a Clerk of Session. To do this, required, of necessity, constant study of law-papers and authorities at home. There was also a great deal of really base drudgery, such as the authenticating of registered deeds by signature, which he had to go through 10 out of Court; he had, too, a Shrievalty, though not a heavy one, all the while upon his hands; — and, on the whole, it forms one of the most remarkable features in his history, that, throughout the most active period of his literary career, he must have devoted a large proportion 15 of his hours, during half at least of every year, to the conscientious discharge of professional duties.

Henceforth, then, when in Edinburgh, his literary work was performed chiefly before breakfast; with the assistance of such evening hours as he could contrive to rescue 20 from the consideration of Court papers, and from those social engagements in which, year after year, as his celebrity advanced, he was of necessity more and more largely involved; and of those entire days during which the Court of Session did not sit — days which, by most of those 25 holding the same official station, were given to relaxation and amusement. So long as he continued quarter-master of the Volunteer Cavalry, of course he had, even while in Edinburgh, some occasional horse exercise; but, in general, his town life henceforth was in that respect as inac- 30 tive as his country life ever was the reverse. He scorned for a long while to attach any consequence to this complete alternation of habits; but we shall find him confessing in the sequel that it proved highly injurious to his bodily health.

CHAPTER V

Marmion — Edition of Dryden's Life and Works — Mr.
Morritt of Rokeby — Domestic Life — Education of
Children — 1806–1809.

DURING the whole of 1806 and 1807 Dryden° continued
to occupy the greater share of Scott's literary hours; but
in November, 1806, he began Marmion.

He was at this time in communication with several
booksellers, each of whom would willingly have engrossed 5
his labour; but from the moment that his undertakings
began to be serious, he seems to have acted on the maxim,
that no author should ever let any one house fancy that
they had obtained a right of monopoly over his works.
Of the conduct of Messrs. Longman, he has attested that it 10
was liberal beyond his expectation; but, nevertheless, a
negotiation which they now opened proved fruitless.
Constable offered a thousand guineas for the poem very
shortly after it was begun, and without having seen one
line of it. It is hinted in the Introduction of 1830, that 15
private circumstances rendered it desirable for Scott to
obtain the immediate command of such a sum; the price
was actually paid long before the book was published;
and it suits very well with Constable's character to suppose that his readiness to advance the money may have 20
outstripped the calculations of more established dealers,
and thus cast the balance in his favour. He was not,
however, so unwise as to keep the whole adventure to
himself. His bargain being concluded, he tendered one-

fourth of the copyright to Miller of Albemarle Street, and another to John Murray, then of Fleet Street; and the latter at once replied, "We both view it as honourable, profitable, and glorious to be concerned in the pub-
5 lication of a new poem by Walter Scott." The news that a thousand guineas had been paid for an unseen and unfinished MS. seemed in those days portentous; and it must be allowed that the man who received such a sum for a performance in embryo, had made a great step in the
10 hazards as well as in the honours of authorship. The bulky appendix of notes, including a mass of curious antiquarian quotations, must have moved somewhat slowly through the printer's hands; but Marmion was at length ready for publication by the middle of February
15 1808.

I shall not say anything more of Marmion in this place, than that I have always considered it as on the whole the greatest of Scott's poems. There is a certain light, easy, virgin charm about the Lay, which we look for in vain
20 through the subsequent volumes of his verse; but the superior strength, and breadth, and boldness both of conception and execution in the Marmion appear to me indisputable. The great blot, the combination of *mean felony* with so many noble qualities in the character of the
25 hero, was, as the poet says, severely commented on at the time by the most ardent of his early friends, Leyden; but though he admitted the justice of that criticism, he chose "to let the tree lie as it had fallen." He was also sensible that many of the subordinate and connecting
30 parts of the narrative are flat, harsh, and obscure — but would never make any serious attempt to do away with these imperfections; and perhaps they, after all, heighten by contrast the effect of the passages of high-wrought en-

thusiasm which alone he considered, in after days, with
satisfaction.

Before quitting Marmion I ought to say that, like the
Lay, this and the subsequent great poems were all first
published in a splendid quarto form. The 2000 of the 5
original Marmion, price a guinea and a half, were disposed
of in less than a month; and twelve octavo editions between 1808 and 1825, had carried the sale to upwards of
30,000 copies, before the author included it in the collection of his poetry with biographical prefaces in 1830; 10
since which period there have been frequent reprints;
making an aggregate legitimate circulation between 1808
and 1848 of about 60,000.

Ere the poem was published, a heavy task, begun earlier,
and continued throughout its progress, had been nearly 15
completed; and there appeared in the last week of April
1808, *The Works of John Dryden, now first collected; with
notes historical, critical, and explanatory, and a Life of the
Author.— Eighteen volumes 8vo.* This was the bold speculation of William Miller of Albemarle Street; and the 20
editor's fee, at forty guineas the volume, was L.756. It
was better received than any one, except perhaps the
courageous bookseller himself, had anticipated. The
entire work was reprinted in 1821; — since then the Life
of Dryden had its place in various editions of Scott's prose 25
miscellanies; nor perhaps does that class of his writings
include any piece which keeps a higher estimation.

On the whole, it is impossible to doubt that the success
of Dryden in rapidly reaching, and till the end of a long
life holding undisputed, the summit of public favour and 30
reputation, in spite of his "brave neglect" of minute
finishing, narrow laws, and prejudiced authorities, must
have had a powerful effect in nervirg Scott's hope and

resolution for the wide ocean of literary enterprise into which he had now fairly launched his bark. Like Dryden, he felt himself to be "amply stored with acquired knowledge, much of it the fruits of early reading and applica-5 tion"; anticipated that though, "while engaged in the hurry of composition, or overcome by the lassitude of continued literary labour," he should sometimes "draw with too much liberality on a tenacious memory," no "occasional imperfections would deprive him of his 10 praise"; in short, made up his mind that "pointed and nicely-turned lines, sedulous study, and long and repeated correction and revision" would all be dispensed with, — provided their place were supplied as in Dryden by "rapidity of conception, a readiness of expressing every idea 15 without losing anything by the way — perpetual animation and elasticity of thought — and language never laboured, never loitering, never (in Dryden's own phrase) *cursedly confined.*"

I believe that Scott had, in 1807, agreed with London 20 booksellers as to the superintendence of two other large collections, the Somers' Tracts° and the Sadler State Papers,° but it seems that Constable first heard of these engagements when he accompanied the second cargo of Marmion to the great southern market; and, alarmed at 25 the prospect of losing his hold on Scott's industry, he at once invited him to follow up his Dryden by an Edition of Swift° on the same scale, — offering, moreover, to double the rate of payment; that is to say, to give him L.1500 for the new undertaking. This munificent tender was 30 accepted; and as early as May 1808, I find Scott writing in all directions for books, pamphlets, and MSS., likely to be serviceable in illustrating the Life and Works of the Dean of St. Patrick's.

It was not long before some of the dull malignants of the Parliament House began to insinuate what at length found a dull and dignified mouthpiece in the House of Commons — that if a Clerk of Session had any real business to do, it could not be done well by a man who found 5 time for more literary enterprises than any other author of the age undertook — "wrote more books," Lord Archibald Hamilton serenely added, "than any body could find leisure to read" — and, moreover, mingled in general society as much as many that had no pursuit but pleasure. 10

He had now reached a period of life after which real friendships are but seldom formed; and it is fortunate that another with an Englishman of the highest class of accomplishments had been thoroughly compacted before death cut the ties between him and George Ellis — be- 15 cause his dearest intimates within Scotland had of course but a slender part in his written correspondence. Mr. Morritt of Rokeby and his wife had long been intimate with Lady Louisa Stuart and Mr. William Rose; and the meeting, therefore, had been well prepared for. It took 20 place at Edinburgh in June. Scott shewed them the lions of the town and its vicinity, exactly as if he had nothing else to attend to but their gratification.

Mr. Morritt's mention of the "happy young family clustered round him" reminds me that I ought to say a 25 few words on Scott's method of treating his children in their early days. He had now two boys and two girls; [1] — and he never had more. He was not one of those who take much delight in a mere infant; but no father ever devoted more time and tender care to his offspring than he did to 30 each of his, as they reached the age when they could

[1] Charlotte Sophia, born in October 1799; Walter, October 1801; Anne, February 1803; Charles, December 1805.

listen to him, and understand his talk. Like their play-
mates, Camp and the greyhounds, they had at all times
free access to his study; he never considered their prattle
as any disturbance; they went and came as pleased their
5 fancy; he was always ready to answer their questions;
and when they, unconscious how he was engaged, entreated
him to lay down his pen and tell them a story, he would
take them on his knee, repeat a ballad or a legend, kiss
them, and set them down again to their marbles or nine-
10 pins, and resume his labour, as if refreshed by the interruption. From a very early age he made them dine at
table, and "to sit up to supper" was the great reward when
they had been "very good bairns." In short, he considered it as the highest duty as well as the sweetest pleasure
15 of a parent to be the companion of his children; he partook all their little joys and sorrows, and made his kind
unformal instructions to blend so easily and playfully
with the current of their own sayings and doings, that so
far from regarding him with any distant awe, it was never
20 thought that any sport or diversion could go on in the right
way, unless *papa* were of the party, or that the rainiest
day could be dull, so he were at home.

Of the irregularity of his own education he speaks with
regret, in the autobiographical fragment written this
25 year at Ashestiel; yet his practice does not look as if that
feeling had been strongly rooted in his mind; — for he
never did shew much concern about regulating systematically what is usually called *education* in the case of his
children. It seemed, on the contrary, as if he attached
30 little importance to anything else, so he could perceive
that the young curiosity was excited — the intellect, by
whatever springs of interest, set in motion. He detested
and despised the whole generation of modern children's

books, in which the attempt is made to convey accurate
notions of scientific minutiæ: delighting cordially, on the
other hand, in those of the preceding age, which, addressing
themselves chiefly to the imagination, obtain through it,
as he believed, the best chance of stirring our graver facul- 5
ties also.   He exercised the memory by selecting for tasks
of recitation passages of popular verse the most likely
to catch the fancy of children; and gradually familiarized
them with the ancient history of their own country, by
arresting attention, in the course of his own oral narra- 10
tions, on incidents and characters of a similar description.
Nor did he neglect to use the same means of quickening
curiosity as to the events of sacred history.   On Sunday
he never rode — at least not until his growing infirmity
made his pony almost necessary to him — for it was his 15
principle that all domestic animals have a full right to
their Sabbath of rest; but after he had read the prayers
and lessons of the day, he usually walked with his whole
family, dogs included, to some favourite spot at a considerable distance from the house — most frequently the 20
ruined tower of Elibank — and there dined with them in
the open air on a basket of cold provisions, mixing his wine
with the water of the brook beside which they all were
grouped around him on the turf; and here, or at home, if
the weather kept them from their ramble, his Sunday 25
talk was just such a series of biblical lessons as that which
we have preserved for the permanent use of rising genera-
tions, in his Tales of a Grandfather on the early history
of Scotland.   I wish he had committed that other series
to writing too; — how different that would have been from 30
our thousand compilations of dead epitome and imbecile
cant!   He had his Bible, the Old Testament especially,
by heart; and on these days inwove the simple pathos or

sublime enthusiasm of Scripture, in whatever story he
was telling, with the same picturesque richness as in his
week-day tales the quaint Scotch of Pitscottie,° or some
rude romantic old rhyme from Barbour's° Bruce or Blind
5 Harry's° Wallace.

By many external accomplishments, either in girl or
boy, he set little store. He delighted to hear his daughters
sing an old ditty, or one of his own framing; but, so the
singer appeared to feel the spirit of her ballad, he was not
10 at all critical of the technical execution. There was one
thing, however, on which he fixed his heart hardly less
than the ancient Persians of the Cyropædia°:   like them,
next to love of truth, he held love of horsemanship for the
prime point of education. As soon as his eldest girl could
15 sit a pony, she was made the regular attendant of his
mountain rides; and they all, as they attained sufficient
strength, had the like advancement. He taught them to
think nothing of tumbles, and habituated them to his own
reckless delight in perilous fords and flooded streams;
20 and they all imbibed in great perfection his passion for
horses — as well, I may venture to add, as his deep reverence for the more important article of that Persian training. "Without courage," he said, "there cannot be truth;
and without truth there can be no other virtue."

25   He had a horror of boarding-schools; never allowed his
girls to learn anything out of his own house; and chose
their governess — Miss Miller — who about this time was
domesticated with them, and never left them while they
needed one, — with far greater regard to her kind good
30 temper and excellent moral and religious principles, than
to the measure of her attainments in what are called
fashionable accomplishments. The admirable system of
education for boys in Scotland combines all the advan-

tages of public and private instruction; his carried their
satchels to the High-School, when the family was in Edinburgh, just as he had done before them, and shared of
course the evening society of their happy home. But he
rarely, if ever, left them in town, when he could himself 5
be in the country; and at Ashestiel he was, for better or
for worse, his eldest boy's daily tutor, after he began
Latin.

CHAPTER VI

The Lady of the Lake — Excursion to the Hebrides — Purchase of Abbotsford — 1809-1812.

Scott had by the end of 1809 all but completed his third great poem; yet this year also was crowded with miscellaneous literary labours. In it he made great progress with Swift, and in it he finished and saw published 5 his edition of the Sadler Papers; the notes copious, curious, lively and entertaining, and the Life of Sir Ralph° a very pleasing specimen of his style. Several volumes of the huge Somers' Collection, illustrated throughout with similar care, were also issued in 1809; and I suppose he re-10 ceived his fee for each volume as it appeared — the whole sum amounting, when the last came out in 1812, to 1300 guineas. His labours on these collections were gradually storing his mind with that minute knowledge of the leading persons and events both of Scotch and English history, 15 which made his conversation on such subjects that of one who had rather lived with than read about the departed. He delighted in them, and never complained that they interrupted disadvantageously the works of his higher genius.

20 Early in May the Lady of the Lake came out — as her two elder sisters had done — in all the majesty of quarto, with every accompanying grace of typography, and with moreover an engraved frontispiece of Saxon's° portrait of Scott; the price of the book two guineas. For the copy-

90

right the poet had nominally received 2000 guineas, but as John Ballantyne° and Co. retained three-fourths of the property to themselves (Miller of London purchasing the other fourth), the author's profits were, or should have been, more than this.   5

Mr. Cadell, the publisher of this Memoir, then a young man in training for his profession, retains a strong impression of the interest which the quarto excited before it was on the counter.   I do not recollect that any of all the author's works was ever looked for with more intense 10 anxiety, or that any one of them excited a more extraordinary sensation when it did appear.   The whole country rang with the praises of the poet — crowds set off to view the scenery of Loch Katrine, till then comparatively unknown; and as the book came out just before the season 15 for excursions, every house and inn in that neighbourhood was crammed with a constant succession of visitors.   It is a well-ascertained fact, that from the date of the publication of the Lady of the Lake, the post-horse duty in Scotland rose in an extraordinary degree, and indeed it 20 continued to do so regularly for a number of years, the author's succeeding works keeping up the enthusiasm for our scenery which he had thus originally created."

In their reception of this work, the critics were for once in full harmony with each other, and with the popular voice. 25 The Lay, if I may venture to state the creed now established, is, I should say, generally considered as the most natural and original, Marmion as the most powerful and splendid, the Lady of the Lake as the most interesting, romantic, picturesque, and graceful of his great poems.   30

Of its success he speaks as follows in 1830 : — "It was certainly so extraordinary as to induce me for the moment to conclude that I had at last fixed a nail in the proverbially inconstant wheel of Fortune. But I can with honest truth exculpate myself from having been at any time a partisan of my own poetry, even when it was in the highest fashion with the million."

5 James Ballantyne has preserved in his *Memorandum* an anecdote strikingly confirmative of the most remarkable statement in this page of Scott's confessions. "I remember," he says, "going into his library shortly after the publication of the Lady of the Lake, and finding Miss 10 Scott (who was then a very young girl) there by herself. I asked her — 'Well, Miss Sophia, how do you like the Lady of the Lake?' Her answer was given with perfect simplicity — 'Oh, I have not read it: papa says there's nothing so bad for young people as reading bad 15 poetry.'"

In fact, his children in those days had no idea of the source of his distinction — or rather, indeed, that his position was in any respect different from that of other Advocates, Sheriffs, and Clerks of Session. The eldest boy 20 came home one afternoon about this time from the High School, with tears and blood hardened together upon his cheeks. — "Well, Wat," said his father, "what have you been fighting about to-day?" With that the boy blushed and hung his head, and at last stammered out — that he 25 had been called *a lassie*. "Indeed!" said Mrs. Scott, "this was a terrible mischief to be sure." "You may say what you please, mamma," Wat answered roughly, "but I dinna think there's a *waufer* (shabbier) thing in the world than to be a lassie, to sit boring at a clout." Upon 30 further inquiry it turned out that one or two of his companions had dubbed him The Lady of the Lake, and the phrase was to him incomprehensible, save as conveying some imputation on his prowess, which he accordingly

vindicated in the usual style of the Yards.   Of the poem
he had never before heard.

On returning from a pleasant expedition to the Hebrides
and establishing himself at Ashestiel, Scott, in searching
an old desk for fishing-flies one morning, found the for- 5
gotten MS. of the first two or three chapters of Waverley.
From a letter of James Ballantyne's on now reading these
chapters, it is plain that he was not their unfavourable
critic of 1805; but though he augured "success" if the novel
were completed, he added that he could not say "how 10
much," and honestly confessed that the impression made on
his mind was far from resembling that he had received from
the first specimen of the Lady of the Lake: and once more
the fated MS. was restored to its hiding-place.   But this
was not the only unwelcome communication from that 15
quarter.   Already their publishing adventure began to
wear a bad aspect.   Between 1805 and the Christmas of
1809, Scott invested in the Ballantyne firms not less than
£9000; by this time probably there had been a farther
demand on his purse; and now the printer's triumph 20
in the fast multiplying editions of the Lady of the Lake
was darkened with ominous reports about their miscellaneous speculations — such as the Beaumont and Flet-
cher° of Weber — the "Tixall Poetry," — and the History of the Culdees° by Dr. Jamieson.°   But a still more 25
serious business was the Edinburgh Annual Register.
Its two first volumes were issued about this time, and expectation had been highly excited by the announcement
that the historical department was in the hands of Southey,
while Scott and other eminent persons were to contribute 30
to its miscellaneous literature and science.   Nevertheless, the public were alarmed by the extent of the history,
and the prospect of two volumes annually, and though

the work was continued during a long series of years, it
never profited the projectors.

Throughout 1811, his serious labour continued to be
bestowed on the Swift; but this and all other literary
5 tasks were frequently interrupted in consequence of a
step which he took early in the year. He had now at
last the near prospect of emolument from his Edinburgh
post. For, connected with the other reforms in the Scotch
judicature, was a plan for allowing the retirement of func-
10 tionaries, who had served to an advanced period of life,
upon pensions — while the effective Clerks of Session were
to be paid not by fees, but by fixed salaries of £1300;
and contemplating a speedy accession of income so considerable as this, he resolved to place himself in the situa-
15 tion to which he had probably from his earliest days
looked forward as the highest object of ambition, that of
a Tweedside Laird. — *Sit mihi sedes utinam senectœ!*°

And the place on which he had fixed his views, though
not to the common eye very attractive, had long been
20 one of peculiar interest for him. I have often heard
him tell, that when travelling in boyhood with his father
from Selkirk to Melrose, the old man desired the carriage
to halt at the foot of an eminence, and said, "We must
get out here, Walter, and see a thing quite in your line."
25 His father then conducted him to a rude stone on the edge
of an acclivity about half a mile above the Tweed, which
marks the spot —

> Where gallant Cessford's life-blood dear
> Reeked on dark Elliot's border spear.

30 This was the conclusion of the battle of Melrose, fought
in 1526, between the Earls of Angus and Home and the
two chiefs of the race of Kerr on the one side, and Buc-

cleuch on the other, in sight of the young King James V., the possession of whose person was the object of the contest. This battle is often mentioned in the Border Minstrelsy, and the reader will find a long note on it, under the lines which I have just quoted from the Lay of the Last 5 Minstrel. In the names of *Skirmish-field, Charge-Law,*° and so forth, various incidents of the fight have found a lasting record; the spot where the retainer of Buccleuch terminated the pursuit by the mortal wound of Kerr of Cessford (ancestor of the Dukes of Roxburghe), has always 10 been called *Turn-again.* In his own future domain the young minstrel had before him the scene of the last great Clan-battle of the Borders.

On the 12th of May 1811, he writes thus to James Ballantyne, — "My lease of Ashestiel is out. I have, 15 therefore, resolved to purchase a piece of ground sufficient for a cottage and a few fields. There are two pieces, either of which would suit me, but both would make a very desirable property indeed. They stretch along the Tweed, on the opposite side from Lord Somerville, and could be had 20 for between £7000 and £8000 — or either separate for about half the sum. I have serious thoughts of one or both, and must have recourse to my pen to make the matter easy. The worst is the difficulty which John might find in advancing so large a sum as the copyright of a new poem; 25 supposing it to be made payable within a year at farthest from the work going to press, — which would be essential to my purpose. Yet the Lady of the Lake came soon home. I have a letter this morning giving me good hope of my Treasury business being carried through: if this 30 takes place, I will buy both the little farms, which will give me a mile of the beautiful turn of Tweed above Galafoot — if not, I will confine myself to one. It is proper

John and you should be as soon as possible apprized of these my intentions, which I believe you will think reasonable in my situation, and at my age, while I may yet hope to sit under the shade of a tree of my own planting. I hope this 5 Register will give a start to its predecessors; I assure you I shall spare no pains. John must lend his earnest attention to clear his hands of the quire stock, and to taking in as little as he can unless in the way of exchange; in short, reefing our sails, which are at present too much spread for 10 our ballast."

It would no doubt have been wise not to buy land at all until he had seen the Treasury arrangement as to his clerkship completed — until he had completed also the poem on which he relied mainly for the purchase-money; 15 above all, until "John reefed his sails"; but he contented himself with one of the farms, that comprising the scene of Cessford's slaughter; the cost being L.4000 — one-half of which was borrowed of his brother, Major John Scott, the other, raised by the Ballantynes on the security of 20 the long-meditated *Rokeby*. The farm consisted of a meadow or *haugh* along the banks of the river, and a tract of undulated ground behind, all in a neglected state, undrained, wretchedly enclosed, much of it covered with the native heath. The house was small and poor, with a 25 common *kail-yard* on one flank, and a staring barn on the other; while in front appeared a filthy pond covered with ducks and duckweed, from which the whole tenement had derived the unharmonious designation of *Clarty Hole*. But the Tweed was every thing to him — a beautiful 30 river, flowing broad and bright over a bed of milkwhite pebbles, unless here and there where it darkened into a deep pool, overhung as yet only by the birches and alders which had survived the statelier growth of the primitive

Forest ; and the first hour that he took possession he claimed
for his farm the name of the adjoining *ford*, situated just
above the influx of the classical tributary Gala.   As might
be guessed from the name of *Abbotsford*, these lands had al!
belonged of old to the great Abbey of Melrose ; and indeed 5
• the Duke of Buccleuch, as the territorial representative
of that religious brotherhood, still retains some seignorial
rights over them and almost all the surrounding district.
Another feature of no small interest in Scott's eyes was an
ancient Roman road leading from the Eildon hills to this 10
ford, the remains of which, however, are now mostly
sheltered from view amidst his numerous plantations.
The most graceful and picturesque of all the monastic
ruins in Scotland, the Abbey of Melrose itself, is visible
from many points in the immediate neighbourhood of the 15
house ; and last, not least, on the rising ground full in view
across the river, the traveller may still observe the chief
traces of that celebrated British barrier, the *Catrail.*°
Such was the territory on which his prophetic eye already
beheld rich pastures, embosomed among flourishing groves, 20
where his children's children should thank the founder.
To his brother-in-law Mr. Carpenter he writes, "I have
bought a property extending along the banks of the river
Tweed for about half-a-mile.   This is the greatest incident
which has lately taken place in our domestic concerns, and 25
I assure you we are not a little proud of being greeted as
laird and *lady* of *Abbotsford.*"

In January 1812, Scott entered upon the enjoyment of
his proper salary as a clerk of Session, which, with his
sheriffdom, gave him from this time till very near the close 30
of his life, a professional income of L. 1600 a-year.

He finally left Ashestiel at Whitsuntide ; and the day
when this occurred was a sad one for many a poor neigh-

H

bour — for they lost, both in him and his wife, very generous protectors. In such a place, among the few evils which counterbalance so many good things in the condition of the peasantry, the most afflicting is the want of 5 access to medical advice. As far as their means and skill would go, they had both done their utmost to supply this want; and Mrs. Scott, in particular, had made it her business to visit the sick in their scattered cottages, and bestowed on them the contents of her medicine-chest as 10 well as of the larder and cellar, with the same unwearied kindness that I observed in her afterwards as lady of Abbotsford. Their children remembered the parting scene as one of unmixed affliction — but it had had its lighter features. To an English friend, on the 25th, Scott 15 wrote:— "The neighbours have been much delighted with the procession of my furniture, in which old swords, bows, targets, and lances, made a very conspicuous show. A family of turkeys was accommodated within the helmet of some *preux* chevalier° of ancient Border 20 fame; and the very cows, for aught I know, were bearing banners and muskets. I assure your ladyship that this caravan, attended by a dozen of ragged rosy peasant children, carrying fishing-rods and spears, and leading poneys, greyhounds, and spaniels, would, as it crossed the 25 Tweed, have furnished no bad subject for the pencil, and really reminded me of one of the gypsey groupes of Callot° upon their march."

The necessary alterations on the old farm-house immediately commenced; and besides raising its roof and pro-30 jecting some of the lower windows, a rustic porch, a supplemental cottage at one end, and a fountain to the south, soon made their appearance.

CHAPTER VII

Publication of Rokeby and the Bridal of Triermain —
Commercial Difficulties — Reconciliation with Constable — Voyage to the Shetland, Orkney, and Hebridean
Islands — Publication of the Life and Works of Swift
— and of Waverley — 1812–1814.

THIS was one of the busiest summers of his busy life.
Till the 12th of July he was at his post in the Court of
Session five days every week; but every Saturday evening
found him at Abbotsford, to observe the progress his
labourers had made within doors and without in his 5
absence; and on Monday night he returned to Edinburgh.
Even before the Summer Session commenced, he appears
to have made some advance in his Rokeby, for he writes
to Mr. Morritt, from Abbotsford, on the 4th of May —
"As for the house and the poem, there are twelve masons 10
hammering at the one, and one poor noddle at the other —
so they are both in progress"; and his literary tasks
throughout the long vacation were continued under the
same sort of disadvantage. That autumn he had, in fact,
no room at all for himself. The only parlour which had 15
been hammered into habitable condition served at once
for dining-room, drawing-room, school-room, and study.
A window looking to the river was kept sacred to his desk;
an old bed-curtain was nailed up across the room close
behind his chair, and there, whenever the spade, the
dibble, or the chisel (for he took his full share in all the
work on hand) was laid aside, he plied his pen, apparently

99

undisturbed and unannoyed by the surrounding confusion of masons and carpenters, to say nothing of the lady's small talk, the children's babble among themselves, or their repetition of their lessons. The truth no doubt
5 was, that when at his desk he did little more, as far as regarded *poetry*, than write down the lines which he had fashioned in his mind while pursuing his vocation as a planter. By and by, he says to Terry° : — "The acorns are coming up fast, and Tom Purdie is the happiest and
10 most consequential person in the world. My present work is building up the well with some *debris* from the Abbey. The worst of all is, that while my trees grow and my fountain fills, my purse, in an inverse ratio, sinks to zero."
15   Scott had promised to spend part of this autumn with Morritt; but now, busied with his planting, and continually urged by Ballantyne to have the Quarto ready by Christmas, he would willingly have trusted his friend's knowledge in place of his own research. Morritt urgently
20 represented, in reply, the expediency of a leisurely personal inspection. This appeal was not to be resisted and he proceeded the week after to Rokeby, travelling on horseback, his eldest boy and girl on their poneys, while Mrs. Scott followed in the carriage.
25   At Rokeby he remained about a week; and how he spent it is well told in Mr. Morritt's *Memorandum:* — "The morning after he arrived he said — 'You have often given me materials for romance — now I want a good robber's cave, and an old church of the right sort.' We
30 rode out, and he found what he wanted in the ancient slate quarries of Brignal and the ruined Abbey of Egglestone. I observed him noting down even the peculiar little wildflowers and herbs on the side of a bold crag near his in-

tended cave of Guy Denzil; and could not help saying, that as he was not to be upon oath in his work, daisies, violets, and primroses would be as poetical as any of the humble plants he was examining. I laughed, in short, at his scrupulousness; but I understood him when he re- 5 plied, 'that in nature herself no two scenes were exactly alike, and that whoever copied truly what was before his eyes, would possess the same variety in his descriptions, and exhibit apparently an imagination as boundless as the range of nature in the scenes he recorded; whereas — 10 whoever trusted to imagination, would soon find his own mind circumscribed and contracted to a few favourite images, and the repetition of these would sooner or later produce that very monotony and barrenness which had always haunted descriptive poetry in the hands of any 15 but the patient worshippers of truth. Besides which,' he said, 'local names and peculiarities make a fictitious story look so much better in the face.' In fact, from his boyish habits, he was but half satisfied with the most beautiful scenery when he could not connect with it some 20 local legend, and when I was forced sometimes to confess with the Knife-grinder, 'Story! God bless you! I have none to tell, sir' — he would laugh and say, 'then let us make one — nothing so easy as to make a tradition.'" Mr. Morritt adds, that he had brought with him about 25 half the Bridal of Triermain — and promised himself particular satisfaction in *laying a trap for Jeffrey*.°

Crowded as this year was with multifarious cares and tasks — the romance of Rokeby was finished before the close of 1812. Though it had been long in hand, the MS. 30 bears abundant evidence of its being the *prima cura*°: three cantos at least reached the printer through the Melrose post — written on paper of various sorts and sizes — full of blots and interlineations — the closing couplets of a despatch now and then encircling the page, and mutilated by the breaking of the seal.

On the day of publication (January 12, 1813), Scott
5 writes gaily enough to Morritt, from his seat at the Clerks' table : — "The book has gone off here very bobbishly ; for the impression of 3000 and upwards is within two or three score of being exhausted, and the demand for these continuing faster than they can be boarded. I am heart-
10 ily glad of this, for now I have nothing to fear but a bankruptcy in the Gazette of Parnassus ; but the loss of five or six thousand pounds to my good friends and school companions would have afflicted me very much."

I have already adverted to the fact that Scott felt it a
15 relief, not a fatigue, to compose the Bridal of Triermain *pari passu°* with Rokeby. In answer, for example, to one of his printer's letters, he says, "I fully share in your anxiety to get forward the grand work ; but, I assure you, I feel the more confidence from coquetting with the
20 guerilla." The quarto was followed, within two months, by the small volume which had been designed for a twin-birth ; — the MS. had been transcribed by one of the Ballantynes themselves, in order to guard against any indiscretion of the press-people ; and the mystification,
25 aided and abetted by Erskine, in no small degree heightened the interest of its reception. Except Morritt, Scott had no English confidant. Whether any of his companions in the Parliament House were in the secret, I have never heard ; but I can scarcely believe that any
30 of those who had known him and Erskine from their youth upwards, could have believed the latter capable either of the invention or the execution of this airy and fascinating romance in little. Mr. Jeffrey, as it happened,

made a voyage that year to America, and thus lost the opportunity of immediately expressing his opinion either of Rokeby or of Triermain. The Quarterly critic seems to have been completely deceived.

The limits of this narrative do not admit of minute 5 details concerning the commercial adventures in which Scott was entangled; and those of the period we have now reached are so painful that I am very willing to spare them. By the spring of 1813 the crisis in the war affected credit universally; and while the oldest firms in every 10 department of the trade of literature had difficulties to contend with, the pressure brought many of humbler resources to extremity. It was so with the house of John Ballantyne & Co. ; which had started with no solid capital except what Scott supplied; and had been entrusted to 15 one who never looked beyond the passing day — availed himself with a blind recklessness of the system of discounting and renewing bills — and, though attached to Scott by the strongest ties of grateful veneration, yet allowed himself to neglect month after month the most 20 important of his duties — that of keeping the only moneyed partner accurately informed as to the actual obligations and resources of the establishment.

Mr. John's loose methods of transacting business had soon cooled the alliance between his firm and the great 25 Tory publisher of London. Murray's Scotch agency was taken away — he retained hardly any connection with Scott himself, except as a contributor to his Review, and from time to time a friendly visitor in Albemarle Street; and under these altered circumstances, I do not see how 30 the whole concern of John Ballantyne & Co. could have escaped the necessity of an abrupt and disastrous exposure within but a few weeks after the appearance of the Trier-

main, had not the personal differences with Constable°
been by that time healed. Mr. Hunter had now retired
from that house; and Constable, released from his influence, had been watching with hope the unconcealable
5 complication in the affairs of this fragile rival. Constable had never faltered in his conviction that Scott must
continue to be the ruling spirit in the literature of their
age : and there were few sacrifices which that sanguine man
would not have made to regain his hold on the unmatched
10 author. The Ballantynes saw the opening for help, and
their advances were well met; but some quite unexpected
calls on Scott compelled him to interfere directly, and he
began in his own person a negotiation which, though at the
time he likened it to that of the treaty of Amiens, was far
15 from being capriciously protracted, or from leading only
to a brief and barren truce. Constable, flattered *in
limine* by the offer, on fair terms, of a fourth part of the
remaining copyright of Rokeby, agreed to relieve the
labouring firm of a mass of its stock : the partners to exert
20 themselves in getting rid of the residue, and then wind
up their publishing concern with all convenient speed.
This was a great relief : on the 18th of May 1813, Scott
writes to Mr. John — "For the first time these many
weeks, I shall lay my head on a quiet pillow" : but there
25 was still much to be achieved.

His preachments of regularity in book-keeping to John,
and of abstinence from good cheer to James, were equally
vain; but, on the other hand, it must be allowed that the
"hard skirmishes," as he calls them, of May 1813, do not
30 seem to have left on himself all the impression that might
have been anticipated. He was in the most vigorous
of his prime : his temperament was buoyant and hopeful :
nothing had occurred to check his confidence in the re-

sources of his own genius and industry. So it was, that
ere many weeks had passed, he was preparing fresh embarrassments for himself by bidding for another parcel
of land. As early as the 20th of June he writes to Constable as being already aware of this matter, and alleges his 5
anxiety "to close at once with a very capricious person,"
as the only reason that could have induced him to offer for
L.5000 the whole copyright of an as yet unwritten poem,
to be called "The Nameless Glen."   A long correspondence
ensued, in the course of which Scott mentions "the Lord 10
of the Isles," as a title which had suggested itself to him
in place of "The Nameless Glen"; but as the negotiation
did not succeed, I may pass its details.   The new property
which he was so eager to acquire, was that hilly tract
stretching from the old Roman road near Turn-again 15
towards the Cauldshiels Loch : a then desolate and naked
mountainmere, which he likens, in a letter of this summer,
to the Lake of the Genie and the Fisherman in the Arabian
Tale.   To obtain this lake at one extremity of his estate,
as a contrast to the Tweed at the other, was a prospect 20
for which hardly any sacrifice would have appeared too
much ; and he contrived to gratify his wishes in the course
of July.

On the 12th of July, as usual, he removed to Tweedside ;
but he had not long enjoyed himself in sketching out woods 25
and walks for the borders of his Fairy Lake before he
received sharp admonishment. Two lines of a letter to
the "little Picaroon," dated July 24th, speak already to a
series of annoyances : — "Dear John, — I sent you the
order, and have only to hope it arrived safe and in good 30
time. I waked the boy at three o'clock myself, having
slept little, less on account of the money than of the time.
Surely you should have written, three or four days before,

the probable amount of the deficit, and, as on former occasions, I would have furnished you with means of meeting it. These expresses, besides every other inconvenience, excite surprise in my family and in the neighbourhood. 5 I know no justifiable occasion for them but the unexpected return of a bill. I do not consider you as answerable for the success of plans, but I do and must hold you responsible for giving me, in distinct and plain terms, your opinion as to any difficulties which may occur, and that in 10 such time that I may make arrangements to obviate them if possible."

Again Constable was consulted; and now a detailed statement was submitted to him. On examining it, he so expressed himself, that all the partners concurred in 15 the necessity of submitting forthwith to steps not less decisive than painful. Constable again relieved them of some of their crushing stock; but he frankly owned that he could not do in that way enough to serve them effectually; and Scott was constrained to have recourse to the 20 Duke of Buccleuch, who with the kindest promptitude gave him a guarantee to the extent of £4000, immediately available in the money market — the poet insuring his life for that sum, and depositing the insurance as security with the Duke; while John Ballantyne agreed, in place of a 25 leisurely winding up of the publishing affair, to terminate it with the utmost possible speed, and endeavour to establish himself as an auctioneer of books, antiquities, and objects of vertu. How bitterly must Scott have felt his situation when he wrote thus to John on the 16th August: 30 — "With regard to the printing, it is my intention to retire from that also so soon as I can possibly do so with safety to myself, and with the regard I shall always entertain for James's interest. Whatever loss I may sustain will be preferable to the life I have lately led, when I seem surrounded by a sort of magic circle, which neither permits me to remain at home in peace, nor to stir abroad with pleasure."

It was in the midst of these distressing occurrences that Scott received two letters — one from Dr. Stanier Clarke, private librarian to the Regent, and another, more formal, from the Marquis of Hertford, Lord Chamberlain, announcing His Royal Highness's desire to nominate him to the office of Poet-laureate, which had just fallen vacant by the death of Mr. Pye. Its emoluments were understood by him to be " L.400, or at least L.300 a-year " ; at that time such an accession of income must have been welcome ; and at any rate, what the Sovereign designed as a favour and a distinction could not be lightly waived by Walter Scott. He felt, however, that holding already two lucrative offices in the gift of the Crown, he could not gracefully accept a third, entirely unconnected with his own legal profession, while so many eminent men remained wholly dependent on their literary exertions ; and the friends whom he consulted, especially the Duke of Buccleuch, all concurring in the propriety of these scruples, he declined the royal offer. It is evident that from the first he had had Mr. Southey's case in his contemplation. The moment he made up his mind as to himself, he wrote to Mr. Croker and others in the Prince Regent's confidence, suggesting that name : and he had soon to congratulate his friend of Keswick on assuming the official laurel, which "had been worn of old by Dryden and more lately by Warton." Mr. Southey, in an essay long subsequent to his death, says — "Sir Walter's conduct was, as it always was, characteristically friendly and generous."

This happened in September. October brought another

succession of John Ballantyne's missives, to one of which
Scott answers : — "For Heaven's sake, treat me as a man,
not as a milch-cow" ; — and a third crisis, at the approach
of the Martinmas term, was again weathered with the
5 narrowest difficulty — chiefly, as before, through the
intervention of Constable. All these annoyances produced no change whatever in his habits of industry. During these anxious months of September, October, and
November, he kept feeding the press from day to day both
10 with the annotated text of the closing volumes of Swift's
works, and with the MS. of his Life of the Dean. He had
also proceeded to mature in his mind the plan of the Lord
of the Isles, and executed such a portion of the First Canto
as gave him confidence to renew his negotiation with
15 Constable for the sale of the whole, or part of its copyright. It was, moreover, at this period, that his eye
chanced to light once more on the Ashestiel fragment of
Waverley. He read over those introductory chapters —
thought they had been undervalued — and determined
20 to finish the story.

On the first of July 1814, the Swift, nineteen volumes
8vo, at length issued from the press. This adventure,
undertaken by Constable in 1808, had been proceeded in
during all the variety of their personal relations, and now
25 came forth when author and publisher felt more warmly
towards each other than perhaps they had ever before
done. The impression was of 1250 copies; and a reprint
of similar extent was called for in 1824.

Before Christmas Erskine had perused the greater part
30 of the first volume, and expressed his decided opinion
that Waverley would prove the most popular of all his
friend's writings. The MS. was forthwith copied by John
Ballantyne, and sent to press. As soon as a volume

was printed, Ballantyne conveyed it to Constable, who did not for a moment doubt from what pen it proceeded, but took a few days to consider of the matter, and then offered L.700 for the copyright. When we recollect what the state of novel literature in those days was, and that 5 the only exceptions to its mediocrity, the Irish Tales of Miss Edgeworth, however appreciated in refined circles, had a circulation so limited that she had never realized a tithe of L.700 by the best of them — it must be allowed that Constable's offer was a liberal one. Scott's answer, 10 however, was, that L.700 was too much in case the novel should not be successful, and too little if it should. He added, "If our fat friend had said L.1000, I should have been staggered." John did not forget to convey this last hint to Constable, but the latter did not choose to 15 act upon it; and ultimately agreed to an equal division of profits between himself and the author.

There was a considerable pause between the finishing of the first volume and the beginning of the second. Constable, eager about an extensive *Supplement* to his Encyclo- 20 pædia Britannica, earnestly requested Scott to undertake a few articles; and, anxious to gratify the generous bookseller, he laid aside his tale until he had finished two essays — those on Chivalry and the Drama. They were written in the course of April and May, and he received for each 25 of them L.100.

A letter of the 9th July to Mr. Morritt gives in more exact detail than the author's own recollection could supply in 1830, the history of the completion of Waverley, which had then been two days published. "I must now " 30 (he says) "account for my own laziness, by referring you to a small anonymous sort of a novel, which you will receive by the mail of this day. It was a very old attempt

of mine to embody some traits of those characters and
manners peculiar to Scotland, the last remnants of which
vanished during my own youth.   I had written great part
of the first volume, and sketched other passages, when I
5 mislaid the MS., and only found it by the merest accident
as I was rummaging the drawers of an old cabinet; and I
took the fancy of finishing it.   It has made a very strong
impression here, and the good people of Edinburgh are
busied in tracing the author, and in finding out originals
10 for the portraits it contains.   Jeffrey has offered to make
oath that it is mine, and another great critic has tendered his affidavit *ex contrario*°; so that these authorities
have divided the Gude Town.   Let me know your opinion
about it.   The truth is that this sort of muddling work
15 amuses me, and I am something in the condition of Joseph
Surface, who was embarrassed by getting himself too
good a reputation; for many things may please people
well enough anonymously, which if they have me in
the title-page would just give me that sort of ill name
20 which precedes hanging — and that would be in many
respects inconvenient, if I thought of again trying a
grande opus."°

Morritt, as yet the only English confidant, conveyed on
volume by volume as he read them his honest criticism:
25 at last vehemently protesting against the maintenance of
the incognito.   Scott in his reply (July 24th) says: — "I
shall *not* own Waverley; my chief reason is, that it would
prevent me the pleasure of writing again.   David Hume,
nephew of the historian, says the author must be of a
30 Jacobite family and predilections, a yeoman-cavalry man,
and a Scottish lawyer, and desires me to guess in whom
these happy attributes are united.   I shall not plead
guilty, however; and as such seems to be the fashion of

the day, I hope charitable people will believe my *affidavit* in contradiction to all other evidence. The Edinburgh faith now is, that Waverley is written by Jeffrey, having been composed to lighten the tedium of his late transatlantic voyage. So you see the unknown infant is like to come to preferment. In truth, I am not sure it would be considered quite decorous for me, as a Clerk of Session, to write novels. Judges being monks, Clerks are a sort of lay brethren, from whom some solemnity of walk and conduct may be expected. So whatever I may do of this kind, 'I shall whistle it down the wind, and let it prey at fortune.' [1] The second edition is, I believe, nearly through the press. It will hardly be printed faster than it was written; for though the first volume was begun long ago, and actually lost for a time, yet the other two were begun and finished between the 4th June and the first July, during all which I attended my duty in Court, and proceeded without loss of time or hindrance of business."

This statement as to the time occupied by the second and third volumes of Waverley, recalls to my memory a trifling anecdote, which, as connected with a dear friend of my youth, whom I have not seen for many years, and may very probably never see again in this world, I shall here set down, in the hope of affording him a momentary, though not an unmixed pleasure, when he may chance to read this compilation on a distant shore — and also in the hope that my humble record may impart to some active mind in the rising generation a shadow of the influence which the reality certainly exerted upon his. Happening to pass through Edinburgh in June 1814, I dined one day with the gentleman in question (now the

---

[1] *Othello*, Act III. Scene 3.

Honourable William Menzies, one of the Supreme Judges at the Cape of Good Hope), whose residence was then in George Street, situated very near to, and at right angles with, North Castle Street.   It was a party of very young

5 persons, most of them, like Menzies and myself, destined for the Bar of Scotland, all gay and thoughtless, enjoying the first flush of manhood, with little remembrance of the yesterday, or care of the morrow.   When my companion's worthy father and uncle, after seeing two or three bottles

10 go round, left the juveniles to themselves, the weather being hot, we adjourned to a library which had one large window looking northwards.   After carousing here for an hour or more, I observed that a shade had come over the aspect of my friend, who happened to be placed immedi-

15 ately opposite to myself, and said something that inti-mated a fear of his being unwell.   "No," said he, "I shall be well enough presently, if you will only let me sit where you are, and take my chair; for there is a confounded hand in sight of me here, which has often bothered me before,

20 and now it won't let me fill my glass with a good will." I rose to change places with him accordingly, and he pointed out to me this hand which, like the writing on Belshazzar's wall, disturbed his hour of hilarity.   "Since we sat down," he said, "I have been watching it — it

25 fascinates my eye — it never stops — page after page is finished and thrown on that heap of MS. and still it goes on unwearied — and so it will be till candles are brought in, and God knows how long after that.   It is the same every night — I can't stand a sight of it when I am not

30 at my books." — "Some stupid, dogged, engrossing clerk, probably," exclaimed myself, or some other giddy youth in our society.   "No, boys," said our host, "I well know what hand it is — 'tis Walter Scott's."   This was the

hand that, in the evenings of three summer weeks, wrote the two last volumes of Waverley.

The gallant composure with which Scott, when he had dismissed a work from his desk, awaited the decision of the public — and the healthy elasticity of spirit with which he could meanwhile turn his whole zeal upon new or different objects — are among the features in his character which will always, I believe, strike the student of literary history as most remarkable. It would be difficult to exaggerate the importance to his fortunes of this his first novel. Yet before he had heard of its reception in the south, except the whisper of one partial friend, he started on a voyage which was likely to occupy two months, and during which he could hardly expect to receive any letters.

He had been invited to accompany the Commissioners of the Northern Light Houses in their annual expedition; and as its programme included the Hebrides, and he had already made some progress in the Lord of the Isles, the opportunity for refreshing and enlarging his acquaintance with that region would alone have been a strong temptation. But there were many others. The trip was also to embrace the isles of Shetland and Orkney, and a vast extent of the mainland coasts, no part of which he had ever seen — or but for such an offer might ever have much chance of seeing. The Commissioners were all familiar friends of his — William Erskine, then Sheriff of the Orkneys, Robert Hamilton, Sheriff of Lanarkshire, Adam Duff, Sheriff of Forfarshire, but the real chief was the Surveyor-General, the celebrated engineer Mr. Stevenson, and Scott anticipated special pleasure in his society. "I delight," he told Morritt, "in these professional men of talent. They always give you some new lights by the

I

peculiarity of their habits and studies — so different from the people who are rounded and smoothed and ground down for conversation, and who can say all that every other person says — and no more."

5 To this voyage we owe many of the most striking passages in the Lord of the Isles, and the noble romance of the Pirate wholly.

After this voyage, as he passed through Edinburgh, the negotiation as to the Lord of the Isles, which had been 10 protracted through several months, was completed: Constable agreeing to give fifteen hundred guineas for one-half of the copyright, while the other moiety was retained by the author. The same sum had been offered at an early stage of the affair, but it was not until now accepted, 15 in consequence of the earnest wish of Messrs. Ballantyne to saddle the publisher of the new poem with another pyramid of their old "quire stock," — which, however, Constable ultimately persisted in refusing. It may easily be believed that John's management during a six weeks' 20 absence had been such as to render it doubly convenient for the Poet to have this matter settled; and it may also be supposed that the progress of Waverley during that interval had tended to put the chief parties in good humour with each other. For nothing can be more unfounded 25 than the statement repeated in various memoirs of Scott's life, that the sale of the first edition of this immortal Tale was slow. It appeared on the 7th of July, and the whole impression (1000 copies) had disappeared within five weeks; an occurrence then unprecedented in the case of 30 an anonymous novel, put forth at what is called among publishers *the dead season*. A second edition of 2000 copies was at least projected by the 24th of the same month : — that appeared before the end of August, and it

too had gone off so rapidly that Scott now, in September,
found Constable eager to treat, on the same terms as
before, for a third of 1000 copies.   This third edition was
published in October; and when a fourth of the like extent was called for in November, I find Scott writing to 5
John Ballantyne : — "I suppose Constable won't quarrel
with a work on which he has netted L.612 in four months,
with a certainty of making it L.1000 before the year is
out."   It would be idle to enumerate subsequent reprints.
Well might Constable regret that he had not ventured to 10
offer L.1000 for the whole copyright of Waverley !

No one of Scott's intimate friends ever had, or could
have had, the slightest doubt as to the parentage of Waverley : nor, although he abstained from communicating
the fact formally to most of them, did he ever affect any 15
real concealment in the case of such persons ; nor, when
any circumstance arose which rendered the withholding of
direct confidence on the subject incompatible with perfect
freedom of feeling on both sides, did he hesitate to make
the avowal.   Nor do I believe that the mystification ever 20
answered much purpose among literary men of eminence
beyond the circle of his personal acquaintance.   But it
would be difficult to suppose that he had ever wished that
to be otherwise; it was sufficient for him to set the mob
of readers at gaze, and above all, to escape the annoyance 25
of having productions, actually known to be his, made
the daily and hourly topics of discussion in his presence
— especially (perhaps) productions in a new walk, to
which it might be naturally supposed that Lord Byron's
poetical successes had diverted him.   30

Loftier romance was never blended with easier, quainter
humour, by Cervantes.   In his familiar delineations he
had combined the strength of Smollett with the native

elegance and unaffected pathos of Goldsmith°; in his darker scenes he had revived that real tragedy which appeared to have left our theatre with the age of Shakspeare; and elements of interest so diverse had been
5 blended and interwoven with that nameless grace, which, more surely perhaps than even the highest perfection in the command of any one strain of sentiment, marks the mastermind cast in Nature's most felicitous mould.

CHAPTER VIII

Publication of the Lord of the Isles and Guy Mannering
— Meeting with Byron — Excursion to Paris — Publication of the Field of Waterloo — Paul's Letters — The
Antiquary — Harold the Dauntless — and the first Tales
of my Landlord — 1815–1816.

HE writes, on the 25th December, to Constable that he
"had corrected the last proofs of the Lord of the Isles,
and was setting out for Abbotsford to refresh the
machine." And in what did his refreshment of the
machine consist? The poem was published on the 15th 5
January; and he says, *on that day*, to Morritt, "I want to
shake myself free of Waverley, and accordingly have
made a considerable exertion to finish an odd little tale
within such time as will mystify the public, I trust — unless they suppose me to be Briareus.° Two volumes are 10
already printed, and the only persons in my confidence,
W. Erskine and Ballantyne, are of opinion that it is much
more interesting than Waverley. It is a tale of private
life, and only varied by the perilous exploits of smugglers
and excisemen." Guy Mannering was published on the 15
24th of February — that is, exactly two months after
the Lord of the Isles was dismissed from the author's
desk; and — making but a narrow allowance for the
operations of the transcriber, printer, bookseller, &c., I
think the dates I have gathered together confirm the 20
accuracy of what I have often heard Scott say, that his

second novel "was the work of six weeks at a Christmas."
Such was his recipe "for refreshing the machine."

I am sorry to have to add, that this severity of labour,
like the repetition of it which had deplorable effects at a
5 later period, was the result of difficulties about the discount of John Ballantyne's bills.

I must not, however, forget that The Lord of the Isles
was published a month before Guy Mannering. The
poem was received with an interest much heightened by
10 the recent and growing success of the mysterious Waverley. Its appearance, so rapidly following that novel, and
accompanied with the announcement of another prose
tale, just about to be published, by the same hand, puzzled
and confounded the mob of dulness. The more sagacious
15 few said to themselves — Scott is making one serious effort
more in his old line, and by this it will be determined
whether he does or does not altogether renounce that
for his new one.

This poem is now, I believe, about as popular as Rokeby;
20 but it has never reached the same station in general
favour with the Lay, Marmion, or the Lady of the Lake.
The instant consumption of 1800 quartos, followed by
8vo reprints to the number of 12,000, would, in the
case of almost any other author, have been splendid
25 success; but as compared with what he had previously
experienced, even in his Rokeby, and still more so as
compared with the enormous circulation at once attained
by Lord Byron's early tales, which were then following
each other in almost breathless succession, the falling off
30 was decided.

If January brought "disappointment," there was abundant consolation in store for February 1815. Guy Mannering was received with eager curiosity, and pronounced

by acclamation fully worthy to share the honours of Waverley. The easy transparent flow of its style; the beautiful simplicity, and here and there the wild solemn magnificence of its sketches of scenery; the rapid, ever heightening interest of the narrative; the unaffected kindliness of feel- 5 ing, the manly purity of thought, everywhere mingled with a gentle humour and a homely sagacity; but, above all, the rich variety and skilful contrast of characters and manners at once fresh in fiction, and stamped with the unforgeable seal of truth and nature; these were charms 10 that spoke to every heart and mind; and the few murmurs of pedantic criticism were lost in the voice of general delight, which never fails to welcome the invention that introduces to the sympathy of imagination a new group of immortal realities. 15

On the rising of the Court of Session in March, Scott went by sea to London with his wife and their eldest girl. Six years had elapsed since he last appeared in the metropolis; and brilliant as his reception had then been, it was still more so on the present occasion. Scotland had been 20 visited in the interim, chiefly from the interest excited by his writings, by crowds of the English nobility, most of whom had found introduction to his personal acquaintance — not a few had partaken of his hospitality at Ashestiel or Abbotsford. 25

And now took place James Ballantyne's "mighty consummation of the meeting of the two bards." "Report," says Scott to Moore,° "had prepared me to meet a man of peculiar habits and a quick temper, and I had some doubts whether we were likely to suit each other in 30 society. I was most agreeably disappointed in this respect. I found Lord Byron° in the highest degree courteous, and even kind. We met for an hour or two almost

daily, in Mr. Murray's drawing-room, and found a great
deal to say to each other. We also met frequently in
parties and evening society, so that for about two months
I had the advantage of a considerable intimacy with this
5 distinguished individual."

During the following summer Scott was received in
France by the distinguished soldiers and statesmen of
Europe, assembled in Paris after the battle of Waterloo.
He gave his impressions of this trip in "Paul's Letters,"
10 published by Constable.

Scott had written verse as well as prose during his travels. "The Field of Waterloo" was published before the
end of October; the profits of the first edition being his
contribution to the fund raised for the relief of the widows
15 and children of the soldiers slain in the battle. This piece
appears to have disappointed those most disposed to sympathize with the author's views and feelings. The descent
is indeed heavy from his Bannockburn to his Waterloo:
the presence, or all but visible reality of what his dreams
20 cherished, seems to have overawed his imagination, and
tamed it into a weak pomposity of movement.

Meanwhile the revision of Paul's Letters was proceeding; and Scott had almost immediately on his return concluded his bargain for the first edition of a third novel
25 — The Antiquary; nor was it much later that he completed rather a tedious negotiation with another bonnet-
laird, and added the lands of *Kaeside* to Abbotsford —
witness the last words of a letter to Miss Baillie,° dated
Nov. 12: — "My eldest boy is already a bold horseman
30 and a fine shot, though only about fourteen years old.
I assure you I was prouder of the first black-cock he killed,
than I have been of anything whatever since I first killed
one myself, and that is twenty years ago. This is all

stupid gossip; but, as Master Corporal Nym° says, 'things must be as they may:' you cannot expect grapes from thorns, or much amusement from a brain bewildered with thorn hedges at Kaeside, for such is the sonorous title of my new possession, in virtue of which I subscribe 5 myself,

ABBOTSFORD & KAESIDE."

The year 1815 may be considered as, for Scott's peaceful tenor of life, an eventful one. That which followed has left almost its only traces in the successive appearance of 10 nine volumes, which attest the prodigal genius and hardly less astonishing industry of the man. Early in January were published Paul's Letters to his Kinsfolk, of which I need not now say more than that they were received with lively curiosity, and general, though not vociferous ap- 15 plause. The first edition was an octavo of 6000 copies; and it was followed in the course of the next two or three years by a second and a third, amounting together to 3000 more. The popularity of the novelist was at its height; and this admitted, if not avowed, specimen 20 of Scott's prose, must have been perceived by all who had any share of discrimination, to flow from the same pen.

Early in May appeared the novel of The Antiquary, which seems to have been begun a little before the close of 25 1815. Scott wrote to his friend at Rokeby: "I sent you some time since, The Antiquary. It is not so interesting as its predecessors — the period did not admit of so much romantic situation. But it has been more fortunate than any of them in the sale, for 6000 went off in the first 30 six days, and it is now at press again; which is very flattering to the unknown author." In a letter of the same date to Terry, Scott says — "It wants the romance of

Waverley and the adventure of Guy Mannering; and yet there is some salvation about it, for if a man will paint from nature, he will be likely to amuse those who are daily looking at it."

5   Considered by itself, this novel seems to me to possess, almost throughout, in common with its two predecessors, a kind of simple unsought charm, which the subsequent works of the series hardly reached, save in occasional snatches : — like them it is, in all its humbler and softer scenes, the transcript of actual Scottish life, as observed by the man himself.   And I think it must also be allowed that he has nowhere displayed his highest art, that of skilful contrast, in greater perfection.   Even the tragic romance of Waverley does not set off its MacWheebles and Callum Begs better than the oddities of Jonathan Oldbuck and his circle are relieved, on the one hand by the stately gloom of the Glenallans, on the other by the stern affliction of the poor fisherman, who, when discovered repairing the "auld black bitch o' a boat" in which his boy had been lost, and congratulated by his visitor on being capable of the exertion, makes answer — "And what would you have me to do, unless I wanted to see four children starve, because one is drowned? *It's weel wi' you gentles, that can sit in the house wi' handkerchers at your een, when ye lose a friend; but the like o' us maun to our wark again, if our hearts were beating as hard as my hammer.*"

It may be worth noting, that it was in correcting the proof-sheets of this novel that Scott first took to equipping his chapters with mottoes of his own fabrication.   On one occasion he happened to ask John Ballantyne, who was sitting by him, to hunt for a particular passage in Beaumont and Fletcher.   John did as he was bid, but did not succeed in discovering the lines. "Hang it, Johnnie," cried Scott, "I believe I can make a motto sooner than you will find one." He did so accordingly; and from that hour, whenever memory failed to suggest an appropriate epigraph, he had recourse to the inexhaustible 5 mines of "*old play*" or "*old ballad*," to which we owe some of the most exquisite verses that ever flowed from his pen.

Unlike, I believe, most men, whenever Scott neared the end of one composition, his spirit seems to have caught a 10 new spring of buoyancy, and before the last sheet was sent from his desk, he had crowded his brain with the imagination of another fiction. The Antiquary was published, as we have seen, in May, but by the beginning of April he had already opened to the Ballantynes the 15 plan of the first Tales of my Landlord; and — to say nothing of Harold the Dauntless which he began shortly after the Bridal of Triermain was finished, and which he seems to have kept before him for two years as a congenial plaything, to be taken up whenever the coach 20 brought no proof-sheets to jog him as to serious matters — he had also, before this time, undertaken to write the historical department of the Register for 1814. He had not yet collected the materials requisite for his historical sketch of a year distinguished for the importance and 25 complexity of its events; but these, he doubted not, would soon reach him, and he felt no hesitation about pledging himself to complete, not only that sketch, but four new volumes of prose romances — and his Harold the Dauntless also, if Ballantyne could make any suitable arrange- 30 ment on that score — between the April and the Christmas of 1816.

Why Scott should have been urgently desirous of seeing

the transaction settled at once, is sufficiently explained by the fact, that though so much of Mr. John's old unfortunate stock still remained on hand — and with it some occasional recurrence of difficulty as to *floating-bills* must be expected — while Mr. James Ballantyne's management of pecuniary affairs had not been very careful — nevertheless, the sanguine author had gone on purchasing one patch of land after another, until his estate had already grown from 150 to nearly 1000 acres. The property all about his original farm had been in the hands of small holders (Scotticè, *cock-lairds*) ; these were sharp enough to understand that their neighbour could with difficulty resist any temptation that might present itself in the shape of acres ; and thus he proceeded buying up lot after lot of unimproved ground, at extravagant prices, — his "appetite increasing by what it fed on"; while the ejected yeomen set themselves down elsewhere, to fatten at their leisure upon the profits — most commonly the anticipated profits — of "The Scotch Novels."

He was ever and anon pulled up with a momentary misgiving, — and resolved that the latest acquisition should be the last, until he could get rid entirely of "John Ballantyne & Co." But, after the first and more serious embarrassments had been overcome, John was far from continuing to hold by his patron's anxiety for the total abolition of their unhappy copartnership. He prompted and enforced the idea of trying other booksellers from time to time, instead of adhering to Constable, merely for the selfish purposes, — first, of facilitating the immediate discount of bills ; — secondly, of further perplexing Scott's affairs, the entire disentanglement of which would have been, as he fancied, prejudicial to his own personal importance.

It was resolved, accordingly, to offer the risk and half profits of the first edition of another new novel — or rather collection of novels — to Mr. Murray of Albemarle Street, and Mr. Blackwood, who was then Murray's agent in Scotland; but it was at the same time resolved, partly 5 because Scott wished to try another experiment on the public sagacity, but partly also, no question, from the wish to spare Constable's feelings, that the title-page of the "Tales of my Landlord" should not bear the magical words "by the Author of Waverley." The facility with 10 which both Murray and Blackwood embraced such a proposal, as no untried novelist, being sane, could have dreamt of hazarding, shews that neither of them had any doubt as to the identity of the author. They both considered the withholding of the avowal on the forthcoming title- 15 page as likely to check very much the first success of the book; but they were both eager to prevent Constable's acquiring a sort of prescriptive right to publish for the unrivalled novelist, and agreed to all the terms, including a considerable burden of the endless "back-stock." 20

Scott's intention originally was to give in the four volumes as many tales, each having its scene laid in a different province of Scotland; but this scheme was soon abandoned: and the series included only the two stories of the Black Dwarf and Old Mortality. On the first of 25 December, the Tales appeared, and notwithstanding the silence of the title-page, the change of publishers, and the attempt which had certainly been made to vary the style both of delineation and of language, all doubts whether they were or were not from the same hand with 30 Waverley had worn themselves out before the lapse of a week. On the 14th, the London publisher was unable to suppress his exultation, and addressed to Scott himself a letter concluding in these words: — "Heber says there are only two men in the world — Walter Scott and Lord Byron. Between you, you have given existence to a THIRD — ever your faithful servant, *John Murray*." To 5 this cordial effusion, Scott returned a dexterous answer. It was necessary, since he had resolved against compromising his incognito, that he should be prepared not only to repel the impertinent curiosity of strangers, but to evade the proffered congratulations of overflowing kind- 'ro ness. Within less than a month, the Black Dwarf and Old Mortality were followed by "Harold the Dauntless, by the author of the Bridal of Triermain." The volume was published by Messrs Constable, and had, in those booksellers' phrase, "considerable success." It has never, 15 however, been placed on a level with Triermain.

CHAPTER IX

Serious Illness — Laidlaw settled at Kaeside and the Fergussons at Huntley Burn — New House begun — Washington Irving — Publication of Rob Roy — and the Heart of Mid-Lothian — Scott in Edinburgh — 1817–1818.

EARLY in 1817, he was visited, for the first time since his childish years, with a painful illness, which proved the harbinger of a series of attacks, all nearly of the same kind, continued at short intervals during more than two years. The reader has been told already how widely his habits of ₅ life when in Edinburgh differed from those of Abbotsford. They at all times did so to a great extent; but he had pushed his liberties with a most robust constitution to a perilous extreme while the affairs of the Ballantynes were labouring.   10

His letters to Terry about this time prove sufficiently that, whatever pain he endured, he had no serious apprehensions as to his health; for a principal theme is the plan of founding a new house at Abbotsford; and by and bye the details of that project wholly engross the correspond-₁₅ ence. The foundation was in part laid early in the ensuing summer: an unfortunate feature in Scott's history; for he was by degrees tempted to extend his design, and the ultimate expense very greatly exceeded all his and his friends' calculations.   20

Shortly before this time, Mr. William Laidlaw had met with misfortunes, which rendered it necessary for him to give up his farm. He was now anxiously looking about

him for some new establishment, and Scott invited him to
occupy a house on his property, and endeavour, under his
guidance, to make such literary exertions as might improve
his income.   The prospect of obtaining such a neighbour
5 was, no doubt, the more welcome to "Abbotsford and
Kaeside," from its opening at this period of fluctuating
health; and Laidlaw, who had for twenty years loved and
revered him, considered the proposal with far greater delight than the most lucrative appointment on any noble
10 domain in the island could have afforded him.   Though
possessed of a lively and searching sagacity as to things in
general, he had always been as to his own worldly interests
simple as a child.   His tastes and habits were all modest;
and when he looked forward to spending the remainder of
15 what had not hitherto been a successful life, under the
shadow of the genius that he had worshipped almost from
boyhood, his gentle heart was all happiness.   He surveyed
with glistening eyes the humble cottage in which his friend
proposed to lodge him, his wife, and his little ones, and
20 said to himself that he should write no more sad songs on
Forest Flittings.

Neither the recurring fits of cramp, nor anything else,
could, as yet, interrupt Scott's literary industry.   Before
Whitsuntide he had made his bargain for another novel.
25 This was at once tendered to Constable, who was delighted
to interrupt in his turn the connection with Murray and
Blackwood, and readily agreed to meet John Ballantyne
at Abbotsford, where all was speedily settled.

As to *Rob Roy*, the title was suggested by Constable,
30 and he told me years afterwards the difficulty he had to get
it adopted by the author.   Constable said the name of the
real hero would be the best possible name for the book.
"Nay," answered Scott, "never let me have to write up

to a name. You well know I have generally adopted a
title that told nothing." — The bookseller, however, persevered; and after the trio had dined, these scruples
gave way.

By this time, the foundations of that part of the existing 5.
house of Abbotsford, which extends from the hall west-
wards to the original court-yard, had been laid; and Scott,.
on reaching home, found a new source of constant occupation in watching the proceedings of his masons. He had,
moreover, no lack of employment further a-field, — for he 10
was now negotiating with another neighbouring landowner
for the purchase of an addition of more consequence than
any he had hitherto made to his estate. In the course of
the autumn he concluded this matter, and became, for the
price of L.10,000, proprietor of the lands of *Toftfield*, on 15
which there had recently been erected a substantial man-
sion-house. This circumstance offered a temptation which
much quickened Scott's zeal for completing his arrangement. The venerable Professor Fergusson had died a year
before; his son Adam had been placed on half-pay; and 20
Scott now saw the means of securing for himself, henceforth, the immediate neighbourhood of the companion of
his youth, and his amiable sisters. Fergusson, who had
written from the lines of Torres Vedras° his hopes of
finding, when the war should be over, some sheltering 25
cottage upon the Tweed, within a walk of Abbotsford, was
delighted to see his dreams realized; and the family took
up their residence next spring at the new house of Toftfield, on which Scott then bestowed, at the ladies' request,
the name of Huntley Burn.
                                                30
A pleasant incident belongs to August 1817. Scott
had read "the History of New York by Knickerbocker,"
shortly after its appearance in 1812; and the admirable

K

humour of this early work had led him to anticipate the
brilliant career which its author has since run.   Campbell,
being no stranger to Scott's estimation of Washington
Irving's° genius, gave him a letter of introduction, which,
5 halting his chaise on the high-road above Abbotsford, he
modestly sent down to the house "with a card on which
he had written, that he was on his way to the ruins of
Melrose, and wished to know whether it would be agreeable to Mr. Scott to receive a visit from him in the course
10 of the morning."

"The noise of my chaise," says Irving, "had disturbed
the quiet of the establishment.   Out sallied the warder
of the castle, a black greyhound, and leaping on one of
the blocks of stone, began a furious barking.   This alarm
15 brought out the whole garrison of dogs, all open-mouthed
and vociferous.   In a little while the lord of the castle
himself made his appearance.   I knew him at once, by
the likenesses that had been published of him.   He came
limping up the gravel walk, aiding himself by a stout
20 walking-staff, but moving rapidly and with vigour.   By
his side jogged along a large iron-grey staghound, of most
grave demeanour, who took no part in the clamour of the
canine rabble, but seemed to consider himself bound, for
the dignity of the house, to give me a courteous reception.
25 — Before Scott reached the gate, he called out in a hearty
tone, welcoming me to Abbotsford, and asking news of
Campbell.   Arrived at the door of the chaise, he grasped
me warmly by the hand: 'Come, drive down, drive down
to the house,' said he, 'ye're just in time for breakfast,
30 and afterwards ye shall see all the wonders of the Abbey.'
I would have excused myself on the plea of having already
made my breakfast.   'Hut, man,' cried he, 'a ride in the
morning in the keen air of the Scotch hills is warrant
enough for a second breakfast.'   I was accordingly whirled
35 to the portal of the cottage, and in a few moments found

myself seated at the breakfast table. There was no one
present but the family, which consisted of Mrs. Scott;
her eldest daughter, Sophia, then a fine girl about seven-
teen; Miss Ann Scott, two or three years younger; Walter,
a well-grown stripling; and Charles, a lively boy, eleven 5
or twelve years of age. — I soon felt myself quite at home,
and my heart in a glow, with the cordial welcome I experienced. I had thought to make a mere morning visit,
but found I was not to be let off so lightly. 'You must
not think our neighbourhood is to be read in a morning 10
like a newspaper,' said Scott; 'it takes several days of
study for an observant traveller, that has a relish for auld-
world trumpery. After breakfast you shall make your
visit to Melrose Abbey; I shall not be able to accompany
you, as I have some household affairs to attend to; but 15
I will put you in charge of my son Charles, who is very
learned in all things touching the old ruin and the neighbourhood it stands in; and he and my friend Johnnie
Bower, will tell you the whole truth about it, with a great
deal more that you are not called upon to believe, unless 20
you be a true and nothing-doubting antiquary. When you
come back, I'll take you out on a ramble about the neighbourhood. To-morrow we will take a look at the Yarrow,
and the next day we will drive over to Dryburgh Abbey,
which is a fine old ruin, well worth your seeing.' — In a 25
word, before Scott had got through with his plan, I found
myself committed for a visit of several days, and it seemed
as if a little realm of romance was suddenly open before
me.''

*   *   *   *   *   *   *

" On the following morning the sun darted his beams from
over the hills through the low lattice of my window. I rose 30
at an early hour, and looked out between the branches of
eglantine which overhung the casement. To my surprise,
Scott was already up, and forth, seated on a fragment of
stone, and chatting with the workmen employed in the new

building. I had supposed, after the time he had wasted upon me yesterday, he would be closely occupied this morning : but he appeared like a man of leisure, who had nothing to do but bask in the sunshine and amuse
5 himself.   I soon dressed myself and joined him.   He talked about his proposed plans of Abbotsford : happy would it have been for him could he have contented himself with his delightful little vine-covered cottage, and the simple, yet hearty and hospitable, style in which he lived at the
10 time of my visit."

These lines to the elder Ballantyne are without date. They accompanied, no doubt, the last proof-sheet of Rob Roy, and were therefore in all probability written about ten days before the 31st of December 1817 — on which
15 day the novel was published.

> "With great joy
> I send you Roy.
> 'Twas a tough job,
> But we're done with Rob."

20   The novel had indeed been "a tough job" — for lightly and airily as it reads, the author had struggled almost throughout with the pains of cramp or the lassitude of opium.

Rob and his wife, Bailie Jarvie and his housekeeper,
25 Die Vernon and Rashleigh Osbaldistone — these boldly drawn and happily contrasted personages — were welcomed as warmly as the most fortunate of their predecessors.   Constable's resolution to begin with an edition of 10,000, proved to have been as sagacious as brave;
30 for within a fortnight a second 3000 was called for.

Scott, however, had not waited for this new burst of applause.   As soon as he came within view of the comple-

tion of Rob Roy, he desired John Ballantyne to propose
to Constable a second series of the Tales of my Landlord,
to be comprised, like the first, in four volumes, and ready
for publication by "the King's birth-day"; that is, the
4th of June 1818. "I have hungered and thirsted," he
wrote, "to see the end of those shabby borrowings among
friends; they have all been wiped out except the good
Duke's L.4000 — and I will not suffer either new offers
of land or anything else to come in the way of that clearance. I expect that you will be able to arrange this resurrection of Jedediah°, so that L.5000 shall be at my order."

Mr. Rigdum used to glory in recounting that he ac-
quitted himself on this occasion with a species of dexterity
not contemplated in his commission. He well knew how
sorely Constable had been wounded by seeing the first
Tales of Jedediah published by Murray and Blackwood — and that the utmost success of Rob Roy would
only double his anxiety to keep them out of the field.
When, therefore, the haughty but trembling bookseller
signified his earnest hope that the second Tales of my
Landlord were destined to come out under the same
auspices with Rob Roy, the plenipotentiary answered
with an air of deep regret, that he feared it would be impossible for the author to dispose of the work — unless
to publishers who should agree to take with it *the whole* of
the remaining stock of "John Ballantyne & Co."; and
Constable, pertinaciously as he had stood out against many
more modest propositions of this nature, was so worked
upon by his jealous feelings, that his resolution at once
gave way. He agreed on the instant to do all that John
seemed to shrink from asking — and at one sweep cleared
the Augean stable in Hanover Street of unsaleable rub-
bish to the amount of L.5270! I am assured by his sur-

viving partner, that when he had finally redisposed of the stock, he found himself a loser by fully two-thirds of this sum. Burthened with this heavy condition, the agreement for the sale of 10,000 copies of the embryo series was 5 signed before the end of November 1817; and on the 7th January 1818, Scott wrote to his noble friend of Buccleuch, — "I have the great pleasure of enclosing the discharged bond which your Grace stood engaged in on my account."

The time now approached when a Commission to examine the Crown-room in the Castle of Edinburgh, which had sprung from one of Scott's conversations with the Prince Regent in 1815, was at length to be acted upon; and the result was the discovery of the long lost regalia of Scotland. Of the official proceedings of the 4th Feb. 15 1818, the reader has a full and particular account in an Essay which Scott penned shortly afterwards; but I may add a little incident of the 5th. He and several of his brother Commissioners then revisited the Castle, accompanied by some of the ladies of their families. His daughter Sophia told me that her father's conversation had worked her feelings up to such a pitch, that when the lid was again removed, she nearly fainted, and drew back from the circle. As she was retiring, she was startled by his voice exclaiming, in a tone of the deepest emotion, 25 "something between anger and despair," as she expressed it, "By G—, No !" One of the Commissioners, not quite entering into the solemnity with which Scott regarded this business, had it seems made a sort of motion as if he meant to put the crown on the head of one of the young 30 ladies near him, but the voice and aspect of the Poet were more than sufficient to make the worthy gentleman understand his error; and respecting the enthusiasm with which he had not been taught to sympathize, he laid down the ancient diadem with an air of painful embarrassment. Scott whispered, "Pray forgive me"; and turning round at the moment, observed his daughter deadly pale, and leaning by the door. He immediately drew her out of the room, and when the air had somewhat recovered her, walked with her across the Mound to Castle Street. "He never spoke all the way home," she said, "but every now and then I felt his arm tremble; and from that time I fancied he began to treat me more like a woman than a child. I thought he liked me better, too, than he had ever done before."

At this moment, his position, take it for all in all, was, I am inclined to believe, what no other man had ever won for himself by the pen alone. His works were the daily food, not only of his countrymen, but of all educated Europe. His society was courted by whatever England could shew of eminence. Station, power, wealth, beauty, and genius, strove with each other in every demonstration of respect and worship, and — a few political fanatics and envious poetasters apart — wherever he appeared in town or country, whoever had Scotch blood in him, "gentle or simple," felt it move more rapidly through his veins when he was in the presence of Scott. To descend to what many looked on as higher things, he considered himself, and was considered by all about him, as rapidly consolidating a large fortune: — the annual profits of his novels alone had, for several years, been not less than £10,000; his domains were daily increased — his castle was rising — and perhaps few doubted that ere long he might receive from the just favour of his Prince some distinction in the way of external rank, such as had seldom before been dreamt of as the possible consequences of a mere literary celebrity. It was about this time that the

compiler of these pages first had the opportunity of observing the plain easy modesty which had survived the many
temptations of such a career; and the kindness of heart
pervading, in all circumstances, his gentle deportment,
5 which made him the rare, perhaps the solitary, example
of a man signally elevated from humble beginnings, and
loved more and more by his earliest friends and connexions,
in proportion as he had fixed on himself the homage of the
great and the wonder of the world.

10 He at this time occupied as his *den* a small square room,
behind the dining parlour in Castle Street. It had but a
single Venetian window, opening on a patch of turf not
much larger than itself, and the aspect of the place was on
the whole sombrous. The walls were entirely clothed with
15 books; most of them folios and quartos, and all in that
complete state of repair which at a glance reveals a tinge
of bibliomania. A dozen volumes or so, needful for immediate purposes of reference, were placed close by him on a
small moveable frame — something like a dumb-waiter.
20 All the rest were in their proper niches, and wherever a
volume had been lent, its room was occupied by a wooden
block of the same size, having a card with the name of the
borrower and date of the loan, tacked on its front. The
old bindings had obviously been retouched and regilt in
25 the most approved manner; the new, when the books were
of any mark, were rich, but never gaudy — a large proportion of blue morocco — all stamped with his *device* of
the portcullis, and its motto, *clausus tutus ero°* — being an
anagram of his name in Latin. Every case and shelf was
30 accurately lettered, and the works arranged systematically;
history and biography on one side — poetry and the drama
on another — law books and dictionaries behind his own
chair. The only table was a massive piece of furniture

which he had had constructed on the
Rokeby; with a desk and all its appurte
side, that an amanuensis might work
when he chose; and with small tiers of drawers, reaching
all round to the floor. The top displayed a goodly array 5
of session papers, and on the desk below were, besides the
MS. at which he was working, sundry parcels of letters,
proof-sheets, and so forth, all neatly done up with red
tape. His own writing apparatus was a very handsome
old box, richly carved, lined with crimson velvet, and con- 10
taining ink-bottles, taper-stand, &c. in silver — the whole
in such order that it might have come from the silver-
smith's window half an hour before. Besides his own huge
elbow-chair, there were but two others in the room, and
one of these seemed, from its position, to be reserved 15
exclusively for the amanuensis. I observed, during the
first evening I spent with him in this *sanctum*, that while
he talked, his hands were hardly ever idle; sometimes he
folded letter-covers — sometimes he twisted paper into
matches, performing both tasks with great mechanical 20
expertness and nicety; and when there was no loose paper
fit to be so dealt with, he snapped his fingers, and the
noble Maida aroused himself from his lair on the hearth-
rug, and laid his head across his master's knees, to be
caressed and fondled. The room had no space for pic- 25
tures except one, a portrait of Claverhouse,° which hung
over the chimneypiece, with a Highland target on either
side, and broadswords and dirks (each having its own
story) disposed star-fashion round them. A few green
tin-boxes, such as solicitors keep title-deeds in, were piled 30
over each other on one side of the window; and on the top
of these lay a fox's tail, mounted on an antique silver
handle, wherewith, as often as he had occasion to take down

a book, he gently brushed the dust off the upper leaves before opening it. I think I have mentioned all the furniture of the room except a sort of ladder, low, broad, well carpeted, and strongly guarded with oaken rails, by which
5 he helped himself to books from his higher shelves. On the top step of this convenience, Hinse of Hinsfeldt (so called from one of the German *Kinder-märchen*°), a venerable tom-cat, fat and sleek, and no longer very locomotive, usually lay watching the proceedings of his master and
10 Maida with an air of dignified equanimity; but when Maida chose to leave the party, he signified his inclinations by thumping the door with his huge paw, as violently as ever a fashionable footman handled a knocker in Grosvenor Square; the Sheriff rose and opened it for him with cour-
15 teous alacrity, — and then Hinse came down purring from his perch, and mounted guard by the footstool, *vice* Maida absent upon furlough. Whatever discourse might be passing, was broken every now and then by some affectionate apostrophe to these four-footed friends. He said
20 they understood everything he said to them — and I believe they did understand a great deal of it. But at all events, dogs and cats, like children, have some infallible tact for discovering at once who is, and who is not, really fond of their company; and I venture to say, Scott was
25 never five minutes in any room before the little pets of the family, whether dumb or lisping, had found out his kindness for all their generation.

Scott managed to give and receive great dinners, at least as often as any other private gentleman in Edinburgh;
30 but he very rarely accompanied his wife and daughters to the evening assemblies, which commonly ensued under other roofs — for *early to rise*, unless in the case of spare-fed anchorites, takes for granted *early to bed*. When he

had no dinner engagement, he frequently gave a few hours
to the theatre; but still more frequently, when the weather
was fine, and still more, I believe, to his own satisfaction,
he drove out with some of his family, or a single friend, in
an open carriage.   5

Whatever might happen on the other evenings of the
week, he always dined at home on Sunday, and usually
some few friends were then with him, but never any person with whom he stood on ceremony. These were, it
may be readily supposed, the most agreeable of his enter- 10
tainments. He came into the room rubbing his hands,
his face bright and gleesome, like a boy arriving at home
for the holidays, his Peppers and Mustards gambolling
about his heels, and even the stately Maida grinning and
wagging his tail in sympathy.   15

*After devoting several interesting pages to a discussion of
the characters of Constable and the Ballantyne brothers,
Lockhart continues:* Why did Scott persist in mixing up
all his most important concerns with these Ballantynes?
The reader of these pages will have all my materials for 20
an answer; but in the meantime let it suffice to say, that
he was the most patient, long-suffering, affectionate, and
charitable of mankind; that in the case of both the
brothers he could count, after all, on a sincerely, nay, a
passionately devoted attachment to his person; that, 25
with the greatest of human beings, use is an all but un-
conquerable power; and that he who so loftily tossed
aside the seemingly most dangerous assaults of flattery,
the blandishment of dames, the condescension of princes,
the enthusiasm of crowds — had still his weak point, upon 30
which two or three humble besiegers, and one unwearied,
though most frivolous underminer, well knew how to direct their approaches. It was a favourite saw of his own,

that the wisest of our race often reserve the average stock of folly to be all expended upon some one flagrant absurdity.

I alluded to James Ballantyne's reading of the famous 5 scene in Richmond Park. According to Scott's original intention, the second series of *Jedediah* was to have included two tales; but his Jeanie Deans soon grew so on his fancy as to make this impossible; and the Heart of Mid-Lothian alone occupied the four volumes which ap-10 peared in June 1818, and were at once placed by acclamation in the foremost rank of his writings.

From the choice of localities, and the splendid blazoning of tragical circumstances that had left the strongest impression on the memory and imagination of every inhabit-15 ant, the reception of this tale in Edinburgh was a scene of all-engrossing enthusiasm, such as I never witnessed there on the appearance of any other literary novelty. But the admiration and delight were the same all over Scotland. Never before had he seized such really noble 20 features of the national character as were canonized in the person of his homely heroine: no art had ever devised a happier running contrast than that of her and her sister, or interwoven a portraiture of lowly manners and simple virtues, with more graceful delineations of polished life, 25 or with bolder shadows of terror, guilt, crime, remorse, madness, and all the agony of the passions.

CHAPTER X

Sketches of Abbotsford — Illness and Domestic Afflictions
— The Bride of Lammermoor — The Legend of Montrose — Ivanhoe — 1818–1819.

THE 12th of July [1818] restored Scott as usual to the
supervision of his trees and carpenters; but he had already
told the Ballantynes, that the story which he had found
it impossible to include in the recent series should be
forthwith taken up as the opening one of a third; and 5
instructed John to embrace the first favourable opportunity of offering Constable the publication of this, on
the footing of 10,000 copies again forming the first edition;
but now at length without any more stipulations connected
with the "old stock." 10

One of his visitors of September was Mr. R. Cadell,
who was now in all the secrets of his father-in-law and
partner Constable; and observing how his host was har-
assed with lion-hunters, and what a number of hours
he spent daily in the company of his work-people, he ex- 15
pressed, during one of their walks, his wonder that Scott
should ever be able to write books at all while in the country. "I know," he said, "that you contrive to get a few
hours in your own room, and that may do for the mere
pen-work; but when is it that you think?" — "Oh," 20
said Scott, "I lie *simmering* over things for an hour or so
before I get up — and there's the time I am dressing to
overhaul my half-sleeping, half-waking, *projet de chapitre*
— and when I get the paper before me, it commonly runs

141

off pretty easily. Besides, I often take a dose in the
plantations, and while Tom marks out a dyke or a drain,
as I have directed, one's fancy may be running its ain riggs
in some other world."

5   Towards the end of this year Scott received from Lord
Sidmouth the formal announcement of the Prince Regent's
desire (which had been privately communicated some
months earlier through the Lord Chief-Commissioner
Adam) to confer on him the rank of Baronet.   When he
10 first heard of the Regent's intention, he signified considerable hesitation; for it had not escaped his observation
that such airy sounds, however, modestly people may be
disposed to estimate them, are apt to entail in the upshot
additional cost upon their way of living, and to affect
15 accordingly the plastic fancies, feelings, and habits of
their children.   But Lord Sidmouth's letter happened
to reach him a few months after he had heard of the sudden
death of Charles Carpenter, who had bequeathed the
reversion of his fortune to his sister's family; and this
20 circumstance disposed Scott to waive his scruples, chiefly
with a view to the professional advantage of his eldest son,
who had by this time fixed on the life of a soldier.   As is
usually the case, the estimate of Mr. Carpenter's property
transmitted on his death to England proved to have been
25 an exaggerated one; and at any rate no one of Scott's
children lived to receive any benefit from the bequest.

His health prevented him from going up to the fountain
of honour for more than a year.   Meantime his building
and other operations continued to tax his resources more
30 than he had calculated upon; and he now completed
an important negotiation with Constable, who agreed
to give him bonds for L.12,000 in consideration of all
his existing copyrights; namely, whatever shares had been

reserved to him in the earlier poems, and the whole property in his novels down to the third series of Tales of my
Landlord inclusive. The deed included a clause by
which Constable was to forfeit L.2000 if he ever "divulged
the name of the Author of Waverley during the life 5
of the said Walter Scott, Esq."

He had now begun in earnest his Bride of Lammermoor, and his amanuenses were William Laidlaw and
John Ballantyne; — of whom he preferred the latter,
when he could be at Abbotsford, on account of the superior 10
rapidity of his pen; and also because John kept his pen to
the paper without interruption, and, though with many
an arch twinkle in his eyes, and now and then an audible
smack of his lips, had resolution to work on like a well-
trained clerk; whereas good Laidlaw entered with such 15
keen zest into the interest of the story as it flowed from
the author's lips, that he could not suppress exclamations
of surprise and delight — "Gude keep us a'! — the like
o' that — eh sirs! eh sirs!" — and so forth — which did
not promote despatch. I have often, however, in the 20
sequel, heard both these secretaries describe the astonish-
ment with which they were equally affected when Scott
began this experiment. The affectionate Laidlaw be-
seeching him to stop dictating, when his audible suffering
filled every pause, "Nay, Willie," he answered, "only 25
see that the doors are fast. I would fain keep all the cry
as well as all the wool to ourselves; but as to giving over
work, that can only be when I am in woolen." John
Ballantyne told me, that after the first day, he always
took care to have a dozen of pens made before he seated 30
himself opposite to the sofa on which Scott lay, and that
though he often turned himself on his pillow with a groan
of torment, he usually continued the sentence in the same

breath. But when dialogue of peculiar animation was in progress, spirit seemed to triumph altogether over matter — he arose from his couch and walked up and down the room, raising and lowering his voice, and as it 5 were acting the parts. It was in this fashion that Scott produced the far greater portion of The Bride of Lammermoor — the whole of the Legend of Montrose — and almost the whole of Ivanhoe. Yet when his health was fairly reëstablished, he disdained to avail 10 himself of the power of dictation, which he had thus put to the sharpest test, but resumed, and for many years resolutely adhered to, the old plan of writing everything with his own hand. When I once, sometime afterwards, expressed my surprise that he did not consult his ease, 15 and spare his eye-sight at all events, by occasionally dictating, he answered — "I should as soon think of getting into a sedan-chair while I can use my legs."

On the 11th of May he returned to Edinburgh, and was present at the opening of the Court; when all who saw 20 him were as much struck as I had been at Abbotsford with the change in his appearance. He was unable to persist in attendance at the Clerks' table — for several weeks afterwards I think he seldom if ever attempted it; and I well remember that, when the Bride of Lammermoor 25 and Legend of Montrose at length came out (which was on the 10th of June), he was known to be confined to bed, and the book was received amidst the deep general impression that we should see no more of that parentage.

I must not forget to set down what Sophia Scott afterwards 30 told me of her father's conduct upon one night in June, when he really did despair of himself. He then called his children about his bed, and took leave of them with solemn tenderness. After giving them, one by one,

such advice as suited their years and characters, he added,
— "For myself, my dears, I am unconscious of ever having
done any man an injury, or omitted any fair opportunity
of doing any man a benefit. I well know that no human
life can appear otherwise than weak and filthy in the eyes 5
of God: but I rely on the merits and intercession of our
Redeemer." He then laid his hand on their heads, and
said — "God bless you ! Live so that you may all hope to
meet each other in a better place hereafter. And now
leave me, that I may turn my face to the wall." They 10
obeyed him; but he presently fell into a deep sleep; and
when he awoke from it after many hours, the crisis of extreme danger was felt by himself, and pronounced by his
physician, to have been overcome.

The Tales of the Third Series would have been read 15
with indulgence, had they needed it; for the painful circumstances under which they must have been produced
were in part known wherever an English newspaper made
its way; but I believe that, except in typical errors, from
the author's inability to correct proof-sheets, no one ever 20
affected to perceive in either work the slightest symptom
of his malady.

These volumes, as was mentioned, came out before the
middle of June; and though at that moment he was unable to quit his room, he did not hesitate to make all arrange- 25
ments as to another romance. Nay, though his condition still required an amanuensis, he had advanced considerably in the new work before the Session closed in
July. That he felt much more security as to his health
by that time, must be inferred from his then allowing his 30
son Walter to proceed to Ireland to join the 18th regiment of Hussars. The Cornet was only in the eighteenth
year of his age; and the fashion of education in Scotland

L

is such, that he had scarcely ever slept a night under a
different roof from his parents, until this separation occurred. The parting was a painful one: but Scott's
ambition centred in the heir of his name, and instead of
5 fruitless pinings and lamentings, he henceforth made it
his constant business to keep up such a frank correspondence with the young man as might enable himself to exert
over him, when at a distance, the gentle influence of kindness, experience, and wisdom. His manly kindness to
10 his boy, whether he is expressing approbation or censure
of his conduct, is a model for the parent; and his practical wisdom was of that liberal order, based on such com-
prehensive views of man and the world, that I am persuaded it will often be found available to the circumstances
15 of their own various cases, by young men of whatever
station or profession.

On the 18th of December, appeared his Ivanhoe.
It was received throughout England with a more clamor-
ous delight than any of the Scotch novels had been. The
20 volumes (three in number) were now, for the first time,
of the post 8vo form, with a finer paper than hitherto,
the press-work much more elegant, and the price accordingly raised from eight shillings the volume to ten; yet
the copies sold in this original shape were twelve thousand.
25 The reader has already been told that Scott dictated the
greater part of this romance. The portion of the MS.
which is his own, appears, however, not only as well and
firmly executed as that of any of the Tales of my Landlord, but distinguished by having still fewer erasures
30 and interlineations, and also by being in a smaller hand.
The fragment is beautiful to look at — many pages together without one alteration. It is, I suppose, super-
fluous to add, that in no instance did Scott re-write his

prose before sending it to the press.   Whatever may have
been the case with his poetry, the world uniformly received
the *prima cura*° of the novelist.

As a work of art, Ivanhoe is perhaps the first of all
Scott's efforts, whether in prose or in verse; nor have the 5
strength and splendour of his imagination been displayed
to higher advantage than in some of the scenes of this romance.   But I believe that no reader who is capable of
thoroughly comprehending the author's Scotch character
and Scotch dialogue will ever place even Ivanhoe, as a 10
work of genius, on the same level with Waverley, Guy
Mannering, or the Heart of Mid-Lothian.

The introduction of the charming Jewess and her father
originated, I find, in a conversation that Scott held with
his friend Skene during the severest season of his bodily 15
sufferings in the early part of this year.   "Mr. Skene,"
says that gentleman's wife, "sitting by his bedside, and
trying to amuse him as well as he could in the intervals
of pain, happened to get on the subject of the Jews, as
he had observed them when he spent some time in Ger- 20
many in his youth.   Their situation had naturally made
a strong impression; for in those days they retained their
own dress and manners entire, and were treated with
considerable austerity by their Christian neighbours, being
still locked up at night in their own quarter by great gates; 25
and Mr. Skene, partly in seriousness, but partly from the
mere wish to turn his mind at the moment upon something that might occupy and divert it, suggested that a
group of Jews would be an interesting feature if he could
contrive to bring them into his next novel."   Upon the 30
appearance of Ivanhoe, he reminded Mr. Skene of this
conversation, and said, "You will find this book owes
not a little to your German reminiscences."

By the way, before Ivanhoe made its appearance, I had myself been formally admitted to the author's secret; but had he favoured me with no such confidence, it would have been impossible for me to doubt that I had been present 5 some months before at the conversation which suggested, and indeed supplied all the materials of, one of its most amusing chapters. I allude to that in which our Saxon terms for animals in the field, and our Norman equivalents for them as they appear on the table, and so on, are ex- 10 plained and commented on. All this Scott owed to the after-dinner talk one day in Castle Street of his old friend Mr. William Clerk, — who, among other elegant pursuits, has cultivated the science of philology very deeply.

About the middle of February — it having been ere 15 that time arranged that I should marry his eldest daughter in the course of the spring, — I accompanied him and part of his family on one of those flying visits to Abbotsford, with which he often indulged himself on a Saturday during term. As we proceeded, he talked without reserve of the 20 novel of the Monastery, of which he had the first volume with him : and mentioned, what he had probably forgotten when he wrote the Introduction of 1830, that a good deal of that volume had been composed before he concluded Ivanhoe. "It was a relief," he said, "to interlay the 25 scenery most familiar to me, with the strange world for which I had to draw so much on imagination."

In giving some of the incidents of this visit to Abbotsford, Lockhart sets forth Tom Purdie, Scott's faithful servant. He continues: I believe Scott has somewhere expressed in 30 print his satisfaction that, among all the changes of our manners, the ancient freedom of personal intercourse may still be indulged between a master and an *out-of- doors'* servant; but in truth he kept by the old fashion even with domestic servants, to an extent which I have hardly seen practised by any other gentleman. He conversed with his coachman if he sat by him, as he often did on the box — with his footman, if he happened to be in the rumble; and when there was any very young lad in the household, he held it a point of duty to see that his employments were so arranged as to leave time for advancing his education, made him bring his copy-book once a-week to the library, and examined him as to all that he was doing. Indeed he did not confine this humanity to his own people. Any steady servant of a friend of his was soon considered as a sort of friend too, and was sure to have a kind little colloquy to himself at coming and going. With all this, Scott was a very rigid enforcer of discipline — contrived to make it thoroughly understood by all about him, that they must do their part by him as he did his by them; and the result was happy. I never knew any man so well served as he was — so carefully, so respectfully, and so silently; and I cannot help doubting if in any department of human operations real kindness ever compromised real dignity.

CHAPTER XI

Scott's Baronetcy — Hospitalities and Sports at Abbotsford — Publication of the Monastery — The Abbot — and Kenilworth — 1820.

THE novel of The Monastery was published in the beginning of March 1820. It appeared not in the post 8vo form of Ivanhoe, but in 3 vols. 12mo, like the earlier works of the series. In fact, a few sheets of The Monas-
5 tery had been printed before Scott agreed to let Ivanhoe have "By the Author of Waverley" on its title-page; and the different shapes of the two books belonged to the abortive scheme of passing off "Mr. Laurence Templeton" as a hitherto unheard of candidate for literary success.
10 At the rising of his Court on the 12th, he proceeded to London, for the purpose of receiving his baronetcy, which he had been prevented from doing in the spring of the preceding year by illness, and again at Christmas by family afflictions. The Prince Regent was now King.
15 The baronetcy was conferred on him, not in consequence of any Ministerial suggestion, but by the King personally, and of his own unsolicited motion; and when the poet kissed his hand, he said to him — "I shall always reflect with pleasure on Sir Walter Scott's having been
20 the first creation of my reign."
The Gazette announcing this was dated March 30, 1820; and the Baronet, as soon afterwards as he could get away, set out on his return to the North; for he had such re-

150

spect for the ancient prejudice (a classical as well as a
Scottish one) against marrying in May, that he was anxious to have the ceremony in which his daughter was concerned, over before that unlucky month should commence.
He reached Edinburgh late in April, and on the 29th of 5
that month he gave me the hand of his daughter Sophia.
The wedding, *more Scotico,*° took place in the evening;
and adhering on all such occasions to ancient modes of
observance with the same punctiliousness which he mentions as distinguishing his worthy father, he gave a jolly 10
supper afterwards to all the friends and connexions of
the young couple.

In May 1820, he received from both the English Uni-
versities the highest compliment which it was in their
power to offer him.   The Vice-Chancellors of Oxford and 15
Cambridge communicated to him, in the same week, their
request that he would attend at the approaching Comme-
morations, and accept the honorary degree of Doctor in
Civil Law.   It was impossible for him to leave Scotland
again in time; and on various subsequent renewals of the 20
same flattering proposition from either body, he was prevented by similar circumstances from availing himself of
their distinguished kindness.

About the middle of August, my wife and I went to
Abbotsford; and we remained there for several weeks, 25
during which I became familiarized to Sir Walter Scott's
mode of existence in the country.   The humblest person
who stayed merely for a short visit, must have departed
with the impression that what he witnessed was an occasional variety; that Scott's courtesy prompted him to 30
break in upon his habits when he had a stranger to amuse;
but that it was physically impossible that the man who
was writing the Waverley romances at the rate of

nearly twelve volumes in the year, could continue, week
after week, and month after month, to devote all but a
hardly perceptible fraction of his mornings to out-of-
doors' occupations, and the whole of his evenings to the
5 entertainment of a constantly varying circle of guests.

I have seen Sir Humphrey Davy in many places, and
in company of many different descriptions; but never to
such advantage as at Abbotsford. His host and he delighted in each other, and the modesty of their mutual
10 admiration was a memorable spectacle. Each strove to
make the other talk — and they did so in turn more
charmingly than I ever heard either on any other occasion whatsoever. I remember William Laidlaw whisper-
ing to me, one night, when their "rapt talk" had kept
15 the circle round the fire until long after the usual bedtime
of Abbotsford — "Gude preserve us ! this is a very superior
occasion ! Eh, sirs !" he added, cocking his eye like a
bird, "I wonder if Shakspeare and Bacon ever met to
screw ilk other up ?"

20 Since I have touched on the subject of Sir Walter's
autumnal diversions in these his latter years, I may as well
notice here two annual festivals, when sport was made
his pretext for assembling his rural neighbours about him
— days eagerly anticipated, and fondly remembered by
25 many. One was a solemn bout of salmon-fishing for the
neighbouring gentry and their families.

The other "superior occasion" came later in the season;
the 28th of October, the birthday of Sir Walter's eldest
son, was, I think, that usually selected for *the Abbotsford
30 Hunt.* This was a coursing-field on a large scale, including, with as many of the young gentry as pleased to attend,
all Scott's personal favourites among the yeomen and
farmers of the surrounding country.

Thus Lockhart concludes his account of the breaking off of the revels that followed the Hunt: How they all contrived to get home in safety, Heaven only knows — but I never heard of any serious accident except upon one occasion, when James Hogg made a bet at starting that he would ⁵ leap over his wall-eyed pony as she stood, and broke his nose in this experiment of "o'ervaulting ambition." °
One comely goodwife, far off among the hills, amused Sir Walter by telling him, the next time he passed her homestead after one of these jolly doings, what her husband's ¹⁰ first words were when he alighted at his own door — "Ailie, my woman, I'm ready for my bed — and oh lass (he gallantly added), I wish I could sleep for a tow mont, for there's only ae thing in this warld worth living for, and that's the Abbotsford hunt !" ¹⁵

In September 1820 appeared The Abbot — the continuation, to a certain extent, of The Monastery, of which I barely mentioned the publication under the preceding March. I have nothing of any consequence to add to the information which the Introduction of 1830 ²⁰ affords us respecting the composition and fate of the former of these novels. It was considered as a failure — the first of the series on which any such sentence was pronounced. Sir Walter himself thought well of The Abbot when he had finished it, and whatever ground he had been supposed ²⁵ to lose in The Monastery, part at least of it was regained by this tale, and especially by its most graceful and pathetic portraiture of Mary Stuart.

For reasons connected with the affairs of the Ballantynes, Messrs Longman published the first edition of the Mon- ³⁰ astery; and similar circumstances induced Sir Walter to associate this house with that of Constable in the succeeding novel. Constable disliked its title, and would

fain have had The Nunnery instead: but Scott stuck
to his Abbot. The bookseller grumbled a little, but
was soothed by the author's reception of his request that
Queen Elizabeth might be brought into the field in his
5 next romance, as a companion to the Mary Stuart of The
Abbot. Scott would not indeed indulge him with the
choice of the particular period of Elizabeth's reign, indi-
cated in the proposed title of The Armada ; but expressed his willingness to take up his own old favourite
10 legend of Meikle's ballad. He wished to call the novel,
like the ballad, Cumnor-Hall, but in further deference
to Constable's wishes, substituted "Kenilworth." John
Ballantyne objected to this title, and told Constable the
result would be "something worthy of the kennel"; but
15 Constable had all reason to be satisfied with the child of
his christening.

About Christmas appeared Kenilworth, in 3 vols.
post 8vo, like Ivanhoe, which form was adhered to with
all the subsequent novels of the series. Kenilworth was
20 one of the most successful of them all at the time of
publication ; and it continues, and, I doubt not, will ever
continue to be placed in the very highest rank of prose
fiction. The rich variety of character, and scenery, and
incident in this novel, has never indeed been surpassed ;
25 nor, with the one exception of the Bride of Lammermoor,
has Scott bequeathed us a deeper and more affecting
tragedy than that of Amy Robsart.

CHAPTER XII

Death of John Ballantyne — Visit of Miss Edgeworth
— Reminiscences by Mr. Adolphus — Halidon Hill
— The Pirate — The Fortunes of Nigel — Peveril of the
Peak — Quentin Durward — and St. Ronan's Well —
1821–1823.

On the 16th of June 1821, died at Edinburgh John
Ballantyne. As we stood together a few days afterwards,
while they were smoothing the turf over John's remains in
the Cannongate churchyard, the heavens which had been
dark and slaty, cleared up suddenly, and the midsummer 5
sun shone forth in his strength.   Scott, ever awake to the
"skiey influences," cast his eye along the overhanging
line of the Calton Hill, with its gleaming walls and towers,
and then turning to the grave again, "I feel," he whispered
in my ear, — "I feel as if there would be less sunshine for 10
me from this day forth."

The coronation of George IV. had been deferred in consequence of the unhappy affair of the Queen's Trial.   The
19th of July 1821 was now announced for this solemnity,
and Sir Walter resolved to be among the spectators.   15

At the close of that brilliant scene, he received a mark
of homage to his genius which delighted him.   Missing
his carriage, he had to return home on foot from Westminster, after the banquet — that is to say, between two
or three o'clock in the morning ; — when he and a young 20

gentleman his companion found themselves locked in the
crowd, somewhere near Whitehall, and the bustle and
tumult were such that his friend was afraid some accident
might happen to the lame limb.   A space for the digni-
5 taries was kept clear at that point by the Scots Greys.°
Sir Walter addressed a serjeant of this celebrated regiment,
begging to be allowed to pass by him into the open ground
in the middle of the street.   The man answered shortly,
that his orders were strict — that the thing was impossible.
10 While he was endeavouring to persuade the serjeant to
relent, some new wave of turbulence approached from
behind, and his young companion exclaimed in a loud
voice, "Take care, Sir Walter Scott, take care!"   The
stalwart dragoon, on hearing the name, said, "What!
• 15 Sir Walter Scott? He shall get through anyhow!"
He then addressed the soldiers near him — "Make room,
men, for Sir Walter Scott, our illustrious countryman!"
The men answered, "Sir Walter Scott! — God bless him!"
— and he was in a moment within the guarded line of
20 safety.

Sir Walter concluded, before he went to town in
November, another negotiation of importance with the
house of Constable.   They agreed to give for the remaining copyright of the four novels published between De-
25 cember 1819 and January 1821 — to wit, Ivanhoe,
The Monastery, The Abbot, and Kenilworth — the
sum of five thousand guineas.   The stipulation about
not revealing the author's name, under a penalty of
L.2000, was repeated.   By these four novels, the fruits
30 of scarcely more than twelve months' labour, he had already cleared at least L.10,000 before this bargain was
completed.   I cannot pretend to guess what the actual
state of his pecuniary affairs was at the time when John

Ballantyne's death relieved them from one great source
of complication and difficulty. But I have said enough
to satisfy every reader, that when he began the second,
and far the larger division of his building at Abbotsford,
he must have contemplated the utmost sum it could cost 5
him as a mere trifle in relation to the resources at his command. He must have reckoned on clearing L.30,000 at
least in the course of a couple of years by the novels written
within such a period. The publisher of his Tales, who
best knew how they were produced, and what they brought 10
of gross profit, and who must have had the strongest
interest in keeping the author's name untarnished by any
risk or reputation of failure, would willingly, as we have
seen, have given him L.6000 more within a space of two
years for works of a less serious sort, likely to be despatched 15
at leisure hours, without at all interfering with the main
manufacture. But alas! even this was not all. Messrs.
Constable had such faith in the prospective fertility of
his imagination, that they were by this time quite ready
to sign bargains and grant bills for novels and romances 20
to be produced hereafter, but of which the subjects and
the names were alike unknown to them and to the man
from whose pen they were to proceed. A forgotten satirist
well says : —

> "The active principle within   25
> Works on some brains the effect of gin ;"

but in Sir Walter's case, every external influence combined
to stir the flame, and swell the intoxication of restless exu-
berant energy. His allies knew indeed, what he did not,
that the sale of his novels was rather less than it had been 30
in the days of Ivanhoe; and hints had sometimes been
dropped to him that it might be well to try the effect of a

pause.   But he always thought — and James Ballantyne
had decidedly the same opinion — that his best things
were those which he threw off the most easily and swiftly;
and it was no wonder that his booksellers, seeing how im-
5 measurably even his worst excelled in popularity, as in
merit, any other person's best, should have shrunk from
the experiment of a decisive damper.   On the contrary,
they might be excused for from time to time flattering
themselves, that if the books sold at less rate, this might
10 be counterpoised by still greater rapidity of production.
They could not make up their minds to cast the peerless
vessel adrift;   and, in short, after every little whisper of
prudential misgiving, echoed the unfailing burden of
Ballantyne's song — to push on, hoisting more and more
15 sail as the wind lulled.

He was as eager to do as they could be to suggest — and
this I well knew at the time.   I had, however, no notion,
until all his correspondence lay before me, of the extent to
which he had permitted himself thus early to build on the
20 chances of life, health, and continued popularity.   Before
The Fortunes of Nigel issued from the press, Scott had
exchanged instruments, and received his booksellers' bills,
for no less than four "works of fiction" — not one of them
otherwise described in the deeds of agreement — to be
25 produced in unbroken succession, each of them to fill at
least three volumes, but with proper saving clauses as to
increase of copy-money in case any of them should run
to four.   And within two years all this anticipation had
been wiped off by Peveril of the Peak, Quentin Dur-
30 ward, St. Ronan's Well, and Redgauntlet;   and the new
castle was by that time complete.   But by that time the
end also was approaching !

The splendid Romance of The Pirate was published

in the beginning of December 1821 ; and the wild freshness
of its atmosphere, the beautiful contrast of Minna and
Brenda, and the exquisitely drawn character of Captain
Cleveland, found the reception which they deserved.

Whoever reads Scott's letters to Terry might naturally 5
suppose that during this winter his thoughts were almost
exclusively occupied with the rising edifice on Tweedside.
The pains he takes about every trifle of arrangement, exterior and interior, is truly most remarkable : it is not
probable that many idle lords or lairds ever took half so 10
much about such matters.   But his literary industry was
all the while unresting.   His Nigel was completed by
April 1822.   Nor had he neglected a promise of the summer before to supply Miss Baillie with a contribution for
a volume of miscellaneous verse, which she had under- 15
taken to compile for the benefit of a friend in distress.
With that view he now produced — and that, as I well
remember, in the course of two rainy mornings at Abbotsford — the dramatic sketch of Halidon Hill; but on concluding it, he found that he had given it an extent quite 20
incompatible with his friend's arrangements for her charitable picnic.   He therefore cast about for another subject
likely to be embraced in smaller compass; and the Blair-
Adam° meeting of the next June supplied him with one in
Macduff's Cross.   Meantime, on hearing a whisper about 25
Halidon Hill, Constable's junior partner, without seeing
the MS., forthwith tendered L.1000 for the copyright —
the same sum that had appeared almost irrationally munificent, when offered in 1807 for the embryo Marmion.
It was accepted, and a letter about to be quoted will shew 30
how well the head of the firm was pleased with this wild
bargain.

The Nigel was published on the 30th of May 1822 ;

and was, I need not say, hailed as ranking in the first class
of Scott's romances. Indeed, as a historical portraiture,
his of James I stands forth preëminent, and almost alone;
nor, perhaps, in reperusing these novels deliberately as a
5 series, does any one of them leave so complete an impression, as the picture of an age. It is, in fact, the best commentary on the old English drama — hardly a single
picturesque point of manners touched by Ben Jonson° and
his contemporaries but has been dovetailed into this story,
10 and all so easily and naturally, as to form the most striking
contrast to the historical romances of authors who *cram*,
as the schoolboys phrase it, and then set to work oppressed
and bewildered with their crude and undigested burden.

On the day after the publication, Constable, then near
15 London, wrote thus to the author: — "I was in town
yesterday, and so keenly were the people devouring my
friend *Jingling Geordie*, that I actually saw them reading
it in the streets as they passed along. I assure you there
is no exaggeration in this. A new novel from the Author
20 of Waverley puts aside — in other words, puts down for
the time, every other literary performance. The smack
Ocean, by which the new work was shipped, arrived at
the wharf on Sunday; the bales were got out by *one* on
Monday morning, and before half-past ten o'clock 7000
25 copies had been dispersed! I was truly happy to hear of
Halidon Hill, and of the satisfactory arrangements made
for its publication. I wish I had the power of prevailing
with you to give us a similar production every three
months; and that our ancient enemies on this side the
30 Border might not have too much their own way, perhaps
your next dramatic sketch might be Bannockburn. It
would be presumptuous in me to point out subjects but
you know my craving to be great, and I cannot resist

mentioning here that I should like to see a battle of Hast-
ings° — a Cressy° — a Bosworth field° — and many
more." — The Nigel was just launched — Constable knew
that Peveril of the Peak was already on the stocks : yet
see how quietly he suggests that a little pinnace of the 5
Halidon class might easily be rigged out once a quarter
by way of diversion, and thus add another L.4000 per
annum to the L.10,000 or L.15,000, on which all parties
counted as the sure yearly profit of the three-deckers *in
fore!* In a letter of the ensuing month, after returning 10
to the progress of Peveril of the Peak under 10,000
copies of which (or nearly that number) Ballantyne's
presses were now groaning, and glancing gaily to the prospect of their being kept regularly employed to the same
extent until three other novels, as yet unchristened, had 15
followed Peveril, he adds a summary of what was then,
had just been, or was about to be, the amount of occupation furnished to the same office by reprints of older
works of the same pen ; — "a summary," he exclaims,
"to which I venture to say there will be no rival in our 20
day !"   And well might Constable say so ; for the result is,
that James Ballantyne and Co. had just executed, or were
on the eve of executing, by his order —

"A new edition of Sir W. Scott's Poetical Works,
　　in 10 vols. (miniature)　　　　　　5000 copies. 25
"Novels and Tales, 12 vols. ditto,　　5000 —
"Historical Romances, 6 vols. ditto,　5000 —
"Poetry from Waverley, &c. 1 vol. 12 mo.　5000 —
"Paper required, .　　.　　.　　.　　7772 reams.
"Volumes produced from Ballantyne's press, 145,000 !"　30

To which we may safely add from 30,000 to 40,000 volumes
more as the immediate produce of the author's daily

M

industry within the space of twelve months. The scale
of these operations was, without question, enough to
turn any bookseller's wits; — Constable's, in his soberest
hours, was as inflammable a head-piece as ever sat on the
5 shoulders of a poet; and his ambition, in truth, had been
moving *pari passu*,° during several of these last stirring and
turmoiling years, with that of *his* poet. He, too, as I
ought to have mentioned ere now, had, like a true Scotchman, concentrated his dreams on the hope of bequeathing
10 to his heir the name and dignity of a lord of acres; he,
too, had considerably before this time purchased a landed
estate in his native county of Fife; he, too, I doubt not,
had, while Abbotsford was rising, his own rural castle *in
petto*°; and alas! for "Archibald Constable of Balniel"
15 also, and his overweening intoxication of worldly success,
Fortune had already begun to prepare a stern rebuke.

Early in October, Scott had another attack of illness.
He says to Terry, in a letter full of details about silk-
hangings, ebony-cabinets, and so forth: — "I have not
20 been very well — a thickness of blood, and a depression
of spirits, arising from the loss of friends, have annoyed me
much; and Peveril will, I fear, smell of the apoplexy. I
propose a good rally, however, and hope it will be a powerful effect. My idea is, *entre nous*,° a Scotch archer in the
25 French king's guard, *tempore*° Louis XI., the most picturesque of all times." This is the first allusion to
Quentin Durward and also the species of malady that ultimately proved fatal to Sir Walter Scott. The depression
of spirits could not, however, have hung over him long.
30 Peveril was completed, and some progress had also been
achieved with Quentin Durward, before the year reached
its close. Nor had he ceased to contemplate future labour
with firmness and hopefulness. He, in October, received

Constable's bills for another unnamed "work of fiction;" and this was the last such work in which the great bookseller was destined to have any concern. The engagement was in fact that redeemed three years afterwards by Woodstock.   5

Peveril of the Peak appeared in January 1823. Its reception was somewhat colder than that of its three immediate predecessors. One morning soon after Peveril came out, one of our most famous wags (now famous for better things), namely Patrick Robertson, commonly 10 called by the endearing Scottish *diminutive* "Peter," observed that tall conical white head advancing above the crowd towards the fire-place, where the usual roar of fun was going on among the briefless, and said, "Hush, boys, here comes old Peveril — I see *the Peak*." A laugh en- 15 sued, and *Peter's* application stuck; to his dying day, Scott was in the Outer-House *Peveril of the Peak*, or *Old Peveril* — and, by and by, like a good Cavalier, he took to the designation kindly. He was well aware that his own family and younger friends constantly talked of him under 20 this *sobriquet*. Many a little note have I had from him (and so probably has *Peter* also), reproving, or perhaps encouraging, Tory mischief, and signed, "Thine, PEVERIL."

It was, perhaps, some inward misgiving towards the completion of Peveril, that determined Scott to break new 25 ground in his next novel; and as he had before awakened a fresh interest by venturing on English scenery and history, try the still bolder experiment of a continental excursion. However this may have been, he was encouraged and strengthened by the return of his friend Skene, about 30 this time, from a tour in France; in the course of which he had kept an accurate and lively journal, and executed a vast variety of clever drawings, representing landscapes

and ancient buildings, such as would have been most
sure to interest Scott had he been the companion of his
wanderings.   Mr. Skene's MS. collections were placed at
his disposal, and he took from one of their chapters the
5 substance of the *original* Introduction to Quentin Durward.
Yet still his difficulties in this new undertaking were frequent, and of a sort to which he had hitherto been a
stranger.   I remember observing him many times in the
Advocates' Library poring over maps and gazetteers with
10 care and anxiety.

The reader of his correspondence will find hints about
various little matters connected with Scott's own advancing edifice, in which he may trace the President of the
Royal Society° and the Chairman of the Gas Company.°
15 But I cannot say that the "century of inventions" at
Abbotsford turned out very happily.   His bells to move by
compression of air in a piston proved a poor succedaneum
for the simple wire; and his application of gas-light to the
interior of a dwelling-house was in fact attended with so
20 many inconveniences, that erelong all his family heartily
wished it had never been thought of.   Moreover, he had
deceived himself as to the expense of such an apparatus
when constructed and maintained for the use of a single
domestic establishment.   The effect of the apparatus was
25 at first superb.   In sitting down to table, in Autumn, no
one observed that in each of three chandeliers there lurked
a tiny bead of red light.   Dinner passed off, and the sun
went down, and suddenly, at the turning of a screw, the
room was filled with a gush of splendour worthy of the
30 palace of Aladdin; but, as in the case of Aladdin, the old
lamp would have been better in the upshot.   Jewelry
sparkled, but cheeks and lips looked cold and wan in this
fierce illumination; and the eye was wearied, and the brow

ached, if the sitting was at all protracted. I confess, however, that my chief enmity to the whole affair arises ∠. from my conviction that Sir Walter's own health was damaged, in his latter years, in consequence of his habitually working at night under the intense and burning glare 5 of a broad star of gas.

In June Quentin Durward was published; and surpassing as its popularity was eventually, Constable, who was in London at the time, wrote in cold terms of its immediate reception. 10

Very shortly before the bookseller left Edinburgh for that trip, he had concluded another bargain (his last of the sort) for the purchase of Waverley copyrights — acquiring the author's property in the Pirate, Nigel, Peveril, and also Quentin Durward, out and out, at the price of 15 five thousand guineas. He had thus paid for the copyright of novels (over and above the half profits of the early separate editions) the sum of L.22,500; and his advances upon "works of fiction" still in embryo amounted at this moment to L.10,000 more. He began, in short, 20 and the wonder is that he began so late, to suspect that the process of creation was moving too rapidly. The publication of different sets of the Tales in a collective shape may probably have had a share in opening his eyes to the fact, that the voluminousness of an author is anything but 25 favourable to the rapid diffusion of his works as library books — the great object with any publisher who aspires at founding a solid fortune. But he merely intimated on this occasion that, considering the usual chances of life and health, he must decline contracting for any more 30 novels until those already bargained for were written. Scott himself appears to have admitted for a moment the suspicion that he had been overdoing in the field of ro-

mance; and opened the scheme of a work on popular
superstitions, in the form of dialogue, for which he had
long possessed ample materials in his curious library of
diablerie. But before Constable had leisure to consider
5 this proposal in all its bearings, Quentin Durward, from
being, as Scott expressed it, *frost-bit*, had emerged into
most fervid and flourishing life. In fact, the sensation
which this novel on its first appearance created in Paris,
was extremely similar to that which attended the original
10 Waverley in Edinburgh, and Ivanhoe afterwards in London. For the first time Scott had ventured on foreign
ground, and the French public, long wearied of the pom-
pous tragedians and feeble romancers, who had alone
striven to bring out the ancient history and manners of
15 their country in popular forms, were seized with a fever of
delight when Louis XI.° and Charles the Bold° started into
life again at the beck of the Northern Magician. The
result of Quentin Durward, as regards the contemporary
literature of the Continent, would open a field for ample
20 digression. As concerns the author himself, the rays of
foreign enthusiasm speedily thawed the frost of Constable's
unwonted misgivings; the Dialogues on Superstition, if he
ever began them, were very soon dropped, and the Novelist resumed his pen. He had not sunk under the short-
25 lived frown — for he wrote to Ballantyne, on first ascer-
taining that a damp was thrown on his usual manufacture,

> "The mouse who only trusts to one poor hole,
>   Can never be a mouse of any soul;"

and, while his publisher yet remained irresolute as to the
30 plan of Dialogues, threw off his excellent Essay on Romance for the Encyclopædia Brittanica; and I cannot
but consider it as another display of his high self-reliance,

that, though he well knew to what influence Quentin owed
its ultimate success in the British market, he, the instant
he found himself encouraged to take up the trade of story-
telling again, sprang back to Scotland — nay, voluntarily
encountered new difficulties, by selecting the compara- 5
tively tame and unpicturesque realities of modern manners
in his native province.

The month of August 1823 was one of the happiest in
Scott's life. Never did I see a brighter day at Abbotsford
than that on which Miss Edgeworth° first arrived there 10
— never can I forget her look and accent when she was
received by him at his archway, and exclaimed, "Everything about you is exactly what one ought to have had wit
enough to dream!" The weather was beautiful, and the
edifice, and its appurtenances, were all but complete; and 15
day after day, so long as she could remain, her host had
always some new plan of gaiety. One day there was fish-
ing on the Cauldshields' Loch, and a dinner on the heathy
bank. Another, the whole party feasted by Sir Thomas
the Rhymer's waterfall in the glen — and the stone on 20
which Maria that day sat was ever afterwards called
Edgeworth's Stone. Thus a fortnight was passed — and
the vision closed; for Miss Edgeworth never saw Abbotsford again during his life; and I am very sure she could
never bear to look upon it now that the spirit is fled. 25

Another welcome guest of the same month was Mr.
Adolphus° — the author of the Letters to Heber°; whose
reminiscences of this and several subsequent visits are
singularly vivid and interesting. He says: —

"No one who has seen him can forget the surprising 30
power of change which his countenance showed when
awakened from a state of composure. In 1823, his face,
which was healthy and sanguine, and the hair about it,

which had a strong reddish tinge, contrasted rather than
harmonized with the sleek, silvery locks above; a contrast
which might seem rather suited to a jovial and humorous,
than to a pathetic expression. But his features were
5 equally capable of both.   The form and hue of his eyes
(for the benefit of minute physiognomists it should be
noted that the iris contained some small specks of brown)
were wonderfully calculated for shewing great varieties of
emotion.   Their mournful aspect was extremely earnest
10 and affecting; and when he told some dismal and mysterious story, they had a doubtful, melancholy, exploring
look, which appealed irresistibly to the hearer's imagination. Occasionally, when he spoke of something very
audacious or eccentric, they would dilate and light up with
15 a tragi-comic, hare-brained expression, quite peculiar
to himself; one might see in it a whole chapter of *Cœur-
de-lion* and the Clerk of Copmanhurst.   Never, perhaps,
did a man go through all the gradations of laughter with
such complete enjoyment, and a countenance so radiant.
20 The first dawn of a humorous thought would shew itself
sometimes, as he sat silent, by an involuntary lengthening
of the upper lip, followed by a shy sidelong glance at his
neighbours, indescribably whimsical, and seeming to ask
from their looks whether the spark of drollery should be
25 suppressed or allowed to blaze out.   In the full tide of
mirth he did indeed 'laugh the heart's laugh,' like Walpole,
but it was not boisterous and overpowering, nor did it
check the course of his words; he could go on telling or
descanting, while his lungs did 'crow like chanticleer,'
30 his syllables, in the struggle, growing more emphatic, his
accent more strongly Scotch, and his voice plaintive with
excess of merriment."

St. Ronan's Well was published in December, and

in its English reception there was another falling off, which of course somewhat dispirited the bookseller for the moment. Scotch readers in general dissented stoutly from this judgment, alleging (as they might well do) that Meg Dods deserved a place by the side of Monkbarns, Bailie Jarvie, and Captain Dalgetty; — that no one, who had lived in the author's own country, could hesitate to recognise vivid and happy portraitures in Touchwood, Mac-Turk, and the recluse minister of St. Ronan's; — that the descriptions of natural scenery might rank with any he had given; — and, finally, that the whole character of Clara Mowbray, but especially its development in the third volume, formed an original creation, destined to be classed by posterity with the highest efforts of tragic romance.

CHAPTER XIII

Publication of Redgauntlet — Abbotsford completed —
Marriage of Captain Scott — Constable's Miscellany
projected — Life of Napoleon begun — Tales of the
Crusaders published — Tour in Ireland — Rumours of
Evil among the Booksellers — 1824–1825.

IMMEDIATELY on the conclusion of St. Ronan's Well, Sir
Walter began *Redgauntlet;* — but it had made considerable progress at press before Constable and Ballantyne
could persuade him to substitute that title for *Herries.*
5 The book was published in June 1824, and was received
at the time somewhat coldly, though it has since, I believe,
found more justice. The reintroduction of the adventurous hero of 1745, in the dulness and dimness of advancing
age and fortunes hopelessly blighted — and the presenting
10 him — with whose romantic portraiture at an earlier period
historical truth had been so admirably blended — as the
moving principle of events, not only entirely, but notori-
ously imaginary — this was a rash experiment, and could
not fail to suggest disadvantageous comparisons; yet, had
15 there been no Waverley, I am persuaded the fallen and
faded Ascanius° of Redgauntlet would have been universally pronounced a masterpiece.
   This year — *mirabile dictu!* ° — produced but one novel;
and it is not impossible that the author had taken deeply
20 into his mind, though he would not *immediately* act upon
them, certain hints about the danger of "overcropping,"

which have been alluded to as dropping from his publishers in 1823. He had, however, a labour of some weight to go through in a second edition of his Swift. The additions to this reprint were numerous, and he corrected his notes, and the "Life of the Dean" throughout, with care. 5

Notwithstanding numberless letters to Terry about his upholstery, the far greater part of it was manufactured at home. The most of the articles from London were only models for the use of two or three neat-handed carpenters whom he had discovered in the villages near him; and he 10 watched and directed their operations as carefully as a George Bullock° could have done; and the results were such as even Bullock might have admired. The great table in the library, for example (a most complex and beautiful one), was done entirely in the room where it now stands, 15 by Joseph Shillinglaw of Darnick — the Sheriff planning and studying every turn as zealously as ever an old lady pondered the development of an embroidered cushion. The hangings and curtains, too, were chiefly the work of a little hunch-backed tailor, by name *William* Goodfellow — 20 (save at Abbotsford, where he answered to *Robin*) — who occupied a cottage on Scott's farm of the Broomielees; one of the race who creep from homestead to homestead, welcomed wherever they appear by housewife and hand-maiden, the great gossips and newsmen of the parish, — in 25 Scottish nomenclature *cardooers*. Proudly and earnestly did all these vassals toil in his service; and I think it was one of them that, when some stranger asked a question about his personal demeanour, answered in these simple words — "Sir Walter speaks to every man as if they were 30 blood-relations." Not long after he had completed his work at Abbotsford, little Goodfellow fell sick, and as his cabin was near Chiefswood, I had many opportunities of

observing the Sheriff's kind attention to him in his affliction.   I can never forget the evening on which the poor
tailor died.   When Scott entered the hovel he found everything silent, and inferred from the looks of the good women
5 in attendance that their patient had fallen asleep, and that
they feared his sleep was the final one.   He murmured
some syllables of kind regret ; — at the sound of his voice
the dying tailor unclosed his eyes, and eagerly and wist-
fully sat up, clasping his hands with an expression of
10 rapturous gratefulness and devotion, that, in the midst
of deformity, disease, pain, and wretchedness, was at once
beautiful and sublime.   He cried with a loud voice,
"The Lord bless and reward you!" and expired with
the effort.

15   In the painting too Sir Walter personally directed everything.   He abominated the commonplace daubing of walls,
panels, doors, and window-boards, with coats of white,
blue, or grey, and thought that sparklings and edgings of
gilding only made their baldness and poverty more notice-
20 able.   Except in the drawing-room, which he abandoned
to Lady Scott's taste, all the roofs were in appearance at
least of antique carved oak, relieved by coats of arms duly
blazoned at the intersections of beams, and resting on
cornices to the eye of the same material, but composed
25 of casts in plaster of Paris, after the foliage, the flowers,
the grotesque monsters and dwarfs, and sometimes the
beautiful heads of nuns and confessors, on which he had
doated from infancy among the cloisters of Melrose
and Roslin.   In the painting of these things, also, he
30 had instruments who considered it as a labour of love.
The master-limner, in particular (Mr. D. R. Hay), had
a devoted attachment to his person ; and this was not
wonderful, for he, in fact, owed a prosperous fortune to

Scott's kind and sagacious counsel tendered at the very outset of his career.

By Christmas the Tales of the Crusaders were begun, and Abbotsford was at last rid of carpenters and upholsterers. Young. Walter arrived to see his father's house complete, and filled with a larger company than it could ever before accommodate. One of the guests was Captain Basil Hall, always an agreeable one: a traveller and a *savant*, full of stories and theories, inexhaustible in spirits, curiosity, and enthusiasm. Sir Walter was surprised and a little annoyed on observing that the Captain kept a note-book on his knee while at table, but made no remark. He kindly allowed me, in 1836, to read his Abbotsford Diaries, &c., and make what use of them I might then think proper. On the present occasion I must give but a specimen : —

"Last night there was a dance in honour of Sir Walter Scott's eldest son, who had recently come from Sandhurst College,° after having passed through some military examinations with great credit. We had a great clan of Scotts. There were no less than nine Scotts of Harden, and ten of other families. There were others besides from the neighbourhood — at least half a dozen Fergussons, with the jolly Sir Adam at their head — Lady Fergusson, her niece Miss Jobson, the pretty heiress of Lochore," &c. But with all his acuteness, Hall does not seem to have caught any suspicion of the real purpose and meaning of this ball. That evening was one of the very proudest and happiest in Scott's brilliant existence. Its festivities were held in honour of the young lady, whom the Captain names cursorily as "the pretty heiress of Lochore." It was known to not a few of the party, and I should have supposed it might have been surmised by the rest, that those

halls were displayed for the first time in all their splendour,
on an occasion not less interesting to the Poet than the
conclusion of a treaty of marriage between the heir of his
name and fortunes, and the amiable niece of his friends
5 Sir Adam and Lady Fergusson. It was the first regular
ball given at Abbotsford, and the last. Nay, I believe
nobody has ever danced under that roof since then. I
myself never again saw the whole range of apartments
thrown open for the reception of company except once —
10 on the day of Sir Walter Scott's funeral.

The lady's fortune was a handsome one, and her guardians exerted the powers with which they were invested,
by requiring that the marriage-contract should settle
Abbotsford (with reservation of Sir Walter's own liferent)
15 upon the affianced parties. To this condition he gave a
ready assent, and the moment he had signed the deed, he
exclaimed — "I have now parted with my lands with more
pleasure than I ever derived from the acquisition or possession of them; and if I be spared for ten years, I think
20 I may promise to settle as much more again upon these
young folks." It was well for himself and his children that
his auguries, which failed so miserably as to the matter of
worldly wealth, were destined to no disappointment as
respected considerations of a higher description.

25 The marriage took place at Edinburgh on the 3d day of
February, and when the young couple left Abbotsford two
or three weeks afterwards, Sir Walter promised to visit
them at their regimental quarters in Ireland in the course
of the summer. Before he fulfilled that purpose he had
30 the additional pleasure of seeing his son gazetted° as Captain in the King's Hussars — a step for which Sir Walter
advanced the large sum of L.3500.

But at this time the chief subject of concern was a grand

scheme of revolution in the whole art and traffic of publishing, which Constable first opened in detail one Saturday
at Abbotsford — none being present except Sir Walter,
Ballantyne, and myself. The reader does not need to be
told that the series of cheap volumes, subsequently issued 5
under the title of "Constable's Miscellany," was the
scheme on which this great bookseller was brooding.
Before he left Abbotsford, it was arranged that the first
number of this collection should consist of one half of
Waverley; the second, of the first section of a "Life of 10
Napoleon Bonaparte by the author of Waverley"; that
this Life should be comprised in four of these numbers;
and that, until the whole series of his novels had been
issued, a volume every second month, in this new and un-
costly form, he should keep the Ballantyne press going 15
with a series of historical works, to be issued on the al-
ternate months.

Some circumstances in the progress of the Tales of the
Crusaders, now on the eve of publication, must have
been uppermost in Scott's mind when he met Constable's 20
proposals with so much alacrity. The story of The Betrothed — (to which he was mainly prompted by the
lively conversation on Welsh antiquities of Archdeacon
Williams) — found no favour as it advanced with Ballantyne; and so heavily did his critical remonstrances 25
weigh on the author, that he at length determined to can-
cel it for ever. The tale, however, all but a chapter or
two, had been printed off, and both publisher and printer
paused about committing such a mass to the flames. The
sheets were hung up meanwhile, and Scott began The 30
Talisman — of which also James criticised the earlier
chapters in such a strain that Scott was deeply vexed.
"Is it wise," he wrote, "to mend a dull overloaded fire by

heaping on a shovelful of wet coals?'' and hinted some
doubts whether he should proceed. He did so, however;
the critical printer by degrees warmed to the story, and
he at last pronounced The Talisman such a masterpiece,
5 that The Betrothed might venture abroad under its
wing. Sir Walter was now reluctant on that subject, and
said he would rather write two more new novels than the
few pages necessary to complete his unfortunate "Betrothed." But while he hesitated, the German news-
10 papers announced "*a new romance by the author of Waverley*" as about to issue from the press of Leipsig. There
was some ground for suspecting that a set of the suspended
·sheets might have been purloined and sold to a pirate, and
this consideration put an end to his scruples. And when
15 the German did publish the fabrication, entitled *Wallad-
mor*, it could no longer be doubtful that some reader of
Scott's sheets had communicated at least the fact that he
was breaking ground in Wales.

Early in June, then, the Tales of the Crusaders were
20 put forth; and, as Mr. Ballantyne had predicted, the
brightness of the Talisman dazzled the eyes of the million
as to the defects of the twin-story. Few of these publications had a more enthusiastic greeting; and Scott's
literary plans were, as the reader will see reason to infer,
25 considerably modified in consequence of the new burst of
applause which attended the brilliant procession of his
Saladin and Cœur de Lion.

He began, without delay, what was meant to be a very
short preliminary sketch of the French Revolution, prior
30 to the appearance of his hero upon the scene of action.
This, he thought, might be done almost *currente calamo°*;
for his recollection of all the great events as they occurred was vivid, and he had not failed to peruse every

book of any considerable importance on these subjects as
it issued from the press. He apprehended the necessity, .
on the other hand, of more laborious study in the way of
reading than he had for many years had occasion for, before he could enter with advantage upon Buonaparte's 5
military career; and Constable accordingly set about
collecting a new library of printed materials, which continued from day to day pouring in upon him, till his little
parlour in Castle Street looked more like an auctioneer's
premises than an author's. The first waggon delivered 10
itself of about a hundred huge folios of the Moniteur°;
and London, Paris, Amsterdam, and Brussels, were all
laid under contribution to meet the bold demands of his
purveyor.

In the meantime he advanced with his Introduction; 15
and, catching fire as the theme expanded before him, had
so soon several chapters in his desk, without having trav-
elled over half the ground assigned for them, that Constable
saw it would be in vain to hope for the completion of the
work within four duodecimos. They resolved that it 20
should be published, in the first instance, as a separate
book, in four volumes of the same size with the Tales of
the Crusaders, but with more pages and more letterpress
to each page. Scarcely had this been settled before it
became obvious, that four such volumes would never 25
suffice; and the number was week after week extended —
with corresponding alterations as to the rate of the author's
payment. Constable still considered the appearance of
the second edition of the Life of Napoleon in his Miscellany as the great point on which the fortunes of that 30
undertaking were to turn; and its commencement was in
consequence adjourned; which, however, must have been
the case at any rate, as the stock of the Novels was greater

N

than he had calculated; and some interval must elapse, before, with fairness to the retail trade, he could throw that long series into any cheaper form.

Before the Court rose in July, Sir Walter had made considerable progress in his Sketch of the French Revolution; but it was agreed that he should make his promised excursion to Ireland before any MS. went to the printers.

On the 1st of August we proceeded from Dublin to Edgeworthstown, the party being now reinforced by Captain and Mrs. Scott. A happy meeting it was: we remained there for several days, making excursions to Loch Oel and other scenes of interest in Longford and the adjoining counties; the gentry everywhere exerting themselves with true Irish zeal to signalize their affectionate pride in their illustrious countrywoman, and their appreciation of her guest; while her brother, Mr. Lovell Edgeworth, had his classical mansion filled every evening with a succession of distinguished friends, the *élite* of Ireland. Here, above all, we had the opportunity of seeing in what universal respect and comfort a gentleman's family may live in that country, and in far from its most favoured district, provided only they live there habitually, and do their duty as the friends and guardians of those among whom Providence has appointed their proper place. Here we found neither mud hovels nor naked peasantry, but snug cottages and smiling faces all about. Here there was a very large school in the village, of which masters and pupils were in a nearly equal proportion Protestants and Roman Catholics — the Protestant squire himself making it a regular part of his daily business to visit the scene of their operations, and strengthen authority and enforce discipline by his personal superintendence. It is a curious

enough coincidence that Oliver Goldsmith and Maria
Edgeworth should both have derived their early love and
knowledge of Irish character and manners from the same
identical district. He received part of his education at
this very school of Edgeworthstown; and Pallasmore 5
(the *locus cui nomen est Pallas* of Johnson's epitaph°),
the little hamlet where the author of the Vicar of Wakefield first saw the light, is still, as it was in his time, the
property of the Edgeworths. It may well be imagined
with what lively interest Sir Walter surveyed the scenery 10
with which so many of the proudest recollections of Ireland must ever be associated, and how curiously he studied
the rural manners it presented to him, in the hope (not
disappointed) of being able to trace some of his friend's
bright creations to their first hints and germs. I was 15
then a young man, and I cannot forget how much I was
struck at the time by some words that fell from one of
them, when, in the course of a walk in the park at Edgeworthstown, I happened to use some phrase which conveyed (though not perhaps meant to do so) the impression 20
that I suspected Poets and Novelists of being a good deal
accustomed to look at life and the world only as materials
for art. A soft and pensive shade came over Scott's
face as he said — "I fear you have some very young ideas
in your head : — are you not too apt to measure things 25
by some reference to literature — to disbelieve that any-
body can be worth much care, who has no knowledge
of that sort of thing, or taste for it? God help us! what
a poor world this would be if that were the true doctrine!
I have read books enough, and observed and conversed 30
with enough of eminent and splendidly cultivated minds,
too, in my time; but I assure you, I have heard higher
sentiments from the lips of poor *uneducated* men and

women, when exerting the spirit of severe yet gentle
heroism under difficulties and afflictions, or speaking their
simple thoughts as to circumstances in the lot of friends
and neighbours, than I ever yet met with out of the pages
5 of the Bible. We shall never learn to feel and respect
our real calling and destiny, unless we have taught ourselves to consider everything as moonshine, compared
with the education of the heart."   Maria did not listen to
this without some water in her eyes — (her tears are always
10 ready when any generous string is touched; — for, as
Pope says, "the finest minds, like the finest metals, dis-
solve the easiest;") — but she brushed them gaily aside,
and said, "You see how it is — Dean Swift said he had
written his books in order that people might learn to treat
15 him like a great lord — Sir Walter writes his in order that
he may be able to treat his people as a great lord ought
to do."

Lest I should forget to mention it, I put down here a
rebuke which, later in his life, Sir Walter once gave in my
20 hearing to his daughter Anne. She happened to say of
something, I forget what, that she could not abide it —
it was *vulgar*. "My love," said her father, "you speak
like a very young lady; do you know, after all, the meaning
of this word *vulgar?* 'Tis only *common;* nothing that is
25 common, except wickedness, can deserve to be spoken of .
in a tone of contempt; and when you have lived to my
years, you will be disposed to agree with me in thanking
God that nothing really worth having or caring about in
this world is *uncommon*."

30   He reached Abbotsford again on the 1st of September.
Without an hour's delay he resumed his usual habits of
life — the musing ramble among his own glens, the
breezy ride over the moors, the merry spell at the wood-

man's axe, or the festive chase of Newark, Fernilee, Hang-
ingshaw, or Deloraine; the quiet old-fashioned content-
ment of the little domestic circle, alternating with the
brilliant phantasmagoria of admiring, and sometimes
admired, strangers — or the hoisting of the telegraph
flag that called laird and bonnet-laird to the burning of
the water, or the wassail of the hall. The hours of the
closet alone had found a change. The preparation for
the Life of Napoleon was a course of such hard reading
as had not been called for while "the great magician,"
in the full sunshine of ease, amused himself, and delighted
the world, by unrolling, fold after fold, his endlessly varied
panorama of romance. That miracle had to all appearance cost him no effort. Unmoved and serene among the
multiplicities of worldly business, and the invasions of
half Europe and America, he had gone on tranquilly
enjoying, rather than exerting his genius, in the production
of those masterpieces which have peopled all our firesides
with inexpensive friends, and rendered the solitary suprem-
acy of Shakspeare, as an all-comprehensive and genial
painter of man, no longer a proverb.

He had, while this was the occupation of his few desk-
hours, read only for his diversion. How much he read
even then, his correspondence may have afforded some
notion. Those who observed him the most constantly,
were never able to understand how he contrived to keep
himself so thoroughly up with the stream of contemporary
literature of almost all sorts, French and German, as well
as English. That a rapid glance might tell him more
than another man could gather by a week's poring, may
easily be guessed; but the grand secret was his perpetual
practice of his own grand maxim, *never to be doing nothing.*
He had no "unconsidered trifles" of time. Every moment

was turned to account; and thus he had leisure for everything — except, indeed, the newspapers, which consume
so many precious hours now-a-days with most men, and
of which, during the period of my acquaintance with him,
5 he certainly read less than any other man I ever knew
that had any habit of reading at all.   I should also except,
speaking generally, the Reviews and Magazines of the
time.   Of these he saw few, and of the few he read
little.
10   He had now to apply himself doggedly to the mastering
of a huge accumulation of historical materials.   He read,
and noted, and indexed with the pertinacity of some pale
compiler in the British Museum; but rose from such employment, not radiant and buoyant, as after he had been
15 feasting himself among the teeming harvests of Fancy,
but with an aching brow, and eyes on which the dimness
of years had begun to plant some specks, before they were
subjected again to that straining over small print and
difficult manuscript which had, no doubt, been familiar
20 to them in the early time, when in (Shortreed's phrase)
"he was making himself."   It was a pleasant sight when
one happened to take a passing peep into his den, to see
the white head erect, and the smile of conscious inspiration
on his lips, while the pen, held boldly, and at a command-
25 ing distance, glanced steadily and gaily along a fast-black-
ening page of The Talisman.   It now often made me
sorry to catch a glimpse of him, stooping and poring with
his spectacles, amidst piles of authorities — a little note-
book ready in the left hand, that had always used to be at
30 liberty for patting Maida.
     Towards the end of September I returned to Scotland
from a visit to London on some personal business.   During
that visit I had heard a great deal more than I understood

about the commercial excitement of the time.   There had
been several years of extravagant speculation.

Among other hints were some concerning a bookselling
establishment in London, with which I knew Constable to
be closely connected.   Little suspecting the extent to 5
which any mischance of Messrs. Hurst and Robinson must
involve Sir Walter's own responsibilities, I transmitted
to him the rumours in question.   Before I could have his
answer, a legal friend told me that people were talking
doubtfully about Constable's own stability.   I thought it 10
probable, that if Constable fell into any embarrassments,
Scott might suffer the inconvenience of losing the copy-
money of his last novel.   Nothing more serious occurred
to me.   But I thought it my duty to tell him this whisper
also; and heard from him, almost by return of post, that, 15
shake who might in London, his friend in Edinburgh was
"rooted, as well as branched, like the oak."

Scott soon convinced himself that it would facilitate, not
impede, his progress with Napoleon, to have a work of
imagination in hand also.   The success of the Tales of 20
the Crusaders had been very high; and Constable, well
aware that it had been his custom of old to carry on two
romances at the same time, was now too happy to encour-
age him in beginning Woodstock, to be taken up whenever
the historical MS. should be in advance of the press.   25

Thenceforth, as the Diary shews, he continued to divide
his usual desk-hours accordingly: but before he had filled
many pages of the private Quarto, it begins to record
alarm — from day to day deepening — as to Constable,
and the extent to which the great publisher's affairs had 30
by degrees come to be connected and bound up with those
of the printing firm.

Till John Ballantyne's death, as already intimated, the

pecuniary management of that firm had been wholly in his hands. Of his conduct in such business I need add no more: the burden had since been on his surviving brother; and I am now obliged to say that, though his deficiencies
5 were of a very different sort from John's, they were, as respected his commercial career and connexions, great and unfortunate.

He was busy, indeed; and inestimably serviceable to Scott was his labour; but it consisted solely in the correc-
10 tion and revisal of proof-sheets. It is most true, that Sir Walter's hurried method of composition rendered it absolutely necessary that whatever he wrote should be subjected to far more than the usual amount of inspection required at the hands of a printer; and it is equally so,
15 that it would have been extremely difficult to find another man willing and able to bestow such time and care on his proof-sheets as they uniformly received from James. But this was, in fact, not the proper occupation of the man who was at the head of the establishment — who had under-
20 taken the pecuniary management. In a letter addressed to John Ballantyne, when the bookselling-house was breaking up, Scott says, — "One or other of you will need to be constantly in the printing-office *henceforth;* it is the sheet anchor." This was *ten* years after that establishment
25 began. Thenceforth James, in compliance with this injunction, occupied, during many hours of every day, a cabinet within the premises in the Canongate; but whoever visited him there, found him at the same eternal business, that of a literator, not that of a printer. He was
30 either editing his newspaper — or correcting sheets, or writing critical notes to the Author of Waverley. Shakespeare, Addison, Johnson, and Burke, were at his elbow; but not the ledger. We may thus understand poor John's

complaint, in what I may call his dying memorandum, of the "large sums abstracted from the bookselling house for the use of the printing-office." Yet that bookselling house was from the first a hopeless one; whereas, under accurate superintendence, the other ought to have pro- 5 duced the partners a dividend of from L.2000 to L.3000 a-year, at the very least.

On the other hand, the necessity of providing some remedy for this radical disorder must very soon have forced itself upon the conviction of all concerned, had not 10 John introduced his fatal enlightenment on the subject of facilitating discounts, and raising cash by means of accommodation-bills. Hence the perplexed *states* and *calendars* — the wildernesses and labyrinths of ciphers, through which no eye but that of a professed accountant 15 could have detected any clue; hence the accumulation of bills and counter-bills drawn by both bookselling and print-ing-house, and gradually so mixed up with other obliga-tions, that John died in utter ignorance of the condition of their affairs. The pecuniary detail then devolved upon 20 James; and I fancy it will be only too apparent that he never made even one serious effort to master the formidable array of figures thus committed to his sole trust.

The reader has been enabled to trace from its beginnings 25 the connexion between Constable and the two Ballantyne firms. It has been seen how much they both owed to his interference on various occasions of pressure and alarm. But when he, in his over-weening self-sufficiency, thought it involved no mighty hazard to indulge his better feel- 30 ings, as well as his lordly vanity, in shielding these firms from commercial dishonour, he had estimated but loosely the demands of the career of speculation on which he was

himself entering. And by and by, when advancing by
one mighty plunge after another in that vast field, he felt
in his own person the threatenings of more signal ruin than
could have befallen them, this "Napoleon of the press" —
5 still as of old buoyed up to the ultimate result of his grand
operations by the most fulsome flatteries of imagination —
appears to have tossed aside very summarily all scruples
about the extent to which he might be entitled to tax
their sustaining credit in requital. The Ballantynes,
10 if they had comprehended all the bearings of the case,
were not the men to consider grudgingly demands of this
nature, founded on service so important; and who can
doubt that Scott viewed them from a chivalrous altitude?
It is easy to see, that the moment the obligations became
15 reciprocal, there arose extreme peril of their coming to be
hopelessly complicated. It is equally clear, that Scott
ought to have applied on these affairs, as their complication thickened, the acumen which he exerted, and rather
prided himself in exerting, on smaller points of worldly
20 business, to the utmost.   That he did not, I must always
regard as the enigma of his personal history; but various
incidents in that history, which I have already narrated,
prove incontestably that he had never done so; and I
am unable to account for this having been the case, except
25 on the supposition that his confidence in the resources
of Constable and the prudence of James Ballantyne was
so entire, that he willingly absolved himself from all duty
of active and thoroughgoing superinspection.
      This is sufficiently astonishing — and had this been all,
30 the result must sooner or later have been sufficiently
uncomfortable; but it must be admitted that Scott could
never have foreseen a step which Constable took in the
frenzied excitement of his day of pecuniary alarm.   Owing

to the original habitual irregularities of John Ballantyne, it had been adopted as the regular plan between that person and Constable, that, whenever the latter signed a bill for the purpose of the other's raising money among the bankers, there should, in case of his neglecting to take 5 that bill up before it fell due, be deposited a counter-bill, signed by Ballantyne, on which Constable might, if need were, raise a sum equivalent to that for which he had pledged his credit. I am told that this is an usual enough course of procedure among speculative merchants; and 10 it may be so. But mark the issue. The plan went on under James's management, just as John had begun it. Under his management also — such was the incredible looseness of it — the *counter-bills*, meant only for being sent into the market in the event of the *primary bills* being 15 threatened with dishonour — these instruments of safeguard for Constable against contingent danger were allowed to lie uninquired about in Constable's desk, until they had swelled to a truly monstrous "sheaf of stamps." Constable's hour of distress darkened about him, and he 20 rushed with these to the money-changers. And thus it came to pass, that, supposing Ballantyne and Co. to have at the day of reckoning, obligations against them, in consequence of bill transactions with Constable, to the extent of L.25,000, they were legally responsible for L.50,000. 25

Scott's friends, and above all posterity, are not left to consider his fate without consoling reflections. They who knew and loved him, must ever remember that the real nobility of his character could not have exhibited itself to the world at large, had he not been exposed in his 30 later years to the ordeal of adversity. And others as well as they may feel assured, that had not that adversity been preceded by the perpetual spur of pecuniary demands, he who began life with such quick appetites for all its ordinary enjoyments, would never have devoted himself to the rearing of that gigantic monument of genius, labour, and power, which his works now constitute.   The imagination which has bequeathed so much to delight and humanize mankind, would have developed few of its miraculous resources, except in the embellishment of his own personal existence.   The enchanted spring might have sunk into earth with the rod that bade it gush, and left us no living waters.   We cannot understand, but we may nevertheless respect, even the strangest caprices of the marvellous combination of faculties to which our debt is so weighty.   We should try to picture to ourselves what the actual intellectual life must have been, of the author of such a series of romances.   We should ask ourselves whether, filling and discharging so soberly and gracefully as he did the common functions of social man, it was not, nevertheless, impossible but that he must have passed most of his life in other worlds than ours ; and we ought hardly to think it a grievous circumstance that their bright visions should have left a dazzle sometimes on the eyes which he so gently reopened upon our prosaic realities.   He had, on the whole, a command over the powers of his mind —I mean, that he could control and direct his thoughts and reflections with a readiness, firmness, and easy security of sway — beyond what I find it possible to trace in any other *artist's* recorded character and history ; but he could not habitually fling them into the region of dreams throughout a long series of years, and yet be expected to find a corresponding satisfaction in bending them to the less agreeable considerations which the circumstances of any human being's practical lot in this world must present in abundance.   The training to which he accustomed himself

could not leave him as he was when he began. He must
pay the penalty, as well as reap the glory of this life-long
abstraction of reverie, this self-abandonment of Fairyland.

This was for him the last year of many things; among
others, of Sybil Grey and *the Abbotsford Hunt*. Towards 5
the close of a hard run on his neighbour Gala's ground,
he adventured to leap *the Catrail* — that venerable relic
of the days of

"Reged wide and fair Strath-Clyde."

He was severely bruised and shattered; and never after- 10
wards recovered the feeling of confidence, without which
there can be no pleasure in horsemanship. He often talked
of this accident with a somewhat superstitious mourn-
fulness.

CHAPTER XIV

Ruin of the Houses of Constable and Ballantyne — Death
of Lady Scott — Publication of Woodstock — Journey
to London and Paris — Publication of the Life of
Napoleon — 1825–1827.

JAMES BALLANTYNE says, in a paper dictated from his
deathbed : — "I need not here enlarge upon the unfortunate facility which, at the period of universal confidence
and indulgence, our and other houses received from the
5 banks.   Suffice it to say that all our appearances of prosperity, as well as those of Constable, and Hurst and
Robinson, were merely shadows, and that from the
moment the bankers exhibited symptoms of doubt, it
might have been easy to discover what must be the ultimate
10 result.   During weeks, and even months, however, our
house was kept in a state of very painful suspense.   The
other two, I have no doubt, saw the coming events more
clearly.   I must here say, that it was one of Sir Walter's
weaknesses to shrink too much from looking evil in the
15 face, and that he was apt to carry a great deal too far —
'sufficient for the day is the evil thereof.'   I do not think
it was more than three weeks before the catastrophe that
he became fully convinced it was impending — if indeed
his feelings ever reached the length of conviction at all.
20 Thus, at the last, his fortitude was very severely tried
indeed."

Mr. Ballantyne had never seen Scott's Diary, and its
entries from the 20th November 1825 (when it begins)

until the middle of January 1826, are in perfect accord-
ance with this statement.   The first on the subject is in
these terms: — "Here is matter for a May morning but
much fitter for a November one.   The general distress
in the city has affected H. and R., Constable's great 5
agents.   Should they *go*, it is not likely that Constable
can stand; and such an event would lead to great distress
and perplexity on the part of J. B. and myself.   Thank
God, I have enough to pay more than 20s. in the pound,
taking matters at the very worst.   But much inconven- 10
ience must be the consequence.   I had a lesson in 1814
which should have done good; but success and abundance
erased it from my mind.   But this is no time for journal-
izing or moralizing either.   Necessity is like a sourfaced
cook-maid, and I a turn-spit she has flogged, ere now, till 15
he mounted his wheel.   If Woodstock can be out by
25th January it will do much, — and it is possible."
  Thus he continued to labour on at his romance; from
time to time arrested amidst his visions by some fresh
omen of the coming reality: but after suggesting or con- 20
curring in the commercial measure that seemed feasible,
immediately commanding his mind into oblivion of whatever must prevent his pursuance of the task that depended
solely on himself.   That down to the 14th of December he
was far indeed from having brought home to himself any- 25
thing like the extent of his danger, is clear enough from
the step recorded in that day's entry — namely, his con-
senting to avail himself of the power he had retained of
borrowing L.10,000 on the lands of Abbotsford, and
advancing that sum to the struggling houses.   Ballantyne 30
hints that in his opinion both Constable and his London
agents must have foreseen more clearly the issue of the
struggle; and it is certain that the only point in Constable's

personal conduct which Scott afterwards considered himself entitled to condemn and resent, was connected with
these last advances.

On the 18th of December he writes thus : — "If things
5 go badly in London, the magic wand of the Unknown will
be shivered in his grasp.   He must then, faith, be termed
the Too-well-known.   The feast of fancy will be over with
the feeling of independence.   He shall no longer have the
delight of waking in the morning with bright ideas in his
10 mind, hasten to commit them to paper, and count them
monthly, as the means of planting such scaurs and purchasing such wastes; replacing dreams of fiction by other
prospective visions of walks by

'Fountain heads, and pathless groves ;
15   Places which pale passion loves.'

This cannot be ; but I may work substantial husbandry,
i.e. write history, and such concerns.   They will not be
received with the same enthusiasm ; at least, I much doubt
the general knowledge that an author must write for his
20 bread, at least for improving his pittance, degrades him
and his productions in the public eye.   He falls into the
second-rate rank of estimation :

'While the harness sore galls, and the spurs his side goad,
The high-mettled racer 's a hack on the road.'

25 It is a bitter thought; but if tears start at it, let them
flow.   My heart clings to the place I have created — there is
scarce a tree on it that does not owe its being to me. —
What a life mine has been ! — half-educated, almost .
wholly neglected, or left to myself; stuffing my head with
30 most nonsensical trash, and undervalued by most of my
companions for a time; getting forward, and held a bold

and a clever fellow, contrary to the opinion of all who thought me a mere dreamer ; broken-hearted for two years ; my heart handsomely pieced again — but the crack will remain till my dying day. Rich and poor four or five times ; once on the verge of ruin, yet opened a new source of wealth almost overflowing. Now to be broken in my pitch of pride, and nearly winged (unless good news should come :) because London chooses to be in an uproar, and in the tumult of bulls and bears, a poor inoffensive lion like myself is pushed to the wall. But what is to be the end of it ? God knows ; and so ends the catechism. — Nobody in the end can lose a penny by me — that is one comfort. Men will think pride has had a fall. Let them indulge their own pride in thinking that my fall will make them higher, or seem so at least. I have the satisfaction to recollect that my prosperity has been of advantage to many, and to hope that some at least will forgive my transient wealth on account of the innocence of my intentions, and my real wish to do good to the poor. Sad hearts, too, at Darnick, and in the cottages of Abbotsford. I have half resolved never to see the place again.. How could I tread my hall with such a diminished crest ? — how live a poor indebted man where I was once the wealthy, the honoured ? I was to have gone there on Saturday in joy and prosperity to receive my friends. My dogs will wait for me in vain. It is foolish — but the thoughts of parting from these dumb creatures have moved me more than any of the painful reflections I have put down. Poor things ! I must get them kind masters ! There may be yet those who, loving me, may love my dog because it has been mine. I must end these gloomy forebodings, or I shall lose the tone of mind with which men should meet distress. I feel my dogs' feet on my knees —

o

I hear them whining and seeking me everywhere. This
is nonsense, but it is what they would do could they know
how things may be. — An odd thought strikes me — When
I die, will the journal of these days be taken out of the
5 ebony cabinet at Abbotsford, and read with wonder,
that the well-seeming Baronet should ever have experienced the risk of such a hitch? — or will it be found in
some obscure lodging-house, where the decayed son of
chivalry had hung up his scutcheon, and where one or two
10 old friends will look grave, and whisper to each other,
'Poor gentleman' — 'a well-meaning man' — 'nobody's
enemy but his own' — 'thought his parts would never
wear out' — 'family poorly left' — 'pity he took that
foolish title.' Who can answer this question? — Poor
15 Will Laidlaw! — poor Tom Purdie! — such news will
wring your hearts, and many a poor fellow's besides, to
whom my prosperity was daily bread.

"Ballantyne behaves like himself, and sinks the prospect
of his own ruin in contemplating mine. I tried to enrich
20 him indeed, and now all — all is in the balance. He will
have the Journal still, that is a comfort, for sure they cannot find a better editor. *They* — alas, who will *they* be —
the *unbekannten obern* [1] who may have to dispose of my
all as they will? Some hard-eyed banker — some of
25 these men of millions! — I have endeavoured to give
vent to thoughts naturally so painful, by writing these
notes — partly to keep them at bay by busying myself
with the history of the French Convention. I thank God
I can do both with reasonable composure. I wonder how
30 Anne will bear such an affliction. She is passionate, but
stout-hearted and courageous in important matters,

[1] *Unbekannten obern* — unknown rulers.

though irritable in trifles. I am glad Lockhart and his
wife are gone. Why? I cannot tell — but I *am* pleased
to be left to my own regrets, without being melted by
condolences, though of the most sincere and affectionate
kind. — *Half-past eight.* I closed this book under the
impression of impending ruin. I open it an hour after
(thanks be to God) with the strong hope that matters
will be got over safely and honourably, in a mercantile
sense. Cadell came at eight to communicate a letter from
Hurst and Robinson, intimating they had stood the
storm. I shall always think the better of Cadell for this —
not merely because 'his feet are beautiful on the mountains
who brings good tidings,'° but because he shewed feeling —
deep feeling, poor fellow. He, who I thought had no
more than his numeration-table, and who, if he had had
his whole counting-house full of sensibility, had yet his
wife and children to bestow it upon — I will not forget
this, if all keeps right. I love the virtues of rough-and-
round men — the others are apt to escape in salt rheum,
sal-volatile, and a white pocket handkerchief."

Scott's Diary has — "*Edinburgh, January* 16. — Came
through cold roads to as cold news. Hurst and Robinson
have suffered a bill to come back upon Constable, which I
suppose infers the ruin of both houses. We shall soon
see. Dined with the Skenes." — Mr. Skene assures me
that he appeared that evening quite in his usual spirits,
conversing on whatever topic was started as easily and
gaily as if there had been no impending calamity; but at
parting he whispered — "Skene, I have something to
speak to you about; be so good as to look in on me as you
go to the Parliament-House to-morrow." When Skene
called in Castle Street, about half-past nine o'clock next
morning, he found Scott writing in his study. He rose,

and said — "My friend, give me a shake of your hand —
mine is that of a beggar." He then told him that Ballantyne had just been with him, and that his ruin was certain
and complete; explaining, briefly, the nature of his con-
5 nexion with the three houses, whose downfall must that
morning be made public. He added — "Don't fancy
I am going to stay at home to brood idly on what can't
be helped. I was at work upon Woodstock when you came
in, and I shall take up the pen the moment I get back
10 from Court. I mean to dine with you again on Sunday,
and hope then to report progress to some purpose." —
When Sunday came, he reported accordingly, that in spite
of all the numberless interruptions of meetings and con-
ferences with his partner and men of business — to say
15 nothing of his anxieties on account of his wife and daughter — he had written a chapter of his novel every intervening day. And the Diary gives the precise detail.
His exertions, he there says, were suspended for the 17th
and 18th; but in the course of the 19th, 20th, and 21st,
20 he wrote 38 pages of his novel — such pages that 70 of
them made "half a volume of the usual size."

The reader may be curious to see what account Ballantyne's memorandum gives of that dark announcement on
the morning of Tuesday the 17th. It is as follows: —
25 "On the evening of the 16th, I received from Mr. Cadell
a distinct message putting me in possession of the truth.
I called immediately in Castle Street, but found Sir Walter
had gained an unconscious respite by being engaged out at
dinner. It was between eight and nine next morning that
30 I made the final communication. No doubt he was greatly
stunned — but, upon the whole, he bore it with wonderful
fortitude. He then asked — 'Well, what is the actual
step we must first take? I suppose we must do some-

thing?' I reminded him that two or three thousand pounds were due that day, so that we had only to do what we must do — refuse payment — to bring the disclosure sufficiently before the world. He took leave of me with these striking words — 'Well, James, depend upon that, I will never forsake you.'"

In the course of that unhappy yet industrious week, Sir Walter's situation as Ballantyne's partner, became universally known. Mr. Ballantyne, as an individual, had no choice but to resolve on the usual course of a commercial man unable to meet engagements: but Scott from the first moment determined to avoid, if by his utmost efforts it could be avoided, the necessity of participating in such steps. He immediately placed his whole affairs in the hands of three trustees (James Jollie, W.S., Alex. Monypenny, W.S., and John Gibson, W.S.), all men of the highest honour and of great professional experience; and declined every offer of private assistance. These were very numerous: — his eldest son and his daughter-in-law eagerly tendered the whole fortune at their disposal, and the principal banks of Edinburgh, especially the house of Sir William Forbes & Co., which was the one most deeply involved in Ballantyne's obligations, sent partners of the first consideration, who were his personal friends, to offer liberal additional accommodation. What, I think, affected him most of all, was a letter from Mr. Poole, his daughters' harp-master, offering L.500, — "probably," says the Diary, "his all." From London, also, he received various kind communications. Among others, one tendering an instant advance of L.30,000 — a truly munificent message, conveyed through a distinguished channel, but the source of which was never revealed to him, nor to me until some years after his death, and even then under conditions of secrecy. To all, his answer was the same. And within a few days he had reason to believe that the creditors would, as a body, assent to let things go in the course which he and his 5 trustees suggested.

His Diary has this entry for the 24th January: — "If I am hard pressed, and measures used against me, I must use all means of legal defence, and subscribe myself bankrupt in a petition for sequestration. It is the 10 course one should, at any rate, have advised a client to take. But for this I would, in a Court of Honour, deserve to lose my spurs. No, — if they permit me, I will be their vassal for life, and dig in the mine of my imagination to find diamonds (or what may sell for such) to make good 15 my engagements, not to enrich myself. And this from no reluctance to be called the Insolvent, which I probably am, but because I will not put out of the power of my creditors the resources, mental or literary, which yet remain to me."

20 *Jan.* 26. — "Gibson comes with a joyful face, announcing that almost all the creditors had agreed to a private trust. This is handsome and confidential, and must warm my best efforts to get them out of the scrape. I will not doubt — to doubt is to lose. Sir William Forbes 25 took the chair, and behaved, as he has ever done, with the generosity of ancient faith and early friendship. That House is more deeply concerned than most. In what scenes have Sir William and I not borne share together! desperate and almost bloody affrays, rivalries, deep 30 drinking matches, and finally, with the kindliest feelings on both sides, somewhat separated by his retiring much within the bosom of his family, and I moving little beyond mine. It is fated our planets should cross, though,

and that at the periods most interesting for me. Down —
down — a hundred thoughts."

There soon, however, emerged new difficulties. It
would indeed have been very wonderful if all the creditors
of three companies, whose concerns were inextricably 5
intertangled, had at once adopted the views of the meeting, composed entirely of eminent citizens of Edinburgh,
over which Sir William Forbes presided on the 26th of
January ; nor, it is proper to add, was Scott himself aware,
until some days later, of the extent to which the debts of 10
the two houses of Constable and Hurst exceeded their
assets ; circumstances necessarily of the greatest importance to the holders of Ballantyne's paper. In point of
fact, it turned out that the obligations of the three firms
had, by what is termed cross-rankings, reached respec- 15
tively sums far beyond the calculations of any of the parties. On the full revelation of this state of things, some of
the printers' creditors felt great disinclination to close
with Scott's proposals ; and there ensued a train of harass-
ment, the detail of which must be left in his Diary, but 20
which was finally terminated according to his own
original, and really most generous suggestion.

The day of calamity revealed the fact that James Ballantyne personally possessed no assets whatever. The
claims against Sir Walter, as the sole really responsible 25
partner in the printing firm, and also as an individual,
settled into a sum of about L.130,000. On much heavier
debts Constable & Co. paid ultimately 2s. 9d. in the pound ;
Hurst & Robinson about 1s. 3d. The Ballantyne firm had
as yet done nothing to prevent their following the same 30
line of conduct. It might still have allowed itself (and not
James Ballantyne merely as an individual) to be declared
bankrupt, and obtained a speedy discharge, like these

booksellers, from all its obligations. But for Scott's being a partner, the whole affair must have been settled in a very short time. If he could have at all made up his mind to let commercial matters take the usual commercial 5 course, the creditors of the firm would have brought into the market whatever property, literary or otherwise, Scott at the hour of failure possessed; they would have had a right to his liferent of Abbotsford, among other things — and to his reversionary interest in the estate, 10 in case either his eldest son or his daughter-in-law should die without leaving issue, and thus void the provisions of their marriage-contract. All this being disposed of, the result would have been a dividend very far superior to what the creditors of Constable and Hurst received; 15 and in return, the partners in the printing firm would have been left at liberty to reap for themselves the profits of their future exertions. Things were, however, complicated in consequence of the transfer of Abbotsford in January 1825. Some creditors now had serious thoughts of con- 20 testing the validity of that transaction; but a little reflection and examination satisfied them that nothing could be gained by such an attempt. On the other hand, Sir Walter felt that he had done wrong in placing any part of his property beyond the reach of his creditors, by entering into 25 that marriage-contract without a previous most deliberate examination into the state of his responsibilities. He must have felt in this manner, though I have no sort of doubt, that the result of such an examination in January 1825, if accompanied by an instant calling in of all *counter-* 30 *bills*, would have been to leave him at perfect liberty to do all that he did upon that occasion. However that may have been, and whatever may have been his delicacy respecting this point, he persisted in regarding the embarrassment of his commercial firm with the feelings not of a merchant but of a gentleman. He thought that by devoting the rest of his life to the service of his creditors, he could, in the upshot, pay the last farthing he owed them. They (with one or two exceptions) ap- 5 plauded his honourable intentions and resolutions, and partook, to a certain extent, in the self-reliance of their debtor. Nor had they miscalculated as to their interest. Nor had Sir Walter calculated wrongly. He paid the penalty of health and life, but he saved his honour and his 10 self-respect: —

"The glory dies not, and the grief is past." [1]

As to the difficulty that occurred in February, a single extract from his Diary must here suffice. On the 16th he writes thus: — " 'Misfortune's growling bark' comes 15 louder and louder. By assigning my whole property to trustees for behoof of creditors, with two works in progress and nigh publication, and with all my future literary labours, I conceived I was bringing into the field a large fund of payment, which could not exist without my exer- 20 tions, and that thus far I was entitled to a corresponding degree of indulgence. I therefore supposed, on selling this house, and various other property, and on receiving the price of Woodstock and Napoleon, that they would give me leisure to make other exertions, and be content 25 with the rents of Abbotsford, without attempting a sale. But Gibson last night came in after dinner, and gave me to understand that the Bank of Scotland see this in a different point of view, and consider my contribution of the produce of past, present, and future labours, as compen- 30

[1] Sonnet on Scott's death, by Sir E. Brydges.

sated *in full* by their accepting of the trust-deed, instead
of pursuing the mode of sequestration, and placing me
in the Gazette. They therefore expect the trustees to
commence a lawsuit to reduce the marriage-settlement
5 which settles the estate upon Walter; thus loading me with
a most expensive suit, and I suppose selling library and
whatever else they can lay hold on. Now this seems
unequal measure, and would besides of itself totally de-
stroy any power of fancy — of genius, if it deserves the
10 name, which may remain to me. A man cannot write
in the House of Correction; and this species of *peine
forte et dure°* which is threatened, would render it impossible for one to help himself or others. So I told Gibson
I had my mind made up as far back as the 24th of January,
15 not to suffer myself to be harder pressed than law would
press me. If they take the sword of the law, I must lay
hold of the shield. If they are determined to consider
me as an irretrievable bankrupt, they have no title to
object to my settling upon the usual terms which the
20 statute requires. They probably are of opinion, that
I will be ashamed to do this by applying publicly for a
sequestration. Now, my feelings are different. I am
ashamed to owe debts I cannot pay; but I am not ashamed
of being classed with those to whose rank I belong. The
25 disgrace is in being an actual bankrupt, not in being made
a legal one. I had like to have been too hasty in this
matter. I must have a clear understanding that I am to
be benefited or indulged in some way, if I bring in two
such funds as those works in progress, worth certainly
30 from L.10,000 to L.15,000."

It was by and bye settled that he should be left in the
undisturbed possession of Abbotsford, on his pledging
himself to dispose immediately of all his other property,

of what kind soever, for the behoof of the creditors — to limit his personal expenses henceforth within his official salary — and, continuing his literary labour with his best diligence, to pay in all its profits until the debt should be wholly obliterated. Excepting from a single London 5 Jew, a creditor originally of Hurst's, no practical interference with this arrangement was ever subsequently threatened.

When the Court of Session was to rise for the spring vacation he had to take farewell of his house in Castle 10 Street. Henceforth, his family were to stay always, as he designed, in the country — and a small hired lodging was to suffice for himself when his duty called him to be in Edinburgh.

Sir Walter's Diary begins to be clouded with a darker 15 species of distress than mere loss of wealth could bring to his spirit. His darling grandson is sinking at a distance from him under incurable disease. At home the misfortunes against which his manhood struggled with stern energy were encountered by his affectionate wife under the 20 disadvantages of enfeebled health, and it seems but too evident that mental pain and mortification had a great share in hurrying her ailments to a fatal end. Nevertheless, all his afflictions do not seem to have interrupted for more than a day or two his usual course of labour. With 25 rare exceptions he appears, all through this trying period, to have finished his daily task — thirty printed pages of Woodstock — until that novel was completed; or, if he paused in it, he gave a similar space of time to some minor production; such as his paper on the Life of Kemble. 30 He also corresponded much as usual (notwithstanding all he says about indolence on that score) with his absent friends; and I need scarcely add, that his duties as Sheriff claimed many hours every week. The picture of resolution and industry which this portion of his Journal presents, is certainly as remarkable as the boldest imagination could have conceived.

5 *"Abbotsford, March* 17. — A letter from Lockhart. My worst augury is verified; — the medical people think poor Johnnie is losing strength; he is gone with his mother to Brighton. The bitterness of this probably impending calamity is extreme. The child was almost too good for 10 this world; — beautiful in features; and though spoiled by every one, having one of the sweetest tempers as well as the quickest intellect I ever saw; a sense of humour quite extraordinary in a child, and, owing to the general notice which was taken of him, a great deal more informa-15 tion than suited his years. The poor dear love had so often a slow fever, that when it pressed its little lips to mine, I always foreboded to my own heart what all I fear are now aware of.

"March 19. — Lady S., the faithful and true compan-20 ion of my fortunes, good and bad, for so many years, has, but with difficulty, been prevailed on to see Dr. Abercrombie, and his opinion is far from favourable. Her asthmatic complaints are fast terminating in hydropsy, as I have long suspected; yet the announcement of the 25 truth is overwhelming. They are to stay a little longer in town to try the effects of a new medicine. On Wednesday, they propose to return hither — a new affliction, where there was enough before; yet her constitution is so good, that if she will be guided by advice, things may 30 be yet ameliorated. God grant it! for really these misfortunes come too close upon each other.

"March 28. — We have now been in solitude for some time — myself nearly totally so, excepting at meals.

One is tempted to ask himself, knocking at the door of his own heart, Do you love this extreme loneliness? I can answer conscientiously, *I do*. The love of solitude was with me a passion of early youth; when in my teens, I used to fly from company to indulge in visions and airy 5 castles of my own, the disposal of ideal wealth, and the exercise of imaginary power. This feeling prevailed even till I was eighteen, when love and ambition awakening with other passions, threw me more into society, from which I have, however, at times withdrawn myself, and 10 have been always even glad to do so. I have risen from a feast satiated; and unless it be one or two persons of very strong intellect, or whose spirits and good humour amuse me, I wish neither to see the high, the low, nor the middling class of society. This is a feeling without the least tinge 15 of misanthropy, which I always consider as a kind of blasphemy of a shocking description. If God bears with the very worst of us, we may surely endure each other. If thrown into society, I always have, and always will endeavour to bring pleasure with me, at least to shew 20 willingness to please. But for all this, 'I had rather live alone,' and I wish my appointment, so convenient otherwise, did not require my going to Edinburgh. But this must be, and in my little lodging I shall be lonely enough. 25

"*April* 3. — I have the extraordinary and gratifying news that Woodstock is sold for L.8228; all ready money — a matchless sale for less than three months' work." [The reader will understand that, the novel being sold for the behoof of J. B. and Co.'s creditors, this sum includes 30 the cost of printing the first edition, as well as paper.] "If Napoleon does as well, or near it, it will put the trust affairs in high flourish. Four or five years of leisure and

industry would, with such success, amply replace my losses.
I have a curious fancy; I will go set two or three acorns,
and judge by their success in growing whether I shall succeed in clearing my way or not.   I have a little toothache
5 keeps me from working much to-day — besides I sent off
copy for Napoleon."

The price received for Woodstock shews what eager competition had been called forth among the booksellers, when,
after the lapse of several years, Constable's monopoly of
10 Sir Walter's novels was abolished by their common calamity.   The interest excited, not only in Scotland and
England, but all over civilized Europe, by the news of
Scott's misfortunes, must also have had its influence in
quickening this commercial rivalry.   The reader need
15 hardly be told, that the first meeting of James Ballantyne
& Company's creditors witnessed the transformation, a
month before darkly prophesied, of the "Great Unknown"
into the "Too-well-known."   Even for those who had
long ceased to entertain any doubt as to the main source
20 at least of the Waverley romances, there would have been
something stirring in the first confession of the author;
but it in fact included the avowal, that he had stood alone
in the work of creation; and when the mighty claim came
in the same breath with the announcement of personal
25 ruin, the effect on the community of Edinburgh was elec-
trical.   It is, in my opinion, not the least striking feature
in his Diary, that it contains no allusion (save the ominous
one of 18th December) to this long withheld revelation.
He notes ˙his painful anticipation of returning to the
30 Parliament-House — *monstrari digito°* — as an insolvent.
It does not seem even to have occurred to him, that when
he appeared there the morning after his creditors had heard
his confession, there could not be many men in the place

but must gaze on his familiar features with a mixture of curiosity, admiration, and sympathy, of which a hero in the moment of victory might have been proud — which might have swelled the heart of a martyr as he was bound to the stake. The universal feeling was, I believe, 5 much what the late amiable and accomplished Earl of Dudley expressed to Mr. Morritt when these news reached them at Brighton. — "Scott ruined!" said he, "the author of Waverley ruined! Good God! let every man to whom he has given months of delight give him a sixpence, 10 and he will rise to-morrow morning richer than Rothschild!"

It is no wonder that the book, which it was known he had been writing during this crisis of distress, should have been expected with solicitude. Shall we find him, asked 15 thousands, to have been master truly of his genius in the moment of this ordeal? Shall we trace anything of his own experiences in the construction of his imaginary personages and events? — I know not how others interpreted various passages in Woodstock, but there were 20 not a few that carried deep meaning for such of Scott's own friends as were acquainted with, not his pecuniary misfortune alone, but the drooping health of his wife, and the consolation afforded him by the dutiful devotion of his daughter Anne, in whose character and demeanour 25 a change had occurred exactly similar to that painted in poor Alice Lee: "A light joyous air, with something of a humourous expression, which seemed to be looking for amusement, had vanished before the touch of affliction, and a calm melancholy supplied its place, which 30 seemed on the watch to administer comfort to others." In several *mottoes*, and other scraps of verse, the curious reader will find similar traces of the facts and feelings

recorded in the author's Diary. As to the novel itself,
though none can pretend to class it in the very highest
rank of his works, since we feel throughout the effects of the
great fundamental error, likened by a contemporary critic
5 to that of the writer who should lay his scene at Rome
immediately after the battle of Philippi, and introduce
Brutus as the survivor in that conflict, and Cicero as his
companion in victory; yet even this censor is forced to
allow that Woodstock displays certain excellencies, not
10 exemplified in all the author's fictions, and which attest,
more remarkably than any others could have done, the
complete self-possession of the mind when composing it.
The success of the book was great: large as the price was,
its publishers had no reason to repent their bargain;
15 and of course the rapid receipt of such a sum as L.8000,
the product of hardly three months' labour, highly gratified
the body of creditors, whose debtor had devoted to them
whatever labour his health should henceforth permit him
to perform.

20   The progress of the domestic story will be best given by
a few more extracts from the Diary : —

"*May* 6. — The same scene of hopeless (almost) and
unavailing anxiety. Still welcoming me with a smile,
and asserting she is better.   I fear the disease is too deeply
25 entwined with the principles of life. I am a tolerable
Stoic, but preach to myself in vain.

> 'Are these things, then, necessities?
> Then let us meet them like necessities.'

"*May* 11. — Charlotte was unable to take leave of me,
30 being in a sound sleep after a very indifferent night.
Perhaps it was as well. Emotion might have hurt her;
and nothing I could have expressed would have been worth

the risk. I have foreseen, for two years and more, that this menaced event could not be far distant. I have seen plainly, within the last two months, that recovery was hopeless. And yet to part with the companion of twenty-nine years, when so very ill — that I did not, could not foresee. It withers my heart to think of it, and to recollect that I can hardly hope again to seek confidence and counsel from that ear to which all might be safely confided."

"*May* 15. — Received the melancholy intelligence that all is over at Abbotsford.

"*Abbotsford, May* 16. — She died at nine in the morning, after being very ill for two days — easy at last. I arrived here late last night. Anne is worn out, and has had hysterics, which returned on my arrival. Her broken accents were like those of a child — the language as well as the tones broken, but in the most gentle voice of submission. 'Poor mamma — never return again — gone for ever — a better place.' Then, when she came to herself, she spoke with sense, freedom, and strength of mind, till her weakness returned. It would have been inexpressibly moving to me as a stranger — what was it then to the father and the husband? For myself, I scarce know how I feel — sometimes as firm as the Bass Rock, sometimes as weak as the water that breaks on it. I am as alert at thinking and deciding as I ever was in my life. Yet, when I contrast what this place now is, with what it has been not long since, I think my heart will break. Lonely, aged, deprived of my family — all but poor Anne; an impoverished, an embarrassed man, deprived of the sharer of my thoughts and counsels, who could always talk down my sense of the calamitous apprehensions which break the heart that must bear them alone. — Even her foibles were

P

of service to me, by giving me things to think of beyond
my weary self-reflections.

"I will go to town on Monday and resume my labours.
Being now of a grave nature, they cannot go against the
5 general temper of my feelings, and in other respects the
exertion, as far as I am concerned, will do me good; besides
I must reëstablish my fortune for the sake of the children,
and of my own character. I have not leisure to indulge
the disabling and discouraging thoughts that press on me.
10 Were an enemy coming upon my house, would I not do my
best to fight, although oppressed in spirits? and shall a
similar despondency prevent me from mental exertion?
It shall not, by Heaven! This day and to-morrow I give
to the currency of the ideas which have of late occupied
15 my mind, and with Monday they shall be mingled at least
with other thoughts and cares. — "

In October he resolved to make a journey to London
and Paris, in both which capitals he had reason to expect
important material would be submitted to him as the
20 biographer of Napoleon. His expedition was a very
seasonable relief; nor was he disappointed as to its direct
object.

Formerly, however great the quantity of work he put
through his hands, his evenings were almost always
25 reserved for the light reading of an elbow-chair, or the
enjoyment of his family and friends. Now he seemed
to grudge every minute that was not spent at the desk.
The little that he read of new books, or for mere amusement, was done by snatches in the course of his meals;
30 and to walk, when he could walk at all, to the Parliament
House, and back again, through the Prince's Street Gardens, was his only exercise and his only relaxation. Every
ailment, of whatever sort, ended in aggravating his lame-

ness; and, perhaps, the severest test his philosophy encountered was the feeling of bodily helplessness that from week to week crept upon him. The winter, to make bad worse, was a very cold and stormy one. The growing sluggishness of his blood shewed itself in chilblains, not 5 only on the feet but the fingers, and his handwriting becomes more and more cramped and confused.

He says on the 30th of December — "Wrote hard. Last day of an eventful year; much evil — and some good, but especially the courage to endure what Fortune sends, 10 without becoming a pipe for her fingers. It is *not* the last day of the year; but to-morrow being Sunday, we hold our festival to-day. The Fergussons came, and we had the usual appliances of mirth and good cheer. Yet our party, like the chariot-wheels of Pharaoh in the Red Sea, dragged 15 heavily. — It must be allowed that the regular recurrence of annual festivals among the same individuals has, as life advances, something in it that is melancholy. We meet like the survivors of some perilous expedition, wounded and weakened ourselves, and looking through 20 diminished ranks to think of those who are no more. Yet where shall we fly from vain repining? — or why should we give up the comfort of seeing our friends, because they can no longer be to us, or we to them, what we once were to each other?"   •   25

That season was further enlivened by one public dinner, and this, though very briefly noticed in Scott's Diary, occupied a large space in public attention at the time, and, I believe I may add, several columns in every newspaper in Europe. His good friend William Murray, manager 30 of the Edinburgh Theatre, invited him to preside at the first festival of a charitable fund for decayed performers. He agreed, and on Friday the 23d February took the chair,

being supported by the Earl of Fife, Lord Meadowbank, Sir John Hope of Pinkie, Admiral Adam, Robert Dundas of Arniston, *Peter* Robertson, and many other personal friends. Lord Meadowbank had come on short notice,
5 and was asked abruptly on his arrival to take a toast which had been destined for a noble person who had not been able to appear. He knew that this was the first public dinner at which the object of the toast had appeared since his misfortunes, and taking him aside in the ante-
10 room, asked him whether he would now consider it indelicate to hazard a distinct reference to the parentage of the Waverley Novels. Sir Walter smiled, and said, "Do just as you like — only don't say much about so old a story." — In the course of the evening the Judge rose
15 accordingly, and said —

"I would beg leave to propose a toast — the health   of one of the Patrons. The clouds have been dispelled — the *darkness visible* has been cleared away — and the Great Unknown — the minstrel of our native land —
20 the mighty magician who has rolled back the current of time, and conjured up before our living senses the men and the manners of days which have long passed away, stands revealed to the eyes and the hearts of his affectionate and admiring countrymen. We owe to him, as a
25 people, a large and heavy debt of gratitude. He it is who has opened to foreigners the grand and characteristic beauties of our country ; — it is to him that we owe that our gallant ancestors and illustrious patriots have obtained a fame no longer confined to the boundaries of a remote
30 and comparatively obscure country — he it is who has conferred a new reputation on our national character, and bestowed on Scotland an imperishable name, were it only by her having given birth to himself. I propose the health of Sir Walter Scott."

Long before Lord Meadowbank ceased speaking, the company had got upon chairs and tables, and the storm of applause that ensued was deafening. When they recovered from the first fever, Sir Walter spoke as follows : —   5

"I certainly did not think, in coming here to-day, that I should have the task of acknowledging before 300 gentlemen, a secret which, considering that it was communicated to more than twenty people, has been remarkably well kept. I am now at the bar of my country, and may 10 be understood to be on trial before Lord Meadowbank as an offender; and so quietly did all who were *airt and pairt°* conduct themselves, that I am sure that, were the *panel°* now to stand on his defence, every impartial jury would bring in a verdict of *Not Proven.* I am willing, however, 15 to plead *guilty* — nor shall I detain the Court by a long explanation why my confession has been so long deferred. Perhaps caprice might have a considerable share in the matter. I have now to say, however, that the merits of these works, if they had any, and their faults, are all 20 entirely imputable to myself. Like another Scottish criminal of more consequence, one Macbeth,

> 'I am afraid to think what I have done :
> Look on't again I dare not.' —

— I have thus far unbosomed myself, and I know that my 25 confession will be reported to the public. I mean, then, seriously to state, that when I say I am the author, I mean the total and undivided author. With the exception of quotations, there is not a single word that was not derived from myself, or suggested in the course of my reading. 30 The wand is now broken, and the book buried. You will allow me further to say, with Prospero, it is your breath that has filled my sails, and to crave one single toast in the capacity of the author of these novels. I would fain

dedicate a bumper to the health of one who has represented several of those characters, of which I had endeavoured to give the skeleton, with a truth and liveliness for
which I may well be grateful.   I beg leave to propose the
5 health of my friend Bailie Nicol Jarvie — and I am sure,
that when the author of Waverley and Rob Roy drinks
to Nicol Jarvie, it will be received with the just applause
to which that gentleman has always been accustomed, —
nay, that you will take care that on the present occasion
10 it shall be PRO — DI — GI — OUS !''   (Long and vehement
applause.)

    Mr. MACKAY. — ''My conscience !   My worthy father
the deacon could never have believed that his son would
hae sic a compliment paid to him by the Great Unknown !''
15   SIR WALTER SCOTT. — ''The Small Known now, Mr.
Bailie !''

    We now reach the completion of that severe task —
the Life of Napoleon: and following instantly, the commencement of the charming Tales of a Grandfather.

20   The Life of Buonaparte, then, was at last published
about the middle of June 1827.   Two years had elapsed
since Scott began it; but, by a careful comparison of dates,
I have arrived at the conclusion that, his expeditions to
Ireland and Paris, and the composition of novels and
25 critical miscellanies, being duly allowed for, the historical
task occupied hardly more than twelve months.   The
book was closely printed; in fact, if it had been printed on
the original model of his novels, the life of Buonaparte
would have filled from thirteen to fourteen volumes: the
30 work of one twelvemonth — done in the midst of pain,
sorrow, and ruin.

    The lofty impartiality with which Scott treats the per-
sonal character of Buonaparte, was of course sure to make
all ultra-politicians both at home and abroad condemn his

representation; and an equally general and better founded exception was taken to the lavish imagery of his historical style. He despised the former clamour — to the latter he bowed submissive. He could not, whatever character he might wish to assume, cease to be one of the greatest of 5 poets. Metaphorical illustrations, which men born with prose in their souls hunt for painfully, and find only to murder, were to him the natural and necessary offspring and playthings of ever-teeming fancy. He could not write a note to his printer — he could not speak to himself 10 in his Diary — without introducing them. Few will say that his historical style is, on the whole, excellent — none that it is perfect; but it is completely unaffected, and therefore excites nothing of the unpleasant feeling with which we consider the elaborate artifices of a far greater 15 historian — the greatest that our literature can boast — Gibbon. The rapidity of the execution infers many inaccuracies as to minor matters of fact; but it is nevertheless true that no inaccuracy affecting the character of the book as a fair record of great events, has to this hour been de- 20 tected by the malevolent ingenuity of Jacobin or Buonapartist.

Woodstock, as we have seen, placed upwards of L.8000 in the hands of Sir Walter's creditors. The Napoleon (first and second editions) produced for them a sum which 25 it even now startles me to mention, — L.18,000. As by the time the historical work was published, nearly half of the First Series of Chronicles of the Canongate had been written, it is obvious that the amount to which Scott's literary industry, from the close of 1825, to the 10th of 30 June 1827, had diminished his debt, cannot be stated at less than L.28,000. Had health been spared him, how soon must he have freed himself from all his encumbrances!

CHAPTER XV

Domestic Life — Publication of the Chronicles of the Canongate and Tales of a Grandfather — Fair Maid of Perth — Anne of Geierstein — Success of the Novels — 1827-1829.

WHEN the Court released him, and he returned to Abbotsford, his family did what they could to keep him to his ancient evening habits; but nothing was so useful as the presence of his invalid grandson. The poor child was at 5 this time so far restored as to be able to sit his pony again; and Sir Walter, who had conceived, the very day he finished Napoleon, the notion of putting together a series of Tales on the history of Scotland, somewhat in the manner of Mr. Croker's on that of England, rode 10 daily among the woods with his "Hugh Littlejohn," and told the story, and ascertained that it suited the comprehension of boyhood, before he reduced it to writing. Sibyl Grey had been dismissed in consequence of the accident at the Catrail; and he had now stooped his 15 pride to a sober, steady creature, of very humble blood; dun, with black mane and legs; by name Douce Davie, *alias* the Covenanter. This, the last of his steeds, by the way, had been previously in the possession of a jolly old laird near Peebles, and acquired a distinguished reputa-20 tion by its skill in carrying him home safely when drunk. Douce Davie, on such occasions, accommodated himself to the swerving balance of his rider with such nice dis-crimination, that on the laird's death the country people expected a vigorous competition for the sagacious animal; but the club-companions of the defunct stood off to a man when it was understood that the Sheriff coveted the succession.

He received about this time a visit from Mr. J. L. Adolphus; who had not seen him since 1824 — and says —

"Calamity had borne heavily upon Sir Walter in the interval; but the painful and anxious feeling with which a friend is approached for the first time under such cir-cumstances, gave way at once to the unassumed serenity of his manner. There were some signs of age about him which the mere lapse of time would scarcely have accounted for; but his spirits were abated only, not broken; if they had sunk, they had sunk equably and gently. It was a declining, not a clouded sun. I do not remember any reference to the afflictions he had suffered, except once, when, speaking of his Life of Napoleon, he said in a quiet but affecting tone, 'I could have done it better, if I could have written at more leisure, and with a mind more at ease.' One morning a party was made to breakfast at Chiefswood; and any one who on that occasion looked at and heard Sir Walter Scott, in the midst of his children and grandchildren and friends, must have rejoiced to see that life still yielded him a store of pleasures, and that his heart was as open to their influences as ever. I was much struck by a few words which fell from him on this subject a short time afterwards. After mentioning an accident which had spoiled the promised pleasure of a visit to his daughter in London, he then added — 'I have had as much happi-ness in my time as most men, and I must not complain now.' I said, that whatever had been his share of happiness, no man could have laboured better for it.   He answered — 'I consider the capacity to labour as part of the happiness I have enjoyed.'"

Such was his life in Autumn 1827.   Before I leave the
5 period, I must note how greatly I admired the manner in which all his dependents appeared to have met the reverse of his fortunes — a reverse which inferred very consider-able alteration in the circumstances of every one of them. The butler, Dalgliesh, had been told when the distress
10 came, that a servant of his class would no longer be re-quired — but the man burst into tears, and said, rather than go he would stay without any wages : So he remained — and instead of being the easy chief of a large establish-ment, was now doing half the work of the house, at prob-
15 ably half his former salary.   Old Peter, who had been for five-and-twenty years a dignified coachman, was now ploughman in ordinary, only putting his horses to the carriage upon high and rare occasions ; and so on with all the rest that remained of the ancient train.   And all, to
20 my view, seemed happier than they had ever done before. Their good conduct had given every one of them a new elevation in his own mind — and yet their demeanour had gained, in place of losing, in simple humility of observance. The great loss was that of William Laidlaw, for whom (the
25 estate being all but a fragment in the hands of the trustees and their agent) there was now no occupation here.   The cottage, which his taste had converted into a loveable re-treat, had found a rent-paying tenant ; and he was living a dozen miles off on the farm of a relation in the Vale of
30 Yarrow.   Every week, however, he came down to have a ramble with Sir Walter over their old haunts — to hear how the pecuniary atmosphere was darkening or brighten-ing ; and to read in every face at Abbotsford that it could

never be itself again until circumstances should permit his reëstablishment at Kaeside.

The first series of Chronicles of the Canongate — (which title supplanted that of The Canongate Miscel- lany or Traditions of the Sanctuary) — was published 5 early in the winter. The contents were, the Highland Widow, the Two Drovers, and the Surgeon's Daughter — all in their styles excellent, except that the Indian part of the last does not well harmonize with the rest; and certain preliminary chapters which were generally considered as 10 still better than the stories they introduce.

These Chronicles were not received with exceeding favour at the time; and Sir Walter was a good deal dis- couraged. Indeed, he seems to have been with some diffi- culty persuaded by Cadell and Ballantyne that it would 15 not do for him to "lie fallow" as a novelist; and then, when he in compliance with their entreaties began a Second Canongate Series, they were both disappointed with his MS., and told him their opinions so plainly that his good- nature was sharply tried. The Tales which they disap- 20 proved of, were those of My Aunt Margaret's Mirror, and the Laird's Jock; he consented to lay them aside, and be- gan St. Valentine's Eve or the Fair Maid of Perth, which from the first pleased his critics.

The first Tales of a Grandfather appeared early in 25 · December, and their reception was more rapturous than that of any one of his works since Ivanhoe. He had solved for the first time the problem of narrating history, so as at once to excite and gratify the curiosity of youth, and please and instruct the wisest of mature minds. The 30 popularity of the book has grown with every year that has since elapsed; it is equally prized in the library, the boudoir, the schoolroom, and the nursery; it is adopted

as the happiest of manuals, not only in Scotland, but where-
ever the English tongue is spoken; nay, it is to be seen in
the hands of old and young all over the civilized world, and
has, I have little doubt, extended the knowledge of Scot-
5 tish history in quarters where little or no interest had ever
before been awakened as to any other parts of that subject,
except those immediately connected with Mary Stuart
and the Chevalier.

There had been serious doubts, in what proportions the
10 copyright of the Novels, &c. was vested, at the moment of
the common calamity, in Scott or in Constable. One of
the ablest of the Scotch Judges, John Irving, Lord Newton,
undertook the settlement of this complicated question, as
private arbiter : and the result of his ultimate award was,
15 that Scott had lost all hold on the copyright of the Novels
from Waverley to Quentin Durward; but that Napoleon
and Woodstock were wholly his. This decision, however,
was not to be expected speedily : it had now become highly
expedient to bring the body of copyrights to sale — and it
20 was agreed to do so, the money to be deposited in bank
until the award were given. This sale (on 19th December
1827) comprised all the Novels from Waverley to Quentin
Durward inclusive, besides a majority of the shares of the
Poetical Works. Mr. Cadell's family and private friends
25 were extremely desirous to secure for him part at least
of these copyrights; and Sir Walter's were not less so
that he should seize this last opportunity of recovering
a share in the prime fruits of his genius. The relations
by this time established between him and Cadell were
30 those of strict confidence and kindness; and both saw
well that the property would be comparatively lost, were
it not ensured that thenceforth the whole should be managed as one unbroken concern. The result was, that

the copyrights exposed to sale were purchased, one-half
for Sir Walter, the other half for Cadell, at the price of
L.8500. Well might the "pockpuddings" — for so the
Diary styles the English booksellers — rue their timidity
on this day; but it was the most lucky one that ever came 5
for Sir Walter's creditors. A dividend of six shillings in
the pound was paid at this Christmas on their whole claims.
The result of their high-hearted debtor's exertions, between January 1826 and January 1828, was in all very
nearly L.40,000. No literary biographer, in all likelihood, 10
will ever have such another fact to record. The creditors
unanimously passed a vote of thanks for the indefatigable
industry which had achieved so much for their behoof.

On returning to Abbotsford at Christmas, after completing these transactions, he says in his Diary — "My 15
reflections in entering my own gate to-day were of a very
different and more pleasing cast than those with which I .
left this place about six weeks ago. I was then in doubt
whether I should fly my country, or become avowedly
bankrupt, and surrender up my library and household 20
furniture, with the liferent of my estate, to sale. A man of
the world will say I had better done so. No doubt, had I
taken this course at once, I might have employed the
money I have made since the insolvency of Constable and
Robinson's houses in compounding my debts. But I 25
could not have slept sound, as I now can under the com-
fortable impression of receiving the thanks of my creditors,
and the conscious feeling of discharging my duty as a man
of honour and honesty. I see before me a long, tedious,
and dark path, but it leads to stainless reputation. If I 30
die in the harrows, as is very likely, I shall die with honour;
if I achieve my task, I shall have the thanks of all concerned, and the approbation of my own conscience."

He now took up in earnest two pieces of work, which
promised and brought great ultimate advantage; namely,
a complete collection of his Poems, with biographical prefaces; the other, an uniform edition of his Novels, each to
5 be introduced by an account of the hints on which it had
been founded, and illustrated throughout by historical and
antiquarian annotations.   On this last, commonly mentioned in the Diary as the *Magnum Opus*,° Sir Walter
bestowed pains commensurate with its importance; —
10 and in the execution of the very delicate task which either
scheme imposed, he has certainly displayed such a combination of frankness and modesty as entitles him to a
high place in the short list of graceful autobiographers.

He finished his novel by the end of March, and imme-
15 diately set out for London, where the last budget of proof-
sheets reached him.   The Fair Maid was, and continues
to be, highly popular, and though never classed with his
performances of the first file, it has undoubtedly several
scenes equal to what the best of them can shew, and is on
20 the whole a work of brilliant variety and most lively interest.

On his return to Edinburgh, Sir Walter was greeted
with the satisfactory intelligence that his plans as to the
Opus Magnum had been considered at a meeting of his
25 trustees, and finally approved *in toto*.°   As the scheme
inferred a large outlay on drawings and engravings, and
otherwise, this decision had been looked for with much
anxiety by him and Mr. Cadell.

During the remainder of this year Sir Walter never
30 opened his "locked book."   Whether in Edinburgh or
the country, his life was such, that he describes himself, in
several letters, as having become "a writing automaton."
He had completed by Christmas the Second Series of

Tales on Scottish History, and made considerable progress in another novel — Anne of Geierstein.

His novel was finished before breakfast on the 29th of
April; and his Diary mentions that immediately after
breakfast he began his compendium of Scottish history for 5
Dr. Lardner's Cyclopædia.   When the proprietors of that
work, in July 1828, offered him L.500 for an abstract of
Scottish History in one volume, he declined the proposal.
They subsequently offered L.700, and this was accepted;
but though he began the task under the impression that he 10
should find it a heavy one, he soon warmed to the subject,
and pursued it with cordial zeal and satisfaction.   One
volume, it by and by appeared, would never do, — in his
own phrase, "he must have elbow-room" — and I believe
it was finally settled that he should have L.1500 for the 15
book in two volumes; of which the first was published before the end of this year.

Anne of Geierstein came out about the middle of
May; and this, which may be almost called the last work
of his imaginative genius, was received at least as well — 20
(out of Scotland, that is) — as the Fair Maid of Perth
had been, or indeed as any novel of his after the Crusaders.   I partake very strongly, I am aware, in the feeling which most of my own countrymen have little shame
in avowing, that no novel of his, where neither scenery nor 25
character is Scottish, belongs to the same preëminent class
with those in which he paints and peoples his native landscape.   I have confessed that I cannot rank even his best
English romances with such creations as Waverley and
Old Mortality; far less can I believe that posterity will 30
attach similar value to this Maid of the Mist.

His Diary has few more entries for this twelvemonth.
Besides the volume of history for Lardner, he had ready

by December the last of the *Scottish* Series of Tales of a
∨ Grandfather; and had made great progress in the prefaces and notes for Cadell's *Opus Magnum*. He had also
overcome various difficulties which for a time interrupted
5 the twin scheme of an illustrated edition of his Poems : and
one of these in a manner honourably characteristic of the
late John Murray of Albemarle Street, who had till now
retained a share in the copyright of Marmion. Scott
having requested him to *sell* that share, he generously re-
10 plied : — "So highly do I estimate the honour of being,
even in so small a degree, the publisher of the author of the
poem, that no pecuniary consideration whatever can induce me to part with it. But there is a consideration of
another kind, which until now I was not aware of, which
15 would make it painful to me if I were to retain it a moment
longer. I mean the knowledge of its being required by
the author, into whose hands it was spontaneously re-
signed in the same instant that I read his request."

The success of the collective novels was far beyond
20 what either Sir Walter or Mr. Cadell had ventured to
anticipate. Before the close of 1829, eight volumes had
been issued ; and the monthly sale had reached as high as
35,000. Should this go on, there was, indeed, every
reason to hope that, coming in aid of undiminished in-
25 dustry in the preparation of new works, it would wipe off
· all his load of debt in the course of a very few years. And
during the autumn (which I spent near him) it was most
agreeable to observe the effects of the prosperous intelligence, which every succeeding month brought, upon his
30 spirits.

CHAPTER XVI

Retirement from the Court of Session — Offers of a
Pension and of Additional Rank declined — Count Robert
of Paris begun — Making of his Will — 1830–1831.

In the course of the Spring Session, circumstances rendered it highly probable that Sir Walter's resignation of
his place as Clerk of Session might be acceptable to the
Government; and it is not surprising that he should have,
on the whole, been pleased to avail himself of this oppor- 5
tunity. He says, in his Diary —"*May* 27. I am agitat-
ing a proposed retirement from the Court. As they are
only to have four instead of six Clerks of Session, it will be
their interest to let me retire on a superannuation. Probably I shall make a bad bargain, and get only two-thirds 10
of the salary, instead of three-fourths. This would be
hard, but I could save between two or three hundred
pounds by giving up town residence. At any rate, *jacta
est alea.*° I think the difference will be infinite in point
of health and happiness. Yet I do not know. It is per- 15
haps a violent change in the end of life to quit the walk
one has trod so long, and the cursed splenetic temper
which besets all men makes you value opportunities and
circumstances when one enjoys them no longer."
In July came the formal intimation that he had ceased 20
to be a Clerk of Session, and should thenceforth have,
in lieu of his salary, &c. (L.1300) an allowance of L.800
per annum. This was accompanied by an intimation
from the Home Secretary, that the Ministers were quite

ready to grant him a pension covering the reduction of his income. Considering himself as the bond-slave of his creditors, he made known to them this proposition, and stated that it would be extremely painful to him to accept
5 of it; and with the delicacy and generosity which throughout characterized their conduct towards him, they without hesitation entreated him on no account to do injury to his own feelings in such a matter as this. Few things gave him more pleasure than this handsome communication.
10   "*Septembr* 5 — Cadell came out here yesterday with his horn filled with good news. He calculates that in October the debt will be reduced to L.60,000. This makes me care less about the terms I retire upon. The efforts by which we have advanced thus far are new in literature,
15 and what is gained is secure."

Mr. Cadell's great hope, when he offered this visit, had been that the good news of the *Magnum* might induce Sir Walter to content himself with working at notes and prefaces for its coming volumes, without straining at more
20 difficult tasks. He found his friend, however, by no means disposèd to adopt such views. He must bend himself to the composition of a romance, founded on a story which he had more than once told cursorily already, and for which he had been revolving the various titles of Robert of the
25 Isle — Count Robert de L'Isle — and Count Robert cf Paris. There was nothing to be said in reply to the decisive announcement of this purpose. The usual agreements were drawn out; and the Tale was begun.

Towards the end of November, Sir Walter had another
30 slight touch of apoplexy. He recovered himself without assistance; but again consulted his physicians in Edinburgh, and by their advice adopted a still greater severity of regimen.

The reader will now understand what his frame and condition of health and spirits were, when he at length received from Ballantyne a decided protest against the novel on which he was struggling to fix the shattered energies of his memory and fancy. He replied thus: 5

"Abbotsford, 8th Dec. 1830.

"My Dear James, — If I were like other authors, as I flatter myself I am not, I should 'send you an order on my treasurer for a hundred ducats,' wishing you all prosperity and a little more taste°; but having never supposed that 10 any abilities I ever had were of a perpetual texture, I am glad when friends tell me what I might be long in finding out myself. Mr. Cadell will shew you what I have written to him. My present idea is to go abroad for a few months, if I hold together as long. So ended the Fathers of the 15 Novel — Fielding and Smollet — and it would be no unprofessional finish for yours — W. S."

This note to the printer, and a letter of the same date and strain to the publisher, "struck both," Mr. Cadell says, "with dismay." They resolved to go out to Abbots- 20 ford, but not for a few days, because a general meeting of the creditors was at hand, and there was reason to hope that its results would enable them to appear as the bearers of sundry pieces of good news.

The meeting of trustees and creditors took place on the 25 17th — Mr. George Forbes (brother to the late Sir William) in the chair. There was then announced another dividend on the Ballantyne estate of three shillings in the pound — thus reducing the original amount of the debt to about L.54,000. It had been not unnaturally appre- 30 hended that the convulsed state of politics might have checked the sale of the *Magnum Opus;* but this does not

seem to have been the case to any extent worth notice.
The meeting was numerous — and, not contented with a
renewed vote of thanks to their debtor, they passed
unanimously a resolution, which was moved by Mr. (now
5 Sir James) Gibson-Craig, and seconded by Mr. Thomas
Allan — both, by the way, leading Whigs : — "That Sir
Walter Scott be requested to accept of his furniture, plate,
linens, paintings, library, and curiosities of every description, as the best means the creditors have of expressing
10 their very high sense of his most honourable conduct, and
in grateful acknowledgment for the unparalleled and most
successful exertions he has made, and continues to make,
for them."

On the 18th, Cadell and Ballantyne proceeded to Ab-
15 botsford, and found Sir Walter in a placid state — having
evidently been much soothed and gratified with the tidings
from Mr. Forbes. His whole appearance was greatly better than they had ventured to anticipate; and deferring
literary questions till the morning, he made this gift from
20 his creditors the chief subject of his conversation. He said
it had taken a heavy load off his mind; he apprehended
that, even if his future works should produce little money,
the profits of the *Magnum*, during a limited number of
years, with the sum which had been insured on his life,
25 would be sufficient to obliterate the remaining part of
the Ballantyne debt : he considered the library and museum now conveyed to him as worth at the least L.10,000,
and this would enable him to make some provision for his
younger children.

30 On the 31st of January, Miss Scott being too unwell
for a journey, Sir Walter went alone to Edinburgh for the
purpose of executing his last will. Of this excursion the
Diary says : " I executed my last will, leaving Walter

burdened with L.1000 to Sophia, L.2000 to Anne, and the
same to Charles.   He is to advance them this money if
they want it; if not, to pay them interest.   All this is his
own choice, otherwise I would have sold the books and
rattletraps.   I have made provisions for clearing my estate 5
by my publications, should it be possible; and should that
prove possible, from the time of such clearance being
effected, to be a fund available to all my children who shall
be alive or leave representatives.   My bequests must,
many of them, seem hypothetical."   10

CHAPTER XVII

Apoplectic Paralysis — Castle Dangerous begun — Departure from Abbotsford — London — Voyage in the Barham — Malta — Naples — Rome — 1831–1832.

AFTER a pause of some days, the Diary has this entry for April 25, 1831 : — "From Saturday 16th April, to Saturday 24th of the same month, unpleasantly occupied by ill health and its consequences. A distinct stroke of paralysis
5 affecting both my nerves and speech, though beginning only on Monday with a very bad cold. Doctor Abercrombie was brought out by the friendly care of Cadell, — but young Clarkson had already done the needful, that is, had bled and blistered, and placed me on a very reduced
10 diet. Whether precautions have been taken in time, I cannot tell. I think they have, though severe in themselves, beat the disease ; but I am alike prepared."

He had resumed, and was trying to recast, his novel. All the medical men had urged him, by every argument,
15 to abstain from any such attempts ; but he smiled on them in silence, or answered with some jocular rhyme. He told me, that in the winter he had more than once tried writing with his own hand, because he had no longer the same "pith and birr" that formerly rendered dictation easy to him ; but that the experiment failed. He was now
20 sensible he could do nothing without Laidlaw to hold the Bramah pen ; adding, "Willie is a kind clerk — I see by

his looks when I am pleasing him, and that pleases me."
And however the cool critic may now estimate Count
Robert, no one who then saw the author could wonder
that Laidlaw's prevalent feeling in writing those pages
should have been admiration. Under the full conscious- 5
ness that he had sustained three or four strokes of apoplexy
or palsy, or both combined, and tortured by various attendant ailments — cramp, rheumatism in half his joints,
daily increasing lameness, and now of late gravel (which
was, though last, not least) — he retained all the energy 10
of his will, struggled manfully against this sea of troubles,
and might well have said seriously, as he more than once
both said and wrote playfully,

" 'Tis not in mortals to command success,
    But we'll do more, Sempronius, we'll deserve it." [1] 15

Some business called me to London about the middle
of June, and when I returned at the end of three weeks,
I had the satisfaction to find that he had been gradually
amending.

But, alas ! the first use he made of this partial renova- 20
tion had been to expose his brain once more to an imaginative task. He began his Castle Dangerous — the
groundwork being again an old story which he had told in
print, many years before, in a rapid manner. And now,
for the first time, he left Ballantyne out of his secret. He 25
thus writes to Cadell on the 3d of July : — "I intend to tell
this little matter to nobody but Lockhart. Perhaps not
even to him; certainly not to J. B., who having turned
his back on his old political friends, will no longer have a
claim to be a secretary in such matters, though I shall 30

[1] Addison's *Cato.*

always be glad to befriend him." James's criticisms on
Count Robert had wounded him — the Diary, already
quoted, shews how severely.

For two or three weeks he bent himself sedulously to his
5 task — and concluded both Castle Dangerous and the
long suspended Count Robert. By this time he had
submitted to the recommendation of all his medical friends,
and agreed to spend the coming winter away from Abbotsford, among new scenes, in a more genial climate, and above
10 all (so he promised), in complete abstinence from all
literary labour. When Captain Basil Hall understood
that he had resolved on wintering at Naples (where, as
has been mentioned, his son Charles was attached to the
British Legation), it occurred to the zealous sailor that on
15 such an occasion as this all thoughts of political difference
ought to be dismissed, — and he, unknown to Scott, addressed a letter to Sir James Graham, then First Lord of
the Admiralty, stating the condition of his friend's health,
and his proposed plan, and suggesting that it would be a
20 fit and graceful thing for the King's Government to place
a frigate at his disposal. Sir James replied that it afforded
his Royal Master, as well as himself, the sincerest satisfaction to comply with this hint; and that whenever Sir
Walter found it convenient to come southwards, a vessel
25 should be prepared for his reception. Nothing could be
handsomer than the way in which all this matter was arranged, and Scott, deeply gratified, exclaimed that things
were yet in the hands of gentlemen; but that he feared
they had been undermining the state of society which
30 required such persons as themselves to be at the head.

He had no wish, however, to leave Abbotsford until the
approach of winter; and having dismissed his Tales,
seemed to say to himself that he would enjoy his dear valley

for the intervening weeks, draw friends about him, revisit all the familiar scenes in his neighbourhood once more; and if he were never to come back, store himself with the most agreeable recollections in his power, and so conduct himself as to bequeath to us who surrounded him a last 5 stock of gentle impressions. He continued to work a little at his notes and prefaces, but did not fatigue himself; and when once all plans were settled, and all cares in so far as possible set aside, his health and spirits certainly rallied most wonderfully. 10

I must not omit to record how gratefully all Sir Walter's family felt the delicate and watchful tenderness of Mr. Cadell's conduct. He so managed that the Novels just finished should remain in types, but not thrown off until the author should have departed; so as to give oppor- 15 tunity for revising and abridging them. He might well be the bearer of cheering news as to their greater concerns, for the sale of the *Magnum* had, in spite of political turbulences and distractions, gone on successfully. But he probably strained a point to make things appear still 20 better than they really were. He certainly spoke so as to satisfy his friend that he need give himself no sort of uneasiness about the pecuniary results of idleness and travel. It was about this time that we observed Sir Walter beginning to entertain the notion that his debts 25 were paid off. By degrees, dwelling on this fancy, he believed in it fully and implicitly. It was a gross delusion — but neither Cadell nor any one else had the heart to disturb it by any formal statement of figures. It contributed greatly more than any circumstance besides to soothe Sir 30 Walter's feelings, when it became at last necessary that he should tear himself from his land and his house, and the trees which he had nursed. And with all that was done and forborne, the hour when it came was a most heavy one.

Early on the 23d of September 1831, Sir Walter left Abbotsford, attended by his daughter Anne and myself, and we reached London by easy stages on the 28th, having spent one day at Rokeby. The following month was spent in London and on the 29th of October the Barham got under weigh.   After a few days, when they had passed the Bay of Biscay, Sir Walter ceased to be annoyed with seasickness, and sat most of his time on deck, enjoying apparently the air, the scenery, and above all the ship itself, the beautiful discipline practised in all things, and the martial exercises of the men.   Italy, especially Naples, gave Scott pleasure, mingled with a great desire for his own Scotland, during this last winter of his life.

CHAPTER XVIII

Return to England — London — Abbotsford — Death
and Funeral of Scott in September 1832 — His Character — Monuments to his Memory.

The last jotting of Sir Walter Scott's Diary — perhaps
the last specimen of his handwriting — records his starting from Naples on the 16th of April. After the 11th of
May the story can hardly be told too briefly.

He reached London about six o'clock on the evening of 5
Wednesday the 13th of June, and was detained there by
illness. At length his constant yearning to return to
Abbotsford induced his physicians to consent to his removal; and the moment this was notified to him, it seemed
to infuse new vigour into his frame. It was on a calm, 10
clear afternoon of the 7th July, that every preparation
was made for his embarkation on board the steam-
boat.

At a very early hour on the morning of Wednesday
the 11th, we again placed him in his carriage, and he 15
lay in the same torpid state during the first two stages
on the road to Tweedside. But as we descended the
vale of the Gala he began to gaze about him, and by degrees it was obvious that he was recognizing the features
of that familiar landscape. Presently he murmured a 20
name or two — "Gala Water, surely — Buckholm —
Torwoodlee." As we rounded the hill at Ladhope, and
the outline of the Eildons burst on him, he became greatly

excited; and, when turning himself on the couch, his eye
caught at length his own towers at the distance of a mile,
he sprang up with a cry of delight. The river being in
flood, we had to go round a few miles by Melrose bridge;
5 and during the time this occupied, his woods and house
being within prospect, it required occasionally both Dr.
Watson's strength and mine, in addition to Nicolson's, to
keep him in the carriage. After passing the bridge, the
road for a couple of miles loses sight of Abbotsford, and
10 he relapsed into his stupor; but on gaining the bank immediately above it, his excitement became again ungov-
ernable.

Mr. Laidlaw was waiting at the porch, and assisted us in
lifting him into the dining-room, where his bed had been
15 prepared. He sat bewildered for a few moments, and then
resting his eye on Laidlaw, said — "Ha! Willie Laidlaw!
O man, how often have I thought of you!" By this time
his dogs had assembled about his chair — they began to
fawn upon him and lick his hands, and he alternately
20 sobbed and smiled over them, until sleep oppressed him.

Something like a ray of hope broke in upon us next
morning. Sir Walter awoke perfectly conscious where
he was, and expressed an ardent wish to be carried out
into his garden. We procured a Bath chair from Huntley
25 Burn, and Laidlaw and I wheeled him out before his door,
and up and down for some time on the turf, and among
the rose-beds then in full bloom. The grandchildren
admired the new vehicle, and would be helping in their
way to push it about. He sat in silence, smiling placidly
30 on them and the dogs their companions, and now and
then admiring the house, the screen of the garden, and the
flowers and trees. By and by he conversed a little, very
composedly, with us — said he was happy to be at home

— that he felt better than he had ever done since he left
it, and would perhaps disappoint the doctors after all.
He then desired to be wheeled through his rooms, and
we moved him leisurely for an hour or more up and down
the hall and the great library : — "I have seen much," he 5
kept saying, "but nothing like my ain house — give me
one turn more !" He was gentle as an infant, and allowed
himself to be put to bed again, the moment we told him
that we thought he had had enough for one day.

Next morning he was still better. After again enjoying 10
the Bath chair for perhaps a couple of hours out of doors,
he desired to be drawn into the library, and placed by the
central window, that he might look down upon the Tweed.
Here he expressed a wish that I should read to him, and
when I asked from what book, he said — "Need you ask ? 15
There is but one." I chose the 14th chapter of St. John's
Gospel ; he listened with mild devotion, and said when I
had done — "Well, this is a great comfort — I have followed you distinctly, and I feel as if I were yet to be myself again." In this placid frame he was again put to bed, 20
and had many hours of soft slumber.

On Monday he remained in bed, and seemed extremely
feeble ; but after breakfast on Tuesday the 17th he appeared revived somewhat, and was again wheeled about on
the turf. Presently he fell asleep in his chair, and after 25
dozing for perhaps half an hour, started awake, and shak-
ing the plaids we had put about him off his shoulders,
said — "This is sad idleness. I shall forget what I have
been thinking of, if I don't set it down now. Take me
into my own room, and fetch the keys of my desk." He 30
repeated this so earnestly, that we could not refuse ; his
daughters went into his study, opened his writing-desk, and
laid paper and pens in the usual order, and I then moved

him through the hall and into the spot where he had always been accustomed to work. When the chair was placed at the desk, and he found himself in the old position, he smiled and thanked us, and said — "Now give me my
5 pen, and leave me for a little to myself." Sophia put the pen into his hand, and he endeavoured to close his fingers upon it, but they refused their office — it dropped on the paper. He sank back among his pillows, silent tears rolling down his cheeks; but composing himself by and
10 bye, motioned to me to wheel him out of doors again. Laidlaw met us at the porch, and took his turn of the chair. Sir Walter, after a little while, again dropt into slumber. When he was awaking, Laidlaw said to me — "Sir Walter has had a little repose." — "No, Willie," said he — "no
15 repose for Sir Walter but in the grave." The tears again rushed from his eyes. "Friends," said he, "don't let me expose myself — get me to bed — that's the only place."

As I was dressing on the morning of Monday the 17th
20 of September, Nicolson came into my room, and told me that his master had awoke in a state of composure and consciousness, and wished to see me immediately. I found him entirely himself, though in the last extreme of feebleness. His eye was clear and calm — every trace of the
25 wild fire of delirium extinguished. "Lockhart," he said, "I may have but a minute to speak to you. My dear, be a good man — be virtuous — be religious — be a good man. Nothing else will give you any comfort when you come to lie here." — He paused, and I said — "Shall I
30 send for Sophia and Anne?" — "No," said he, "don't disturb them. Poor souls! I know they were up all night — God bless you all." — With this he sunk into a very tranquil sleep, and, indeed, he scarcely afterwards gave

any sign of consciousness, except for an instant on the arrival of his sons.

They, on learning that the scene was about to close, obtained anew leave of absence from their posts, and both reached Abbotsford on the 19th. About half-past 5 one P.M. on the 21st of September, Sir Walter breathed his last, in the presence of all his children. It was a beautiful day — so warm, that every window was wide open — and so perfectly still, that the sound of all others most delicious to his ear, the gentle ripple of the Tweed over its 10 pebbles, was distinctly audible as we knelt around the bed, and his eldest son kissed and closed his eyes. No sculptor ever modelled a more majestic image of repose.

Almost every newspaper that announced this event in Scotland, and many in England, had the signs of mourning 15 ∠ usual on the demise of a king. With hardly an exception, the voice was that of universal, unmixed grief and veneration.

His funeral was conducted in an unostentatious manner, but the attendance was very great. Few of his old friends 20 then in Scotland were absent, — and many, both friends and strangers, came from a great distance. His domestics and foresters made it their petition that no hireling hand might assist in carrying his remains. They themselves bore the coffin to the hearse, and from the hearse 25 to the grave.

The wide enclosure at the Abbey of Dryburgh was thronged with old and young; and when the coffin was taken from the hearse, and again laid on the shoulders of the afflicted serving-men, one deep sob burst from a thou- 30 sand lips. Mr. Archdeacon Williams read the Burial Service of the Church of England; and thus, about half-past five o'clock in the evening of Wednesday the 26th

September 1832, the remains of Sir Walter Scott were
laid by the side of his wife in the sepulchre of his ancestors
—*"in sure and certain hope of the resurrection to eternal
life, through our Lord Jesus Christ: who shall change our*
5 *vile body that it may be like unto his glorious body, according
to the mighty working, whereby he is able to subdue all things
to himself."*

Of the persons closely connected with Sir Walter Scott,
and often named accordingly in these pages, few remain.
10 James Ballantyne was on his deathbed when he heard of
his great friend and patron's death. Of his own children
none now survive. Miss Anne Scott received at Christmas 1832 a grant of L.200 per annum from the privy purse
of King William IV. But her name did not long burden
15 the pension list. Her constitution had been miserably
shattered in the course of her long and painful attendance,
first on her mother's illness, and then on her father's; and
perhaps reverse of fortune, and disappointments of various sorts connected with that, had also heavy effect.
20 From the day of Sir Walter's death, the strong stimulus of
duty being lost, she too often looked and spoke like one

"Taking the measure of an unmade grave."

After a brief interval of disordered health, she contracted
a brain fever, which carried her off abruptly. She died in
25 my house in the Regent's Park on the 25th June 1833,
and her remains are placed in the New Cemetery in the
Harrow Road.

The adjoining grave holds those of her nephew John
Hugh Lockhart, who died 15th Dec. 1831; and also
30 those of my wife Sophia, who expired after a long
illness, which she bore with all possible meekness and
fortitude, on the 17th of May 1837. Of all the race she

most resembled her father in countenance, in temper,
and in manners.

Charles Scott, whose spotless worth had tenderly endeared him to the few who knew him intimately, and whose
industry and accuracy were warmly acknowledged by his 5
professional superiors, on Lord Berwick's recall from the
Neapolitan Embassy resumed his duties as a clerk in the
Foreign Office, and continued in that situation until the
summer of 1841. Sir John M'Neill, G. C. B., being
then entrusted with a special mission to the Court of 10
Persia, carried Charles with him as attaché and private
secretary; but the journey on horseback through Asia
Minor was trying for his never robust frame; and he con-
tracted an inflammatory disorder, which cut him off at
Teheran, almost immediately on his arrival there — 15
October 28, 1841. He had reached his 36th year.

Walter, who succeeded to the baronetcy, proceeded to
Madras in 1839, as Lieutenant-Colonel of the 15th Hussars; and subsequently commanded that regiment. He
was beloved and esteemed in it by officers and men as 20
much, I believe, as any gentleman ever was in any corps
of the British army; and there was no officer of his rank
who stood higher in the opinion of the heads of his profession. He had begun life with many advantages — a very
handsome person, and great muscular strength — a sweet 25
and even temper, and talents which in the son of any
father but his would have been considered brilliant. Though
neglectful of extra-professional studies in his earlier days,
he had in after-life read extensively, and made himself,
in every sense of the term, an accomplished man. The 30
library for the soldiers of his corps was founded by him:
the care of it was a principal occupation of his later years.
His only legacy out of his family was one of L.100 to this

R

library; and his widow, well understanding what he felt towards it, directed that a similar sum should be added in her own name.   Sir Walter having unwisely exposed himself in a tiger-hunt in August 1846, was on his return to his 5 quarters at Bangalore, smitten with fever, which ended in liver disease.   He was ordered to proceed to England, and died near the Cape of Good Hope, on board the ship Wellesley, February the 8th, 1847.   Lady Scott conveyed his remains to this country, and they were interred in the 10 paternal aisle at Dryburgh on the 4th of May following, in the presence of the few survivors of his father's friends and many of his own.   Three officers who had served under him, and were accidentally in Britain, arrived from great distances to pay him the last homage of their respect. 15 He had never had any child; and with him the baronetcy expired.

The only descendants of the Poet now alive are my son, Walter Scott Lockhart (a lieutenant in the army), who, as his uncle's heir of entail, has lately received permission 20 to assume the additional surname of Scott; — and his sister, Charlotte Harriet Jane, married in August 1847 to James Robert Hope, Barrister, second son of the late General the Honourable Sir Alexander Hope, G. C. B.[1]

---

[1] Walter Scott Lockhart Scott died at Versailles, on the 10th of January 1853, and was buried in the cemetery of Notre Dame there.

John Gibson Lockhart, his father, and the author of this Biography, died at Abbotsford on the 25th of November 1854, and was buried in Dryburgh Abbey, at the feet of Walter Scott.

Mrs. Hope, on the death of her brother, succeeded to the estate of Abbotsford, and, with her husband, assumed the name of Scott, in addition to that of Hope.   She died

In the winter succeeding the Poet's death, his sons and myself, as his executors, endeavoured to make such arrangements as were within our power for completing the great object of his own wishes and fatal exertions.

We found the remaining principal sum of commercial 5 debt to be nearly L.54,000. L.22,000 had been insured upon his life; there were some monies in the hands of the Trustees, and Mr. Cadell very handsomely offered to advance to us the balance, about L.30,000, that we might without further delay settle with the body of creditors. 10
This was effected accordingly on the 2d of February 1833; Mr. Cadell accepting, as his only security, the right to the profits accruing from Sir Walter's copyright property and literary remains, until such time as this new and consolidated obligation should be discharged. Besides 15 his commercial debt, Sir Walter left also one of L.10,000,

---

at Edinburgh on the 26th of October 1858, leaving three children, viz. : —

"Mary Monica," born on the 2d of October 1852.

"Walter Michael," born on the 2d of June 1857.

"Margaret Anne," born on the 17th of September 1858.

Of these, Margaret died on the 3d, and Walter on the 11th of December 1858, and their remains lie beside those of their mother (and of their father, J. R. Hope-Scott, who died April 29, 1873) in the vaults of St. Margaret's Convent, Edinburgh. "Mary Monica," who thus became the only surviving descendant of Walter Scott, married in 1874 the Hon. J. C. Maxwell, who assumed the name of Scott, and has, with other issue, Walter Joseph, born 1875.

As an officer in the English army this Walter Scott saw service in the Boer War. Mr. J. R. Hope-Scott added a west wing to Abbotsford and made many other improvements.

contracted by himself as an individual, when struggling to support Constable in December 1825, and secured by mortgage on the lands of Abbotsford. And, lastly, the library and museum, presented to him in free gift by his 5 creditors in December 1830, were bequeathed to his eldest son, with a burdèn to the extent of L. 5000, which sum he designed to be divided between his younger children, as already explained in an extract from his diary. His will provided that the produce of his literary property, in case 10 of its proving sufficient to wipe out the remaining debt of the firm, should then be applied to the extinction of these mortgages; and thereafter, should this also be accomplished, divided equally among his surviving family.

15	Various meetings were held soon after his death with a view to the erection of Monuments to his memory; and the records of these meetings, and their results, are adorned by many of the noblest and most distinguished names both of England and of Scotland. In London, the Lord Bishop 20 of Exeter, Sir Robert Peel, and Sir John Malcolm, took a prominent part as speakers: and the result was a subscription amounting to about L.10,000; but a part of this was embezzled by a young person rashly appointed to the post of secretary, who carried it with him to America, 25 where he soon afterwards died. The noblemen and gentlemen who subscribed to this fund adopted a suggestion — (which originated, I believe, with Lord Francis Egerton, now Earl of Ellesmere, and the Honourable John Stuart Wortley, now Lord Wharncliffe) — that, in place of 30 erecting a cenotaph in Westminster Abbey, or a statue or pillar elsewhere, the most suitable and respectful tribute that could be paid to Sir Walter's memory would be to discharge all the encumbrances upon Abbotsford, and entail the House, with its library and other articles of curiosity collected by him, together with the lands which he had planted and embellished, upon the heirs of his name for ever. The sum produced by the subscription, however, proved inadequate to the realization of such a scheme; and after much consultation, it was at length's settled that the money in the hands of the committee (between L.7000 and L.8000), should be employed to liquidate the debt upon the library and museum, and whatever might be over, towards the mortgage on the lands. This arrangement enabled the Lieutenant-Colo- 10 nel Sir Walter Scott to secure, in the shape originally desired, the permanent preservation at least of the house and its immediate appurtenances, as a memorial of the tastes and habits of the founder.

Such was the state of matters when the Lieutenant- 15 Colonel embarked for India : and in his absence no further steps could well be taken. Upon his death, it was found that, notwithstanding the very extensive demand for his father's writings, there still remained a considerable debt to Mr. Cadell, and also the greater part of the old 20 debt secured on the lands. Mr. Cadell then offered to relieve the guardians of the young inheritor of that great name from much anxiety and embarrassment, by accepting, in full payment of the sum due to himself, and also in recompense for his taking on himself the final oblitera- 25 tion of the heritable bond, a transference to him of the remaining claims of the family over Sir Walter's writings, together with the result of some literary exertions of the only surviving executor. This arrangement was completed in May 1847 ; and the estate, as well as the house 30 and its appendages, became at last unfettered. The rental is small ; but I hope and trust, that as long as any of the blood remains, reverent care will attend over the guardianship of a possession associated with so many

high and noble recollections. On that subject the gallant soldier who executed the entail expressed also in his
testament feelings of the devoutest anxiety : and it was,
I am well assured, in order that no extraneous obstacle
5 might thwart the fulfilment of his pious wishes, that Mr.
Cadell crowned a long series of kind services to the cause
and the memory of Sir Walter Scott, by the very handsome proposition of 1847.

Abbotsford, after his own immortal works, is the best
10 monument of its founder. But at Edinburgh also, soon
after his death, a meeting was held with a view to the
erection of some visible memorial in his native city; the
prominent speakers were the late Marquess of Lothian,
the late Earl of Dalhousie, the Earl of Rosebery, Lord
15 Jeffrey, and Professor Wilson; and the subscription then
begun realized a sum of L.8000, which by subsequent
exertions reached no less than L.15,000. The result may
now be seen in a truly magnificent monument, conspicuous to every visitor of Scott's "own romantic town" —
20 a lofty Gothic cross, enclosing and surmounting a marble
statue of the Poet, which, as well as many happy relievos
on the exterior, does great honour to the chisel of Mr.
Steele.

In Glasgow, also, there was a meeting in 1832 : the sub-
25 scriptions there reached L.1200 : and in the chief square of
that city, already graced with statues of two illustrious
natives, James Watt and Sir John Moore, there is now
a lofty pillar, surmounted with a statue of Sir Walter
Scott.

30   Finally, in the market-place of Selkirk there has been set
up, at the cost of local friends and neighbours, a statue in
freestone, by Mr. Alexander Ritchie of Musselburgh, with
this inscription : —

"ERECTED IN AUGUST 1839,

IN PROUD AND AFFECTIONATE REMEMBRANCE,

OF

SIR WALTER SCOTT, BARONET,

SHERIFF OF THIS COUNTY   5

FROM 1800 TO 1832

By Yarrow's stream still let me stray,
Though none should guide my feeble way;
Still feel the breeze down Ettrick break,
Although it chill my withered cheek."°   10

In what manner to cover the grave itself at Dryburgh
required some consideration, in consequence of the state of
the surrounding and overhanging ruins. Sir F. Chantrey
recommended a block of Aberdeen granite, so solid as to
resist even the fall of the ivied roof of the aisle, and kindly 15
sketched the shape; in which he followed the stone coffin
of the monastic ages — especially the "marble stone" on
which Deloraine awaits the opening of the wizard's vault
in the Lay. The inscriptions on this simple but graceful
tomb are merely of name and date.   20
On the whole, I have no doubt that, the more the details of his personal history are revealed and studied, the
more powerfully will they be found to inculcate the same
great lessons with his works. Where else shall we be
taught better how prosperity may be extended by be- 25
neficence, and adversity confronted by exertion? Where
can we see the "follies of the wise" more strikingly re-
buked, and a character more beautifully purified and ex-
alted in the passage through affliction to death? I have
lingered so long over the details, that I have, perhaps, 30

become, even from that circumstance alone, less qualified than more rapid surveyors may be to seize the effect in the mass. But who does not feel that there is something very invigorating as well as elevating in the contemplation? His character seems to belong to some elder and stronger period than ours; and, indeed, I cannot help likening it to the architectural fabrics of other ages, which he most delighted in, where there is such a congregation of imagery and tracery, such endless indulgence of whim
10 and fancy, the sublime blending here with the beautiful, and there contrasted with the grotesque — half, perhaps, seen in the clear daylight, and half by rays tinged with the blazoned forms of the past — that one may be apt to get bewildered among the variety of particular impressions,
15 and not feel either the unity of the grand design, or the height and solidness of the structure, until the door has been closed upon the labyrinth of aisles and shrines, and you survey it from a distance, but still within its shadow.

NOTES AND SUGGESTIONS

1:19. Robert **Burns**, 1759–1796. Scott calls him " the boast of Scotland." Can you report incidents in the poet's life to justify Scott's estimate of the value of his memoirs?

1:20. Thomas **Chatterton**, 1752–1770. Committed suicide at the age of nineteen years. Perhaps you can explain how this boy gained a place in literature.

1:20. Richard **Savage**, 1698–1743. Scott may have had in mind Dr. Samuel Johnson's " Life of Savage " of which Macaulay wrote, " No finer specimen of literary biography existed in any language, living or dead." Macaulay's comment on Savage in his essay on Samuel Johnson, originally published in the Encyclopædia Britannica, will be found most interesting.

2:28. **Teviotdale.** The valley of the river Teviot, near the southeastern border of Scotland.

3:2. **Yarrow.** A parish and stream in the county of which Scott was for many years the honored sheriff. " Yarrow Revisited," a poem by William Wordsworth, describes the beauties of the border country and is rich in references to the Mighty Minstrel.

3:6. **Stuart.** In 1371 Robert Stuart became Robert II of Scotland. Different members of this family take leading parts in many of Scott's tales. Especially interesting are " Waverley " and " The Fortunes of Nigel."

4:18. Hermann **Boerhaave**, 1668–1738. A Dutch

physician and scientist whose genius gave the university of Leyden great fame.

6 : 27. Jacobites. " Jacobus " is the Latin form of " James." The last Stuart king was James II. For many years after his flight from England the Stuart family had ardent supporters in England and Scotland. The supporters of James.

6 : 30. Culloden. The decisive battle of April 15th, 1746, in which the Stuart cause was finally overthrown by a son of King George II, the Duke of Cumberland, then a distinguished general though but twenty-four years old.

7 : 12. Robin Hood was a legendary outlaw, famed to have lived in the forest of Sherwood in the fourteenth century, who robbed the rich and befriended the poor and became the hero of ballad and story. **Little John** was one of his retainers. Both are characters in Scott's " Ivanhoe."

7 : 19. Automathes. " The capacity and extent of the human understanding; exemplified in the extraordinary case of Automathes, a young nobleman, who was accidentally left in infancy upon a desolate island, and continued nineteen years in that solitary state, separate from all human society." Written by John Kirby, a tutor of the historian, Gibbon, and published at London in 1745.

7 : 19. Allan Ramsay, 1685–1758. Scottish poet.

7 : 21. Josephus, 37–100. Jewish historian of the last war between the Jews and the Romans.

7 : 33. La Mancha. The home of Don Quixote, the hero of Cervantes' great Spanish novel.

8 : 8. Bath. A beautiful city of Somerset, England, in the valley of the Avon. It was famous for its baths at the time of the Roman occupation of Britain and has for over two centuries been the chief watering place of England.

8 : 12. Bladud. An ancient British prince who was afflicted with leprosy. Tradition says he discovered the medicinal qualities of the Bath waters by observing their effect on some swine that seemed to have a disease similar to his own.

8 : 29. Non sine diis animosus infans. The Latin way of expressing, A sturdy child, thanks to the gods.

9 : 20. John **Home,** 1722–1808. Minister, soldier, and author. His military exploits made him a national character and offset in a measure the criticism that came upon him as a minister of the gospel for his connection with theatrical productions, notably his tragedy, " Douglas."

9 : 24. Downs. Rounded hills.

11 : 20. John **Bunyan,** 1628–1688. His " Pilgrim's Progress " is the greatest work of its class in our language.

11 : 21. Solomon **Gesner,** 1730–1788. Swiss painter and poet. The " Death of Abel " is an idyllic pastoral.

11 : 21. Nicholas **Rowe,** 1674–1718. English poet and dramatist.

11 : 30. Alexander Pope, 1688–1744.

11 : 30. Homer. Tradition tells us that the Greek poet, Homer, was blind. Pope's translations of his great poems will give you some of the pleasure that came to the boy Scott.

15 : 9. Pare and burn a muir. The cutting of peat in the moors was work for a strong man.

16 : 22. Ossian. An interesting literary forgery by James Macpherson.

16 : 22. Edmund Spenser, 1552–1599. Which of Spenser's poems is Scott referring to?

18 : 8. Tasso, 1544–1595. Italian poet. John **Hoole,** 1727–1803. English translator.

18 : 11. Bishop **Percy,** 1729–1811. English bishop of

Dromore, Ireland.   While a vicar in Northamptonshire he did his literary work.

18 : 17.   Delilahs.   The sixteenth chapter of the Book of Judges will give the story of Samson and Delilah.   Can you explain Scott's figurative use of the name?

19 : 5–7.   Richardson, Fielding, Smollett.   The fathers of the English novel.

19 : 6.   Henry Mackenzie.   Frequently referred to as " The Man of Feeling," the title of his first novel.

22 : 3.   George Buchanan, 1506–1582.   One of Scotland's greatest scholars.   He wrote Latin with all but classic ease.   Scott doubtless refers to his " Rerum Scoticarum Historica."

22 : 4.   Matthew of Paris.   An English monk of the thirteenth century who may have studied in France. Scott read parts of his " Historia Anglorum."

24 : 3.   Menus plaisirs.   French for " amusements."

24 : 21.   Jemmy and Jenny Jessamy.   Jemmy and Jenny are characters noted for their cunning and treachery in Gay's " The Beggar's Opera,"   Jessamy, a fop in Bickerstaff's opera, " Lionel and Clarissa."   They gave their names to a tribe of imitations.

24 : 22.   Frances Burney, 1752–1840.   Better known as Madame D'Arblay, English novelist and friend of Dr. Samuel Johnson.   What class of novel did she introduce ?

24 : 23.   Mackenzie.   Henry Mackenzie, 1745–1831, author of " The Man of Feeling " and other novels.   Some critics think his works the most sentimental of all English novels.

26 : 5.   Andrew Macdonald, 1755–1790.   Unfortunate because a failure in almost everything he attempted except his tragedy, " Vimonda," which had successful productions in both Edinburgh and London.

26 : 17. Preston. Battle of 1715, fought in behalf of the first Stuart pretender.

26 : 18. Tiled haddocks. This use of " tiled," in the sense of " dried " as applied to fish, seems to be peculiar to Scotland.

26 : 33. Immortal general. General Sir Ralph Abercrombie, 1734–1801, is credited with having restored the ancient discipline and military success of the British soldier, much impaired by reverses in America.

27 : 21. Autolycus. Make his acquaintance in "Winter's Tale."

28 : 1. Bannockburn. June 24, 1314, saw the defeat at Bannockburn of Edward II and 100,000 English by Robert Bruce and 30,000 Scotch.

29 : 9. Falkland. The summer palace of the Stuart kings of Scotland, located in Fifeshire.

29 : 10. Holy-Rood. The royal residence at Edinburgh. The story of the application of the name, Holy Cross, to this palace is an interesting one.

29 : 11. Queen Mary's yew tree at Crookston. Crookston castle was the property of the Darnley family at the time of the murder of Lord Darnley, the husband of Mary Queen of Scots, in 1567.

32 : 1. Civil law. The laws derived from the Romans. For centuries the Scotch were allied with the French as the natural enemies of the English. This explains the popularity in Scotland of the laws of the Latin countries. Much of the civil law came into England by way of the equity courts.

32 : 17. Tony Lumpkin. If you do not know Tony, make his acquaintance in Goldsmith's delightful comedy, " She Stoops to Conquer."

35 : 3. Hercules. The national hero of ancient Greece.

He was the son of Jupiter and a mortal mother. The story of his twelve labors and countless adventures is full of interest.

37 : 24. Michaelmas. The feast of Saint Michael, September 29, one of the four quarter days of the business year. This was the autumn term of the court.

37 : 29. Liddesdale. In Scott's day a wild district near the southeastern border of Scotland.

37 : 31. Riding Ballad. A ballad celebrating a Border raid. It was sung by the horsemen as they rode.

37 : 32. Moss-troopers. Border horsemen of Scotland, so called because of the mossy or boggy character of much of the border country.

37 : 33. Douglasses. Robert the Bruce gave the Douglas of his day charge over the borders. The power of the Douglas family increased until at times it was a menace to the power of the kings.

40 : 20. Parliament House. The building formerly used by the Scotch Parliament, which was at this time the meeting place of the supreme courts of Scotland.

41 : 1. Outer-House. The supreme court of Scotland consists of two courts of appeal, called the Inner-House, and five courts of original jurisdiction, the Outer-House.

41 : 5. Mountain. The extreme revolutionary party in the French National Assembly at the time of the French revolution was called the Mountain because of the position it occupied in the upper part of the hall.

41 : 30. Duns Scotus. Scottish theologian of the thirteenth century.

42 : 26. Bean Lean. To be met in Scott's first novel.

45 : 1. Queen Guenever. As King Arthur's queen she has a place in immortal story, told for our age by Tennyson.

45 : 7. Balmawhapples. See Scott's " Waverley."

48 : 30. Lenore. The heroine of a ballad composed by Bürger. Scott liked to surround himself by material reminders of the world of fancy, which was in many respects his real world.

58 : 30. George Ellis, 1753–1815. English poet and antiquarian. Scott held him in high regard ; and it was from the many letters to Ellis that Lockhart drew much of the material for his biography.

63 : 6. William Wordsworth, 1770–1850. As an interpreter of the spirit in nature he holds a place in the first rank of English poets.

63 : 7. Sir John Stoddart. English journalist and jurist.

64 : 26. Reged. One of the localities named in the Arthurian legends. Scott identified it with Tweeddale, the region about Ashestiel. Modern scholarship favors Dunbartonshire.

65 : 25. James Hogg. A rude shepherd of Ettrick Forest in whom Scott discovered a brother poet of not inconsiderable natural gifts. The district known as Ettrick Forest was at this time almost treeless.

66 : 25. Galled my kibes. Hurried me. A Shakespearean expression with the literal meaning, Irritated my chilblains ; figuratively, Stepped on my frost-bitten heels.

70 : 10. Dis aliter visum. The gods saw otherwise.

74 : 16. Robert Southey, 1774–1843. English poet.

75 : 32. Out damned spot. Scott was playing with the tragic expression of Lady Macbeth.

78 : 11. Sir Humphry Davy, 1778–1829. English scientist. For what is he especially noted ?

79 : 9. Teind. tithe.

81 : 1. John Dryden, 1631–1701. English poet and dramatist.

84 : 21. Somers' Tracts. John Somers, 1651–1716, Lord Chancellor of England. His library furnished the materials for the collection known as the "Somers' Tracts," published in London about 1750.

84 : 22. Sadler State Papers. Sir Ralph Sadler, 1507–1587. Diplomat in the service of Henry VIII and later in the service of Elizabeth. His despatches are among the most reliable and most interesting records of his time. In editing these papers Scott was again "making himself" for his romances.

84 : 27. Jonathan Swift, 1667–1745. Dean of St. Patrick's. How do many children first make his acquaintance?

88 : 3. Piscottie. Robert Lindsay of Piscottie lived from 1500 to 1565. He was an interesting but inaccurate historian of Scotland.

88 : 4. John **Barbour.** Scottish poet, 1316–1395.

88 : 5. Blind Harry. A minstrel who died about the time of the discovery of America. His fame rests on his poem, "Wallace." See Scott's "Fair Maid of Perth."

88 : 12. Cyropædia. A Greek prose romance by Xenophon describing the education of the older and greater Cyrus.

90 : 6. Sir Ralph. Sir Ralph Saddler.

90 : 23. James Saxon. English portrait painter.

91 : 2. John Ballantyne. A younger brother of James Ballantyne. The book-selling concern of John Ballantyne & Co. was established in 1809 as a part of Scott's dealings with the Ballantynes in opposition to Constable. See Note on **Differences with Constable** on page 257.

93 : 24. Beaumont and Fletcher. English playwrights of Shakespeare's time who worked together in writing a number of plays.

93 : 25. Culdees. An ancient monastic order that had settlements in Ireland and Scotland.

93 : 25. John Jamieson, D.D., 1759–1838. Antiquary and philologist.

94 : 17. Sit mihi sedes utinam senectæ! Would that I might have a home for my old age.

95 : 6. Charge-Law. In some districts of Scotland " law " has the meaning, " hill."

97 : 18. Catrail. A ditch, some forty miles in length, of doubtful origin, but supposed to have been a work of defence built by the Picts in their opposition to the Romans.

98 : 19. Preux chevalier. A valiant knight.

98 : 27. Jacques Callot, 1592–1635. French painter.

101 : 27. Jeffrey. By publishing the "Bridal of Triermain" anonymously Scott hoped to puzzle Jeffrey, the brilliant editor of the *Edinburgh Review*, as well as the reading public.

102 : 16. Pari passu. With equal step; at the same speed.

104 : 1. Differences with Constable. Some rather unfair criticisms of Scott's work appeared in Constable's *Edinburgh Review*. Scott was not easily offended in this way, but he noticed with some bitterness the Whig principles the *Review* was advancing, and determined to assist in the establishment of a rival, the *Quarterly Review*. These differences continued for some years, but mutual interests finally brought the greatest writer and the greatest publisher of the time back to their old alliance.

110 : 12. Ex contrario. On the contrary.

110 : 22. Grande opus. A great work; another poem like " Marmion." It is interesting to note that at this time Scott did not consider his prose work a grande opus.

116 : 1. Oliver Goldsmith, 1728–1774. Irish poet,

s

dramatist, novelist, and historian. Irving's "Life of Goldsmith" is one of the most fascinating of books.

117 : 10. Briareus. In Greek mythology a monster with an hundred hands.

119 : 28. Thomas **Moore,** 1780–1852. Irish poet.

119 : 32. Lord Byron, 1789–1824. Though Byron's poetry crowded Scott's from its first place in popular favor in their day, a hundred years later we find more readers of Scott than of Byron.

120 : 28. Joanna Baillie, 1762–1851. Her first work of importance, "Plays on Passions," was published anonymously and ascribed by some critics to Scott. This resulted in their meeting and becoming warm friends. Scott considered her the greatest poet of his time. This opinion must be classed with his belief that Dr. Samuel Johnson was one of the greatest poets of our language.

121 : 1. Corporal Nym. A rogue of Shakespeare's creation in "Merry Wives of Windsor" and "King Henry Fifth."

127 : 11. Daniel **Terry,** 1780–1829. Actor and playwright. He admired Scott to the extent of imitating his facial mannerisms and his handwriting. Scott said that if called on to take oath concerning a page of his own writing he could only swear that it was either his own or Terry's. Terry dramatized several of Scott's novels; "Terrifications" Scott called them.

129 : 24. Torres Vedras. A town in Portugal. In what war did English troops fight in Portugal?

130 : 4. Washington Irving, 1783–1859. One of the first Americans to place our country on the literary map of the world. You will enjoy his essay on Abbotsford, giving a full account of this visit at the home of Scott. He fails to tell us one of the most interesting incidents of the visit, from our point of view, an incident with which Lockhart seems to have been unfamiliar. It was Irving who gave to Scott the original of the Rebecca of "Ivanhoe." Scott sent Irving one of the first copies of "Ivanhoe" and wrote, "How do you like your Rebecca? Does the Rebecca I have pictured compare with the pattern given?"

The pattern was the beautiful Rebecca Gratz of Philadelphia, a dear friend of Miss Hoffman to whom Irving was engaged at the time of her early death. Rebecca Gratz loved a Christian, but her Jewish piety would not allow her to marry him. However, she steadfastly refused to marry any other and devoted her life to good works. When Irving learned that Scott planned to introduce a group of Jews in his next novel, he told him the story of the charming American Jewess. That he does not mention this in his account of his visit is but proof that he rarely opened to others the memories of his great loss: Scott's was a nature that invited and won the best and deepest from all who knew him.

133 : 11. Jedediah. Scott playfully presented the "Tales of my Landlord" as the work of Jedediah Cleishbotham, a Scotch schoolmaster.

136 : 28. Clausus tutus ero. Closed I shall be safe. Gualterus Scotus is the Latin form of Scott's name. Remembering that "Gu" is the Latin equivalent of our double "u" you can trace the anagram.

137 : 26. Graham of Claverhouse. Viscount Dundee, in 1689, declared for James II and with an army of Highlanders defeated the government forces under General Mackay at the battle of Killiecrankie, but was himself mortally wounded.

138 : 7. Kinder-märchen. German nursery tale.

147 : 3. Prima cura. First work.

151 : 7. More Scotico. In the Scottish manner.

153 : 7. ﹁ **O'ervaulting ambition** ﹂: Shakespeare has Macbeth use the line, ﹁ Vaulting ambition, which o'erleaps itself.﹂

156 : 5. Scots Greys. The Second Royal Dragoons, a regiment with an honorable record since its organization in 1681.

159 : 24. Blair-Adam. In the summer of 1816 Scott and William Clerk with several friends were the guests of Judge Adam at his country seat, Blair-Adam. It was agreed that they should have an annual reunion at the same place. Hence the Blair-Adam club, devoted to the study of the rich historical legends of Scotland.

160 : 8. Ben Jonson, 1573–1637. English poet and playwright.

161 : 1. Hastings. In 1066 the Normans under Duke William, the Conqueror, defeated the Saxons under their last king, Harold, in the battle of Hastings. **Cressy** (Crécy). Great victory of the English over the French in 1346 at Crécy in France. **Bosworth Field.** In 1485 Henry, Earl of Richmond, defeated King Richard III in the battle of Bosworth Field, and became Henry VII of England.

162 : 6. Pari passu. With equal speed.

162 : 14. In petto. Italian for, " In the breast." We would say, " In his mind," or, possibly, " In Spain."

162 : 24. Entre nous. Between us.

162 : 25. Tempore. At the time of.

164 : 14. President of the Royal Society. The Royal Society, though a scientific body, delighted in honoring their great countryman. Because of his executive ability as shown in the management of the festivities in honor of the king's visit to Edinburgh, Scott was offered a number of commercial positions and accepted the Chairmanship of the Edinburgh Gas Company.

166 : 16. Louis XI. King of France from 1461 to 1483. He is known in history as the shrewd and false king who overcame the great barons and laid the foundations for absolutism in France. **Charles the Bold,** Duke of Burgundy, rather successfully opposed the encroachments of Louis until the battle of Nancy, where he was slain in 1477.

167 : 10. Maria Edgeworth, 1767–1849. Her "Castle Rackrent" and other Irish novels were much admired by Scott.

167 : 27. Mr. Adolphus — Letters to Heber. John Leycester Adolphus, 1795–1862. His "Letters to Richard Heber" conclusively fixed the authorship of the Waverley novels on Scott.

167 : 27. Richard Heber, 1773–1833. English book collector.

170 : 16. Ascanius. The son of Trojan Æneas. In our text it simply means the aged son of a banished prince.

170 : 18. Mirabile dictu. Wonderful to tell.

171 : 12. George Bullock. His factory in Tenterden street, London, turned out all sorts of building materials. He made some of the plans for Abbotsford and gave many suggestions concerning its furnishings. Scott held him in high regard.

173 : 19. Sandhurst College. The royal military college was settled at Sandhurst in 1812.

174 : 30. Gazetted. The *Gazette* is the official biweekly government newspaper of London, Edinburgh, and Dublin, in which are announced appointments, promotions, honors, etc. Promotions frequently depended on the retirement of a superior, and it was the custom to pay an agreed sum to the one leaving the army.

176 : 31.   Currente calamo.   With a running pen.

177 : 11.   Le Moniteur.   The official journal of France during the rule of the great Napoleon.

179 : 6.   Locus cui nomen est Pallas.   In Westminster Abbey there is a bust of Goldsmith and beneath it a white marble tablet bearing the Latin epitaph written by Dr. Johnson. It contains the line, *In loco cui nomen Pallas.* In a place called Pallas. Some of the friends of Goldsmith preferred an English epitaph, but the "Pope of the English Language" declared that it was absurd to think of using English inscriptions in Westminster Abbey.

195 : 13.   His feet are beautiful, etc.   A comparison of this sentence with the fifteenth verse of the first chapter of the Book of Nahum and with the seventh verse of the fifty-second chapter of the Book of Isaiah will show how Old Testament thought and phrase entered into Scott's writing.

202 : 12.   Peine forte et dure.   Very severe punishment.

206 : 30.   Monstrari digito.   To be pointed out.

213 : 12.   Airt and pairt.   Scotch for "aiding and abetting."

213 : 13.   Panel.   A prisoner at the bar.

222 : 8.   Magnum Opus.   The great work.

222 : 25.   In toto.   Entirely.

225 : 14.   Jacta est alea.   The die is cast. Do you recall the important historical event with which this expression is connected?

227 : 10.   A little more taste.   Quoting the Archbishop of Granada in "Gil Blas," the French romance by Le Sage, novelist and dramatist, 1668–1747.

247 : 10.   "By Yarrow's stream, etc."   From stanza II, Canto VI, of "The Lay of the Last Minstrel."

The Tudor Shakespeare Series

An unexpurgated edition for library and general use. Under the general editorship of Professor WILLIAM ALLEN NEILSON of Harvard University and Professor ASHLEY HORACE THORNDIKE of Columbia University. Notes, glossaries, and introductions scholarly and unobtrusive.

Pocket Classics Edition, cloth, 25 cents each
Superior Cloth Edition, 35 cents each
De Luxe Edition, leather, 55 cents each

All's Well That Ends Well. (Lowes.)

Antony and Cleopatra. (Benedict.)

As You Like It. (Shackford.)

Comedy of Errors. (Padelford.)

Coriolanus. (Sherman.)

Cymbeline. (Howe.)

Hamlet. (Baker.)

Henry IV, Part I. (Chandler.)

Henry IV, Part II. (Hanscom.)

Henry V. (Mott.)

Henry VI, Part I. (Pound.)

Henry VI, Part II. (Barnwell.)

Henry VI, Part III. (Law.)

Henry VIII. (Dunlap.)

Julius Cæsar. (Lovett.)

King John. (Belden.)

King Lear. (Gildersleeve.)

Love's Labour's Lost. (Royster.)

Macbeth. (Brown.)

Measure for Measure. (Morris.)

Merchant of Venice. (Ayres.)

Merry Wives of Windsor. (Emery.)

Midsummer-Night's Dream. (Cunliffe.)

Much Ado About Nothing. (Lawrence.)

Othello. (Parrott.)

Pericles. (Smith.)

Richard II. (Craige.)

Richard III. (Churchill.)

Romeo and Juliet. (Neilson and Thorndike.)

The Sonnets. (Alden.)

Taming of the Shrew. (Tupper.)

The Tempest. (Greene.)

Timon of Athens. (Fletcher.)

Titus Andronicus. (Stoll.)

Troilus and Cressida. (Tatlock.)

Twelfth Night. (Hart.)

Two Gentlemen of Verona. (Sampson.)

Venus and Adonis, and Lucrece. (Brown.)

Winter's Tale. (Wylie.)

Facts about Shakespeare. (Neilson and Thorndike.)

Elements of English Composition

By Professor HENRY S. CANBY, Sheffield Scientific School,
Yale University, and Mr. JOHN B. OPDYCKE, High
School of Commerce, New York City

Cloth, 12mo, 593 pages, $1.00

The characteristic feature of this book is that the authors see
the end from the beginning and never lose sight of it. That
end is the ability on the part of the pupil to write clearly, correctly,
and intelligently. From start to finish the appeal is to the intelligence rather than to mere form. The fact that before all else there
must be something to say is emphasized in the first two chapters on
Composition and Shaping the Material. The remainder of the book
is simply a study of different ways and the best ways of saying what
you want to say.

The manner of approach is psychological. Part I contains
(1) choice of subject; (2) arrangement of what you want to say;
(3) the use of the sentence as the expression of a single thought;
(4) the use of the paragraph; (5) the structure of the whole composition; (6) the choice of the right word to express meaning
nicely. Part II is a study of the recognized forms of composition,
exposition, argument, description, narration, the story. In Part III,
Aids to Composition, there are given for reference necessary details
concerning spelling, punctuation, capitalization, grammatical forms,
figures of speech, etc. Throughout the book there are abundant
exercises and illustrative excerpts that serve to emphasize the point
under consideration. The book is a unit, the plan works.

THE MACMILLAN COMPANY

Publishers   **64-66 Fifth Avenue**   **New York**

Studies in Literature

By FREDERICK MONROE TISDEL

Assistant Professor of English in the University of Missouri.

Cloth, 12mo, illustrated, 333 pages, list price $ .90

In Part I of this book the author introduces the student to more than twenty standard English classics, giving in connection with each a brief explanatory introduction, suggestions for study and topics for oral and written discussion. These classics are grouped with respect to the different types of literature which they represent, — epic, drama, essay, novel, etc., and there is a brief exposition of the type. The result is that in the mind of the reader the individual masterpiece and the type with its characteristics are inseparably connected.

Part II consists of a brief but masterly survey of English literature. The book as a whole serves to systematize and unify the study of secondary school literature, — a most desirable end.

Professor E. A. Cross, State Teachers College, Greeley, Colo. " It meets with my heartiest approval. It is brief, considers all the writers high school students need to know, touches the interesting features in the lives and works of these men, — about all you could want it to do."

Mr. John B. Opdycke, English Department of the High School of Commerce, New York City. " I like it very much indeed. It has just enough in its review of the history of English literature, and its treatment of the classics is restrained and dignified. So far as I have seen, this is the only book that combines the two in one volume. I am all against the use of an abstract History of English Literature in the high school and I am all in favor of putting into the hands of the students some book that analyzes classics fully and yet with restraint. This book seems to have combined the two in just the right proportions and treated them in just the right manner."

THE MACMILLAN COMPANY

Publishers   64-66 Fifth Avenue   New York

Boston   Chicago   Atlanta   Dallas   San Francisco

Oral English for

Secondary Schools

By WILLIAM PALMER SMITH

Instructor in Oral English in Stuyvesant High School, New York City

Cloth, 12mo, Ill., 358 pages, $1.00

It is the purpose of this volume to outline graded lessons in enunciation and pronunciation; to indicate how the speaking voice may be improved by appropriate exercise and proper use; to explain and illustrate the most important principles of expression; to point out the relation of oral reading to conversation and public speaking; and to furnish appropriate selections which are unhackneyed, interesting, and of literary merit.

PUBLISHED BY

THE MACMILLAN COMPANY

64–66 Fifth Avenue, New York City

Boston   Chicago   Atlanta   San Francisco   Dallas

Milton Keynes UK
Ingram Content Group UK Ltd.
UKHW021401261124
3143UKWH00044B/526